THE COMMUNIST CONSPIRACY

by Stephen King-Hall and Ann Dewar

HISTORY IN HANSARD
1803–1900

An Anthology of wit, wisdom and nonsense uttered in Parliament during the nineteenth century

Sunday Times: " This volume is not merely interesting; it is highly instructive and entertaining.
" This is necessarily potted history in a form that makes it curiously alive. Some present-day M.P.s could profit from a study of the diction of members long dead."

Scotsman: " It is a well varied assortment, ranging from the sublime to the ridiculous, and reminding the reader frequently that, human nature being what it is, our M.P.s have not changed a great deal since those times."

Manchester Guardian: " An entertaining anthology. The wise and the foolish, the short-sighted and the prescient, the philistine and the sider with the angels are all there."

Liverpool Post: " Very few books nowadays offer such fascinating variety and absorbing interest as this amusing and amazing volume."

STEPHEN KING-HALL

THE
COMMUNIST
CONSPIRACY

CONSTABLE & COMPANY LTD LONDON

LONDON

PUBLISHED BY
Constable and Company Ltd.
10-12 Orange Street, W.C.2

INDIA
Orient Longmans Ltd.
BOMBAY MADRAS CALCUTTA

CANADA
Longmans, Green and Company Ltd.
TORONTO

SOUTH *and* EAST AFRICA
Longmans, Green and Company Ltd.
CAPE TOWN NAIROBI

First published 1953

Printed in Great Britain by
RICHARD CLAY AND COMPANY, LTD,
BUNGAY
SUFFOLK

"War consisteth not in Battle only, or in the act of fighting; but in a tract of time, wherein the Will to contend by Battle is sufficiently known: and therefore the notion of *Time* is to be considered in the nature of War, as it is in the nature of Weather. For as the nature of foul weather lieth not in a shower or two of rain, but in and inclination thereto of many days together, so the nature of war consisteth not in actual fighting, but in the known disposition thereto during all the time there is not assurance to the contrary. All other time is PEACE.

"Whatsoever therefore is consequent to a time of War, where every man is Enemy to every man, the same is consequent to the time wherein men live without other security than what their own strength and their own invention shall furnish them withal.

"In such condition there is no place for Industry, because the fruit thereof is uncertain: and consequently no Culture of the Earth; no Navigation, nor use of the commodities that may be imported by sea; no commodious Building; no Instruments or moving and removing such things as require much force; no Knowledge of the face of the Earth; no account of Time; no Arts; no Letters; no Society; and, which is worst of all, continual fear and danger of violent death; and the life of man solitary, poor, nasty, brutish, and short."

Leviathan, Thomas Hobbes, 1688–1779.

"The Communists disdain to conceal their views and aims. They openly declare that their ends can be attained only by the forcible overthrow of all existing conditions."

(From the Communist Manifesto, 1848.)

"Since becoming Secretary-General, Comrade Stalin has concentrated huge power in his hands, and I am not at all sure he knows how to use that power with sufficient circumspection."

LENIN (December 1922, when he lay stricken with paralysis).

"Everything is not good in Russia. Do not forget to talk about the bad things as well as the good ones when you return to England."

(Advice given to a group of British M.P.s in the Kremlin by Stalin, January, 1945.)

M. MOLOTOV (*referring to M. Stalin's remark*) : "What do you consider the worst thing you have seen in Russia?"

A BRITISH M.P. : "The fact that I believe M. Stalin is the only man in the U.S.S.R. who could have given us this advice."

(At a reception in Moscow, 1945.)

"There is no force capable . . . of halting the advance of society towards Communism . . . the guiding and organizing force in our advance towards Communism is the Communist Party of the Soviet Union, the militant union of like-minded persons, Communists who are striving to transform human society in accordance with the theory of Marxism–Leninism. Many long years of life and health to our dear teacher and leader, great Stalin (*tumultuous, prolonged applause reaching an ovation. All rose*). Under the banner of Lenin and Stalin, forward to Communism! (*The concluding words of the report were followed by an ovation in honour of great Stalin, the wise leader and teacher, the organizer and inspirer of the historic victories of the Soviet people, the genius leading all progressive mankind.*)"

(*Soviet News*, account of M. G. Pervukhin's report 6th November, 1952, at the celebration meeting of the Moscow Soviet.)

CONTENTS

INTRODUCTION

THIS book, entitled *The Communist Conspiracy*, has been written in order to make available to the English speaking world some information about the world conflict which began in 1917, when the Communist Party, with its objective of world revolution, secured control over the minds and bodies of the Russian people and the material resources of the Russian Empire. Until about 1946 the existence, and therefore the nature, of this stupendous struggle was concealed from most people living in democratic States by two circumstances.

First, the Communists in Russia realised that before they could safely embark upon their programme of world revolution they must consolidate themselves in Russia and develop the resources of that nation so that world Communism would have as a spring-board an adequate amount of military and industrial strength.

Secondly, the existence of the world struggle was temporarily obscured by events arising out of the Second World War. The decision of the Communists to spend some time consolidating their position in Russia—a decision for resistance to which Leon Trotsky was first overthrown and subsequently murdered in Mexico—led to a tactical retreat on the part of the Communists during the period between the two world wars.

How long this period of retreat (more or less) from the policy of actively promoting world revolution and substituting Communism for liberal democracy was intended to last it is impossible to say. The time-table, whatever it may have been, was upset by the rise in Germany of Hitler and his Nazi movement. From the point of view of the Kremlin, the struggle between the democracies and the Nazis and Fascists was an event full of promise.

This conflict, which culminated in 1939 in the outbreak of military operations, was from the Communist point of view a civil war within the capitalist camp. This was a correct diagnosis. The Nazi movement, and still more so the papier-mâché Fascist movement in Italy, were outbreaks of extreme nationalism inside the Western world, and not world revolutionary religions. Although both Hitler and Mussolini

invented philosophies in support of what were gangster operations on a grand scale, the theories were puerile. Hitler's strange
mixture of anti-Semitism and Nordic racial theory was scientific-
ally as ridiculous as ex-Socialist Benito Mussolini's attempts to
span the centuries and link his 20th-century condottièri with
the glories of ancient Rome.

The facts were that Hitler and Mussolini were megalo-
maniacal tyrants whose appeal to their dupes—the German
and Italian peoples—was based on crude 19th-century nationalism. Neither Nazi-ism nor Fascism was an exportable product. Although nothing can excuse the filthy excesses of
both these totalitarian régimes, or the miseries they inflicted
on mankind, the democracies are not without responsibility
for the growth of these monstrosities within the Western
world. In both cases firm action, instead of appeasement at
early stages in the careers of Mussolini and Hitler, would have
brought both dictators to ruin. Furthermore, in the case of
Hitler, the behaviour of the victors of World War I towards
the Germans, especially at the time of the world economic
crisis of 1931, made a substantial contribution to the economic
conditions in Germany which provided the Nazis with a fertile
field in which to sow the seeds of their abominable plans.

To write this is not to infer that the Western way of life
can dissociate itself from responsibility for the growth of Communism. It can be argued, and in the opinion of this author,
with force, that it was a failure on the part of democracy to
realise sufficiently soon that changes were morally (i.e.
politically) needed in the economic structure of society, which
gave Communism its opportunity (see page 27).

We now know that Stalin was determined to keep out of the
internal struggle of the West; he hoped, no doubt, that if the
Germans and the Italians on the one hand, and the British
and French on the other, fought each other to a standstill, a
wrecked and ruined Western Europe would become Communist almost over-night, and if it hesitated, then Russia, un-
touched by war, could easily provide the persuasive force.
We therefore find that in 1939 Stalin made a pact with the
Nazis and actively assisted them with supplies of raw material,
including oil up to 1940. At the same time he secured half
Poland. We find that on 28th September, 1939, Molotov and
Ribbentrop issued a joint communique in which they implied

that the continuation of the war was the responsibility of the British and French, now that Poland had been liquidated, and on 30th November Stalin confirmed this analysis of the war in *Pravda* (see p. 94 of this book).

All this in spite of the fact that a few years previously Hitler, in some of his saner moments, had declared that the Communists in Russia were a world menace. But although the Communists—as we shall see in this book—are masters of the strategy and tactics of political warfare, there is no infallible formula for dealing with a lunatic, and it was undoubtedly a great shock to Stalin and his advisers when the warning they received from London that Hitler was about to attack them turned out to be correct.

From that moment the Russians became our gallant allies. The Russian armed forces were gallant, but the régime was a peculiar ally. The position from the British (and American) point of view seemed simple enough. Hitler, the Nazis and the Germans were over-running Europe, and anyone who would fight against these enemies was a friend. Sufficient unto the day was the menace thereof.

The position of the Russians after the treacherous attack by Hitler was more complicated. On the one hand, they were desirous of receiving as much help as possible from the Allies, in order to save Russia (the womb of the world revolution) from conquest by the Nazis. On the other hand, it must also have interested Stalin to observe that a situation had been created by Hitler in which the democracies were doing their utmost to save from destruction the group of men in the Kremlin whose life-task was the elimination of the democracies!

The Russian alliance with the Western Powers was therefore the second reason why men of intelligence in the West failed to realise that Communism was a deep-seated and well established menace to the free way of life. The long record of Russian refusal to co-operate in many different ways culminated in the tremendous Russian diplomatic victory at Yalta and—as we can now see—the farce of the Potsdam Conference. One example will be quoted from many to show how lamb-like and honestly trusting we were with men who were our arch-enemies. We took it for granted that we could rely on free communications between our zone in Berlin and the West.

By 1946–47 a situation had arisen in which it became

increasingly clear, except to those unwilling to recognise unpleasant facts, that the Russian Communists had discarded the ill-fitting masks of co-operation with the democracies and had begun an all-out offensive against the democratic world. Their misuse of the veto in the U.N.; their seizure of power in the East European States; their attempt—frustrated largely by Marshall Aid—to obtain control of France and Italy; their virtual annexation of Eastern Germany; their support of the Chinese and North Koreans in the Korean aggression, are only some of the items in the dossier of evidence in support of the charge that the war has been ON in active form between the Communists and the democracies since 1945.

To-day (1953) a large number of people in the Western world appreciate that the Russian-controlled Communists mean them no good. Even so, there are still large numbers of persons, especially in Great Britain, who hesitate to admit that " we are at war " with the Communists. These doubts are less widespread in the U.S.A., where the bereaved mourn 30,000 dead in the far-off peninsula of Korea : young Americans who would be alive to-day if it were not for the policies of Communism. Nor, it is to be feared, is the tragic chapter of Korea yet at its end. It has become a war of attrition.

In Western Germany, and in general on the continent of Europe, there is a better realisation—for obvious reasons—of the reality of the struggle between West and East. If in Great Britain the whole of the United Kingdom north of a line from the Humber to Bristol was under Communist control directed from Moscow, and if Manchester was cut in half as an isolated island in Communist territory (as is Berlin), the facts of life in this affair would be better realised by the British.

But there is another and more complex reason why the reality of what is going on is only partially understood by sincere and genuine liberal-democratic opinion in the West, and this is due to the great delusion of the day, which is concerned with the word war and its antithesis PEACE.

Words which are the carriers of ideas are perhaps the most powerful instruments ever invented by men, and by this invention Man has signally distinguished himself from the beasts, even if he has on occasions used words to convey ideas which for ferocity and animal-like quality are unmatched in the jungle, But, like all powerful instruments, words can be as great a danger as a blessing, and when they mislead instead of inform, when they seem to mean one thing but in fact mean something else, when they are used with different meanings by different people, much damage can result.

The word WAR has become *a false word*, and this has produced a most dangerous state of affairs in the minds of liberal democrats.

In its original form, " WERRE ", the word meant conflict or strife, and that is what WAR ought to mean. It is of the utmost importance, and absolutely essential to any clear understanding of the present world situation, to grasp the fact that if we attribute to the word WAR its true meaning of conflict or strife, it at once represents a *far more comprehensive idea* than it denotes in the minds of most people.

First, it is necessary to start with the understanding that all action depends upon ideas. Without ideas there can be no action, even as there can be no thunder without lightning. It is worth noting that ignorant people are more frightened of the thunder, which is harmless, than of the lightning, which is dangerous. From this it follows that if one can control men's ideas, the control automatically extends to their actions.

Secondly, it therefore follows that strife or controversy, whether between individuals or groups of persons organised as nations—*i.e.* WAR—must be at bottom a conflict of ideas.

If there is not conflict of ideas there is harmony of ideas, and that is Peace.

If there is conflict of ideas, the conflict or strife—*i.e.* War—will be expressed in some form of action. We can exclude from our argument the case of conflict between individuals (or private war, as the jurists call it), and confine our attention to public wars—*i.e.* conflicts between States or groups of States.

But before we leave the subject of private wars, which were common enough in Western Europe during the early Middle Ages, it is worth noting for future reference that it is a principle of liberal democracy that society forbids unrestricted private wars. Since, however, conflict or strife is inevitable in human society, and indeed has an important value insomuch as progress depends upon the clash of ideas, some method has to be provided in order to restrict private war. This is provided by the LAW (itself a product of parliamentary conflict in democratic countries), and the citizen is obliged to wage his private war, be it against another citizen, a corporation, or even his own State, in the Law Courts. It is the aim of the democratic States to extend this limitation of war into the field of international relationships; hence the International Court at the Hague, and the Judicial Courts attached to the new-supra-national bodies in Europe.

Public wars between sovereign States or groups of States reach their extreme form of violence when military operations begin, for this introduces the dramatic issue of life and death. For several centuries after the rise in Western Europe of the sovereign State, when wars—*i.e.* conflict of ideas—became so acute that physical force was resorted to by the combatants, the military operations were undertaken by a relatively small percentage of the population. There were the professional fighters supplemented by volunteers and/or conscripts in the hour of battle. But as civilisation became more complex, so did the ways and means whereby nations waged war with each other become more complicated, and involved the whole resources of the nation. This state of affairs made new demands upon the overworked word WAR, and so people began to talk of Total War, without realising that it was partially at least a contradiction in terms.

Moreover, because during the 18th and 19th centuries most of the nation sat back and watched their gladiatorial champions die for their country, the word WAR became synonymous with the military operations which were relatively simple, being confined chiefly to battles between armies and navies.

Later on in the 20th century the same error persisted because military operations had now become so frightful and all-embracing that their drama completely obscured the undoubted fact that they were means to an end, and not ends in themselves. But in the 20th century military operations (even with the addition of the air arm) were clearly not the whole story. New terms had to be invented to describe *economic* war; *sabotage* war; and, most curious of all, POLITICAL WAR! This is a curiosity, because the object of political warfare is to change the enemy's mind, and this, as we shall now see, happens to be the object of WAR.

It has already been pointed out that men's actions reflect their ideas and that a conflict or war occurs because of a clash of ideas. Clearly the object of war is to change the enemy's mind and persuade or force him to abandon his ideas and accept those of his opponent. There are two ways of changing a person's mind. One is by persuasion, and the other is by force. The disadvantage of the second method is that there is no certainty about the permanence of a change of mind brought about by force. These two operations can be described as the Battle of the Brains and the Battle of the Bodies.

In the case of the Battle of the Brains, an attempt is made to reason with the enemy, to put our ideas forward as being better than his, to persuade him that it will be better for him if he abandons his ideas and adopts or accepts our own. It is essentially a process of argument, and when an ultimatum is sent from nation A to nation B, the argument for the time being is at an end, since nation A in effect says to nation B, " Accept my ideas or face the consequences of physical violence ".

The Battle of the Bodies is the concern of military operations. In such a case an endeavour is made to inflict so much suffering upon the enemy people by blockade, aerial bombardment and battle casualties that the enemy finds the physical strain intolerable. His resistance collapses.

Action being the consequence of an idea, the enemy's desire to escape further suffering is reflected in the act of surrender. For the moment the victor has imposed his will on his van-quished enemy, but history is littered with examples showing (not surprisingly) that the vanquished, not having been con-verted to the justice of the victor's point of view, begins forth-with to plan revenge.

For example, the First World War (the war to end war) was fought between the allies and the German and Austro-Hungarian Empires in order to prove that " might was not right ". The Treaty of Versailles, signed by the German delegates at the point of a pistol, merely convinced a great many Germans that might obviously was right and the error of the Germans consisted in not having had enough might when they began their aggression in 1914.

A military victory—it is almost superfluous to remark—does not provide any guarantee of peace; the most it can certainly do is to provide an armistice. Moreover, recent experience has shown that the victors in modern military operations are then obliged, owing to the interdependent nature of modern economic society, to spend a lot of time, money and effort restoring the damage they have done to their enemy. Wars (conflict or strife) between national States do not immediately begin with military operations. There is a diplomatic phase, perhaps ushered in by some trivial incident. Notes are exchanged, possibly succeeded or accompanied by non-military hostile actions, such as discriminatory tariffs or the closing of frontiers. This is part of the Battle of Brains, or political warfare as it is sometimes called. Then comes the moment when the first shot is fired, and then a most curious and illogical phenomenon is to be observed. Obviously, the most sensible thing to do is " to win the war " without fighting, since however great may be one's military strength relative to that of the enemy, a shooting war is bound to cause some loss of life and property. But what happens in practice, so far as the democracies are concerned, is that in the period prior to military operation, very little money or effort is spent on political war. On the other hand, as the strife becomes more acute, an increasingly large amount of the national effort is devoted to armaments. Why are not efforts made to change the enemies' ideas *before* these ideas are translated into military action?

For example, round about 1936–37 it became apparent—at any rate to some people, of whom Mr Churchill was the most notable in Britain—that Hitler and the Nazis were becoming a world menace. In successive years Parliament voted increased sums for armaments, but the notion that in, say, 1936 or even 1937 or 1938 a Ministry of Information should be created and given 1% of the revenue devoted to armaments was regarded as ludicrous.

This was not the view of Hitler when he put Dr Goebbels in charge of the Ministry of Press and Propaganda with enormous funds at his disposal. Obviously the ability of the Nazi leaders to carry out their expansionist plans depended upon the support of the mass of the German nation. In order to secure the maintenance of this activity, certain ideas and beliefs had to be rooted in the minds of the Germans. For the small minority not susceptible to the drum-fire treatment of Dr Goebbels via the Press, the radio and the showmanship of the Nazi rallies, anti-Semitism, chauvinistic patriotism, etc., etc., there was the concentration camp. Particular attention was, of course, paid to the youth, the citizens of to-morrow.

It never appears to have occurred to anyone in authority that the existence of Dr Goebbels and all his works, and the important place he and they held in the Nazi programme, revealed with startling clarity to anyone who could think clearly that the chink in the Nazi armour was the relationship between the group of gangsters and the mass of the German people (who were no better nor worse than any other national mass of 70,000,000), without whose willing support the Nazis were nothing. As this was true—and it cannot be denied that it was true—the threatened democracies should have devoted a great deal of time, trouble and (say) £50,000,000 a year to driving a wedge in the field of ideas between the Nazis and the Germans.

What in fact happened was almost exactly the reverse. In the years immediately preceding 1939, when a few heroic Germans were resisting Hitler and being tortured in the concentration camps such as Buchenwald, British Ministers would get up and make speeches saying that the pogroms against the Jews were deplorable, that the concentration camps were really most unfortunate, but after all " it was not our business what a government did within its own frontiers ". Events were to prove that such statements were as idiotic as they were immoral and undemocratic.

Just as disease cannot be confined to territories arbitrarily defined by man, so tyranny in one part of the world cannot be isolated morally or physically from the rest of humanity, as the developments of modern science cause the world to shrink in terms of Time and space. Litvinov said that peace was indivisible; Stalin has taken the Soviet Union out of the World Health Organization and sabotaged the United Nations. Liberal democracy should know no frontiers.

I have summarised the lessons of the past; now for the present and the future.

We, and by that word is meant all men, wherever they live, who believe in the freedoms, are engaged to-day in a desperate and epoch-making struggle with the most ruthless, highly organised and powerful conspiracy against freedom which has ever darkened the pages of human history. It is of the first importance to understand that this vast conspiracy cannot be defeated by military force, although such force, as we shall see, has a place in our defences. The reasons for the inability of physical force to do the job are as follows:

B

(*a*) All the indications are that if, for one reason or another, the Western world and its enemies became involved in a third world war, the destruction and chaos which would result from this event would be so enormous that military victory by the Western Powers would be meaningless in a positive sense. There would be no room for freedoms or liberty in a western Europe devastated by atomic warfare. This, of course, is a speculation, but hard to dismiss as likely to be wrong. Modern developments in military warfare, and the hydrogen bomb is now more than a nightmare, are such that the means will destroy the ends.

(*b*) As already explained, one idea can only be decisively defeated by another idea.

What, then, is the rôle of force in all this affair? As we shall see in this book, the armed forces of the Soviet Union and its satellites play an important part in the whole vast conspiracy. They may even be used, as in Korea and in Greece, to hot up the cold war in certain chosen localities. But their main purpose would appear to be: First, to oblige the Western Powers to re-arm, and thus strain their economies; second, to act as a menace which can always move in to any part of the Western world in which, by the various methods described in this book, a successful revolution has been engineered. Finally, there is always the possibility that for one of several reasons the Soviet Union might decide to try to over-run the West by a large-scale attack. Such reasons might be a need for an external adventure in order to distract attention from weaknesses and dissatisfactions on the home front, or a belief on the part of the men in the Kremlin that an attack on the West would be a " push-over ". From these considerations we can deduce the rôle of armed force from the point of view of the democracies.

Its purpose is to act as a deterrent in case the Soviet Union be tempted to abandon what appears to be its chosen strategy of victory through political warfare.

In short, the main rôle of the Western defence forces is to gain time, with the subsidiary rôle of demonstrating that force will be met by force.

But to gain time can be a barren achievement unless something constructive is done in the time which is gained.

The use which should be made of the time which has been

gained since 1945 is the overthrow of Communism by political warfare methods. This is the only form of victory which will be decisive, and it is the only form of offensive which can be deployed against the special type of aggression being practised by this vast conspiracy.

The statement made above usually produces the question: " Yes, but how does one do it? "

This is a question of tactics, and usually indicates that the enquirer does not understand the difference between strategy and tactics. For at least fifteen years the author has endeavoured to bring home to anyone who would read or listen to him the vital importance of the Battle of Ideas. Others have been doing the same thing, and a little progress has been made, but it is apparent that before informed public opinion in the Western world can be persuaded to give serious attention to positive action on the part of democracy in the ideological battle with Communism, it must be better informed than it is at present about the nature of the menace which must be overthrown.

It is therefore NOT the purpose of this book to describe the measures required to put in motion a democratic movement of a positive character against Communism.

It is the purpose of this book to analyse and expose the nature and machinations of the conspiracy which must be defeated. This book is an *unmasking* operation and, as the reader will discover, most of its contents come from what the Communists say about themselves.

When the truths in this book are common property, then we shall have accomplished the first step in the renaissance of democracy and its awakening from apathy. Then thoughtful men and women will perhaps begin to realise that Peace can only be achieved through a passionate and sincere effort to make world-wide the practices and principles of liberal democracy.

It may, however, be appropriate to remark here that those who conceive of such a movement as an organised campaign doing through some cut-and-dried plan or blue-print for democracy what the Communists do for their creed are approaching dangerous territory with totalitarian frontiers. Perhaps it is even dangerous to use the word " movement ", lest it conjure up visions of too much planning of freedom. Finally, a word of warning to and condemnation of all those who in the belief that they are fighting Communism attempt to restrict the free expression of opinion. Such behaviour is the mark of an enemy of democracy.

I am indebted to Mr Carew Hunt for some valuable help and criticism in connection with certain passages and to Miss Ann King-Hall for many useful suggestions which were adopted, and to Mr R. E. Thompson for the index.

STEPHEN KING-HALL

January 21, 1953.

CHAPTER I

THE SAFETY OF THE DEMOCRATIC STATE

WE are living in a period in human history marked by a world-wide controversy popularly known as the cold war. It is a conflict between groups of States, one group being adherents to the democratic or free way of life; the other representing a totalitarian theory of the relation between the individual and the State.

The purpose of the democratic State is that of providing a framework within which the individual can express his or her personality to the fullest extent. This type of State is by definition a means to an end. The totalitarian State is an end in itself; the citizens in such States are the means to the end. The safety of both types of State is liable to be jeopardised by internal and external factors.

As regards the internal factors, the democratic State is perpetually having to grapple with the problem of how to combine a proper regard and priority for the essential freedoms whose exercise it is the function and *raison d'être* of this kind of State to promote and preserve, and the inescapable fact that, for a variety of reasons, of which probably the chief is the complexity of modern civilisation in its technical manifestations, the State is obliged to intervene to an ever-increasing degree in social and economic life.

Politicians may shout aloud that it is their purpose (if elected) to set the people free from the irritating mass of controls and regulations within which the individual citizen resembles the chrysalis in a cocoon, but the individual often finds that the inconveniences of some freedoms outweigh their theoretical advantages.

A simple example will illustrate this point. The traveller by road in a motor car in a modern State is subject to a series of controls (licences, driving tests, highway code, traffic signals, roundabouts, speed limits, one-way routes, signs and directions, compulsory third-party insurance, etc., etc.) which would have been incomprehensible to the man of 1880, but even with the controls of 1952 the death rate on the roads increases and movement becomes more difficult. The only rational answer to this problem is the construction of special motor roads to which long-distance traffic would be compulsorily directed.

The totalitarian State is menaced by an internal danger of a different character. It may be supposed that men and women in such States also find modern controls irksome, but these people suffer from the additional and fundamental master-control of ideas. Democratic peoples are allowed to say what they think about controls; they may express the opinion that some controls are needless or are being inefficiently operated by one set of people who should be replaced by an alternative collection of politicians. More than this, the democratic citizens can give practical effect to their opinion. In the totalitarian State this privilege of criticism is severely limited—although it is significant that it has to be permitted, and may even be encouraged, within limits. These limits are reached should any suggestion be made that a change of régime might be desirable.

One may generalise with reasonable accuracy by saying that in a totalitarian State the troops (citizens) may voice their opinion at company and possibly battalion level on matters of detail, but any criticism of the strategy or high command is a mortal sin.

It is a belief at the very centre of the democratic creed that MAN the individual is by nature a freedom-loving creature and has a desire to express his personality.

It is argued by some that this is not so, or for example that if human beings are from youth onwards subjected to rigid controls designed to canalise their thoughts in one direction, they will not wish to express any other opinion. It is argued, for instance, that to-day beyond the Iron Curtain a generation is growing up which, never having experienced democracy, will not want it, and will remain happily within the mental strait-jacket prescribed by the Communist Party.

The facts seem to disprove this theory, since it can easily be proved that one of the obvious characteristics of the totalitarian State is the extraordinary and elaborate measures taken by the dictators to prevent the people having access to uncensored information, coupled with an enormous output of prejudiced propaganda. The opinion sometimes expressed to the effect that " dictators do not have to bother about public opinion " is the exact opposite of the truth. They bother about it a great deal, and spend very large sums of money and an enormous amount of time (with punishments in the background) in order to control the opinions of their victims.

Why do they bother so much about public opinion? It is not unreasonable to suppose that they are concerned with this question because they know that if it were left free, public opinion would manifest the normal critical faculties of MAN the democratic creature.

Turning now to the external factors which menace the security of each type of State, the position is as follows.

The totalitarian State is menaced by the " danger " that its people will hear the truth from without. But a totalitarian State is not menaced by physical attack from a democratic State (although it may be expected to say it is thus menaced) because a democratic State which launches an aggressive military operation against a totalitarian State (or another democratic State) is simply not being true to its own principles. For instance, there is to-day a fairly wide measure of agreement that the Boer War in 1899 lacked much justification from a democratic point of view, even if, looked at from the British standpoint, the provocation may have been considerable. This war was, in the opinion of the author, the end of an era in British policy (so-called Imperialist), and since that date the British have certainly anchored their policy to the principle that the relationships between sovereign States should be governed by due processes of law and that military operations are only justified as sanctions against the aggressive inter-national law-breaker.

The external menace to the democratic State is under no such restraints. Indeed, history is full of examples in which tyranny, in order to justify its existence, has indulged in foreign adventures. These general observations are introductory to an examination of the dangers facing the free States of to-day from the principal despotism now in existence, which is the government of the Soviet Union.

Concerning this despotism it should be noted that the modern totalitarian State, in which the ruling party identifies itself *with* the State, is, as Mr Plamenatz has written, " the creation of the Bolsheviks. Mussolini and Hitler were imitators." Although in theory one of the ultimate objects of

Communism is that " the state shall wither away ", it is a plain statement of fact that during the three decades of its existence the Russian Communist State has shown no signs of withering, or even liberalising itself. Compared to Stalin, Lenin was quite a democrat, though he said in 1917 : " The State is indispensable to the proletariat, not to ensure the freedom of the people but solely to ensure the destruction of their enemies."

The dangers menacing the democratic States can best be considered under two headings. The first of these is the use of force by the Soviet Union. It is the responsibility of the Governments of free States which have the best information at their disposal to assess this risk, tell the people of the danger and call upon them to support the measures necessary to provide sufficient force to deter the aggressor.

In a democracy the final responsibility for security against straightforward military aggression lies upon the shoulders of the electorate, provided the Government has given them the facts and taken the necessary measures against sabotage and subversive actions of a type which fall within the category of underground military operations. It is, however, in the nature of things that free men are disinclined to make the effort and sacrifices for defence against aggression, since such sacrifices impinge upon the normalities of a peaceful life. This fact—which can be used as a proof of the fundamentally peaceful nature of free men if they are not incited otherwise by appeals to fear, and perhaps cupidity—leads to the second aspect of the danger we are considering.

In a free society, in which the people through the right to vote, a free Press and freedom of speech and discussion have a power to control the general policy and the particular acts of their Government, the very breadth of their freedom and the diversity of viewpoints make it all the more difficult for them to make the right decision. The wrong decision may be as fatal as the victorious advance of an invading army.

Public opinion upon political issues, trade union affairs and matters of general public interest is not determined by equal contributions to the general viewpoint. Life is too complicated and too short for each single man and woman to examine all the evidence and all sources of opinion before making up his or her mind.

Much of our thinking is partially done for us by those whose opinions we trust and whose guidance and leadership we respect. Yet, in a free society, when it comes to the vote or the crucial decision, the opinion of each one counts equally, no matter whence that opinion came. So we have the apparent paradox that the people who take the decisions which govern their lives are many, and those who furnish the evidence and the advice are comparatively few.

This fact can be a grave danger to the freedom and independence of the State. A free society solves its problems by ensuring that all opinions, however contradictory, are permitted to find expression; but it also relies on the integrity of the originators of opinion, supported by the good sense and maturity of the vast mass of ordinary people.

The most effective way to ensure control of a community is to control the sources of knowledge and the moulders of opinion; thus the first steps towards dictatorship are control of the Press, broadcasting, films and education, the imposition of censorship, control of the police, control of the trade unions and, as far as possible, of the Church.

But in a free society these are all activities which are jealously kept outside Government control, or if, as in the case of education, they are within the purview of the Government, their independence is jealously watched over and guarded by all parties in the State. Therefore, if a dictatorship wishes to destroy a free society, *it must contrive to insert its agents in those key positions in the community which are outside Government control but are answerable to public opinion alone.* Naturally if they can be infiltrated into the Government or its administrative machine, so much the better, but this is not necessary for the success of the early stages of the operation.

The obstacles in the way of such an operation are formidable. By definition, free society is bitterly opposed to despotism, and is therefore going to resist any attempt of which it is conscious to bring it under the control of a despot, be he foreign or domestic.

How, then, is a free society to be captured through what we have described as the second aspect of its danger : the influence upon the body politic of the free State of persons who will rot it from within?

CHAPTER II

AGGRESSION FROM WITHIN—OR " PEACEFUL " AGGRESSION

IF the Government of a totalitarian State decides to establish its control over another State, it is unlikely openly to declare its intention, even if in the last resort it intends to use military force. In modern times no dictator will bluntly inform his own people that he proposes to undertake an act of naked aggression in the course of which casualties may be expected, and not only on one side.

The operation must be called something else, and in the case we are considering, in which a totalitarian State endeavours to exploit the nature of democracy in order to destroy democracy, it is essential that important parts of the operation be entrusted to nationals of the State to be controlled. Another way of looking at this operation is to regard it as an attempt to hypnotise a democracy into destroying itself.

These agents must first be recruited. But there is a universal prejudice against those persons who deliberately, out of conviction or for money, assist an enemy to achieve his aims. They are normally known as traitors, and their influence upon public opinion is extensive, but unfavourable. Such agents have therefore to be presented in a different guise; and the task they are called upon to perform has to be explained in different terms.

The task confronting these agents is complicated, so that there has to be a considerable subdivision of functions between them.

At the centre there must be a directing body, devising the local tactics and methods of operation in the light of the instructions it receives. The members of this body have several functions. They must present the Power they are serving as a peace-loving friend of all nations, and interpret its policy and actions in a friendly and favourable light. They must insert themselves or persons they can control in those relatively few positions in the community which can be most influential in moulding public opinion.

These agents must exploit the positions they have won, in political, Press, trade union and other circles, in order to lead public opinion in the direction required by the Government whom they are secretly serving. Since by definition the interests of the community in which they are operating conflict with those of the State whose agents they are, it follows that an elaborate scheme of deception is necessary. Whatever they do or say has to be portrayed as serving the interest of the community they seek to influence, and any prejudice, special interest or trend of opinion must be exploited for this purpose.

The other side of this manœuvre is to spread confusion and doubt about the existing policies of the elected Government and uncertainty about the structure and the foundations of the community, in order that whatever alternative they profess to offer shall appear the more attractive. The more genuine grievances they can exploit the easier their task becomes.

The difficulty that only a handful of citizens in any community are prepared consciously to lend themselves to such a task can partly be circumvented by the exploitation of misplaced idealism, fanaticism and the desire to serve; but it is unlikely that enough persons can be found for the vast task to be done. Some link, therefore, has to be found between these agents and the great mass of the general public. " Fellow-travellers " are necessary.

The link is created by the skill of the agents in selecting certain aspects of what they are doing, and presenting these matters—which in themselves and in isolation may seem harmless—to men of known integrity, respected and eminent in some walk of life, in such a way that these men will lend their co-operation.

The aspect chosen may be " peace " or " racialism ", displayed in such a manner that it makes an appeal to a person who would be repelled if he realised that the policy which attracts him is only part of a vast conspiracy.

By this time the whole subversive manœuvre has become so complicated that only those who study it as a whole can realise its true aim and method. The general public, having neither time nor inclination to study in detail so confusing and cunning a jigsaw, form superficial and possibly mistaken opinions about it in the light of whatever evidence is presented to them. If the situation is allowed to develop unchecked, it becomes a relatively simple matter, in a climate of benevolent public opinion, to recruit new members for the movement and lead public opinion gently towards accepting more and more completely the objectives of the aggressive State.

The point is then reached where public opinion exerts more and more pressure on its Government to pursue policies sympathetic to those of the aggressor until ultimately a mixture of fear and uncertainty, plus acceptance of the blandishments and arguments offered, leave the way clear for a change of Government, and its replacement by one totally subservient to the aggressor.

This is a straightforward simplified account of how an operation of political warfare can be conducted in such a way as to achieve a bloodless revolution without publicly observed foreign intervention, and without resort to force. It is safe to say that any member of a free society who studied this account and was then asked whether he would like to see such things happen in his own country, would reply emphatically that he would not.

Nevertheless, such things have happened: free societies have let themselves be rotted from within and brought under foreign despotic domination.

Put in more popular language, the policy of " appeasement ", when stimulated from within the democracy by the agents of the aggressor, has paid substantial dividends—from the point of view of the aggressor. Moreover, what makes the situation so confusing is that the appeasers are not in the mass the conscious agents of the aggressor. They are the tools of a few people and the victims of their own wishful thinking.

Now, to anyone who has read this far it may be apparent that it is outrageous and absurd that a free community should allow itself to be thus destroyed. The campaign against it would be defeated if the facts were sufficiently well known and the consequences adequately appreciated. Therefore some conditions must be fulfilled if the plot is to succeed.

First acts likely to be regarded as aggressive must be given a convincing justification. They must appear to be serving high interests, and to be benefiting the greater part of humanity.

Second, the explanation given for the policy of aggression must exploit certain universal and praiseworthy human instincts —idealism, hope for the future, love of service. There is no need for the " message " to have much foundation in fact, provided that means can be found for creating an atmosphere of enthusiasm which can be exploited to influence and deceive others.

Next, inevitable weaknesses and shortcomings of human society must be exaggerated in propaganda and if possible made worse by political and diplomatic action. Potential opposition to the operation will thus be disunited, and incapable of collective action against aggression.

By these means the true nature of the aggressor will be concealed from those it is sought to conquer by persuasion. An elaborate façade of deception will be built up, so that only trusted agents or those who can be relied upon to be deceived ever have the chance to see behind the real structure.

The campaign will be helped if the fact can be glossed over that the parties concerned—the aggressor and his victim—are individual States. Once they are seen in this light, aggression becomes obvious. Therefore, the sinister operation must be presented as a local manifestation of a world-wide event transcending national frontiers. Or, failing that, the aggressor must appear as the agent of a world-wide movement serving the true interests even of its potential victims.

An account as to how this psychological assault operates is to be found in the second interim report of the Canadian Royal Commission (15th March, 1946), which investigated the Gouzenko case. This man, the Soviet Military Attaché in Ottawa, had the duty of organising a group of spies in order to obtain information about the atom bomb. It was done through members of the local Communist Party, and the Royal Commission reported *inter alia*:—

> ". . . the evidence has revealed the existence of an organisation constituting at least a threat to the safety and interests of the State, as evidenced by the fact that some witnesses holding strategic positions have made the significant statement under oath that they had a loyalty which took priority over the loyalty owed by them to their country and for that reason they acted as they did and would unquestionably have continued so to act had they not been detected . . ."

Explaining the developments of this loyalty the Royal Commission stated (Section II 6 (*b*) of its Report):—

> ". . . in the great majority of cases the motivation [of agents] was inextricably linked with courses of psychological development . . . These secret ' development ' courses are very much more widespread than the espionage

network itself . . . the Canadian members of the espionage
network themselves took an active part in directing and
furthering such courses for other Canadians, which were
calculated to allow them to draw suitable ' developed '
persons later into active participation and thus to expand
the network itself.

" It has been established, for example, that Sam Carr
and Fred Rose, M.P., both Moscow-trained, not only
designated Canadians for recruiting into the espionage ring,
but took an active part in fostering the courses or study
courses wherein suitable motivation for espionage was
gradually developed. . . ."

Later in the same section of its report the Royal Commission
states :—

". . . a sense of internationalism seems in many cases to
play a definite rôle in one stage of the [development]
courses. In these courses the Canadian sympathiser is first
encouraged to develop a sense of loyalty not directly to a
foreign State but to what he conceives to be an international ideal . . ."

II

In addition to all these dark and subtle manœuvrings in the
realm of men's minds the aggressor must have physical force.
There must be armies waiting near the frontiers of the intended
victim, and air forces near enough to bomb him, in order to
ensure that fear and intimidation can exercise the decisive
influence on the political scene and in order that, should the
moment and the circumstances appear propitious, a direct act
of military aggression may be launched.

At home the aggressor Government must also be prepared to
threaten the use of force. It has to take quick decisions without
regard to the interests or wishes of its people, who must therefore
be controlled by force, according to the well-known pattern of
police States. Finally, the aggressor's agents serving abroad
must be subjected to equally rigid discipline, for which purpose
the threat must be held over them of savage penalties forcibly
imposed, both upon themselves and their dependants and
relatives.

But even if all these conditions are satisfied, the aggressor can
only succeed if there is in the victim State a climate of public

opinion which is so tolerant, indifferent and easily deceived that when it awakens to the danger it is already too late.

Modern history provides us with at least one classic example of this type of operation by an aggressor State to impose its will on its neighbours. The political achievements of the Nazi régime in Germany started with the occupation of the Rhineland and ended with the total subjugation of Czechoslovakia. Then came the gamble of open aggression against Poland.

In many respects it was an unsatisfactory political campaign, since, although most of the other conditions were sufficiently met, the basic appeal—namely, justice to rectify the wrongs of Versailles—was too blatantly associated with German nationalism, and the threat of force was too openly displayed.

Nevertheless, the Nazi campaign succeeded to the extent that it created a situation in which the prospective victims in Britain and France found, to their shocked alarm, that they were faced with the choice of fighting for their existence or being the clients of the Nazi Empire. From 1936 to 1939 Mr Churchill on the Parliamentary platform and in the press together with others of lesser influence, including the author in his weekly *News-Letter*, endeavoured in vain to arouse the British people to the mortal danger gathering around them. If Mr Churchill persistently and eloquently drew attention to the plain evidence of the growth of the Nazi armaments, the author and his friends endeavoured to concentrate in the *News-Letter* upon the fact that a compromise, other than an uneasy armistice, between the Nazis and the Democracies was theoretically and practically impossible, if the Democracies intended to remain Democracies and if Hitler and his Nazis *meant what they said*.

Hitler in his *Mein Kampf*, which was elevated amongst the Nazis to that status of holy writ now enjoyed by the works of Lenin and Stalin so far as Communists are concerned, said in unmistakable if turgid language what Nazism was and what it intended to do.

Was he speaking the truth as he saw it—or romancing? Was *Mein Kampf* a political programme ostensibly based on a mass of nonsense disguised as philosophy and absurd anthropological theories, or was it the outpourings of an irresponsible lunatic?

Events showed that it was both, but the lunatic controlled the resources of the German nation.

If as late as 1936, *Mein Kampf* had been taken seriously by the Democracies World War II could have been prevented.

A question of far greater interest and importance to-day, and one to which an answer must be found, is whether the policy of the Soviet Government from 1917 to the present day conforms to the pattern of aggression outlined in this chapter.

This question is far too serious in its implication for the entire world to be decided on a basis of ignorance, prejudice and sentimental attachments that have survived from 1917. It is essential to ascertain the facts, weigh the evidence and then decide which is the correct interpretation of the aims and the methods of the Soviet Government.

CHAPTER III

RUSSIAN POLICY—IS IT " PEACEFUL " AGGRESSION?

IN the preceding chapter we analysed the technique of aggression without direct military operations: the technique of destroying democracy from within; of using some of the principles and practices of democracy to make democracy destroy itself—a technique of implanting, as it were, a cancer growth in the body politic of a democratic State.

In this third chapter we shall relate theory to practice, and see whether the facts about Soviet policy are such that they justify any reasonable person in declaring that the Soviet Union is devoted to an aggressive policy of this kind against the democratic world.

What are the facts about the Soviet Union and its foreign policy? Where are they to be found?

There are obvious difficulties in the quest for truth in this matter. The present conflict is not only between the Soviet Government and the non-Communist world; it is between the Communist doctrine as now interpreted and exemplified by the Soviet Government, and the whole mass of non-Communist creeds, opinions, philosophies and systems which together comprise the free world.

The Communists have always shown themselves willing to use falsehood and misrepresentation as a political weapon. Also, the Soviet Government has so shut itself off from the free world that the true facts about its domestic policy and situation and about its attitude to the non-Communist world are very hard to discover. We have, therefore, to seek sources of knowledge which are not tainted.

We have four sources of information: the statements of theory and policy made by the Soviet leaders themselves; the constitution, laws, edicts and acts of the U.S.S.R.; the evidence, after every possible attempt has been made to eliminate inaccuracy and bias, of those who have known the Soviet Union and experienced its system of government at first hand; there is also the evidence of a general character provided by the observed behaviour of the Soviet Government in world affairs.

Another possible source—statements by Communists about Russia—has to be treated with the utmost reserve, since they have a vested interest in the Soviet propaganda version.

Using these sources of information, this book contains some of the evidence which is available to anyone who has the time and patience to collect it. The evidence has been analysed, and this analysis has led to certain conclusions, which will be stated. If they are correct, or even partially correct, their implications for the modern world are formidable and far-reaching.

In considering what follows in these pages it must be remembered that the evidence is being added to every day, and therefore no book on this subject can be completely up to date.

Secondly, it is dangerous and self-deceiving to pay too much attention to any piece of evidence in isolation. For example, Mr Stalin has in the past given interviews to journalists in which he has made conciliatory and not unreasonable statements; a few months later Soviet action (whether it was the blockade of Berlin, or the instigation of the Korean aggression, etc.) has revealed that whatever tactical retreats may from time to time be considered advisable, the main strategical advance towards an objective which, as we shall see, is world wide extension of Communism, remains the policy of the men in the Kremlin.

II

A vital requirement of the campaign of aggression of the type we are considering is, as we have remarked on page 7, a plausible motive to conceal the truly aggressive aim. The Soviet Government long enjoyed, and in certain quarters is still enjoying, the advantages of the confusion caused by the fact that the October Revolution was a *Communist* revolution, and that its theoretical origins are to be found in the writings of Karl Marx.

The Russian revolution was the first practical application of ideals which had long animated progressive elements in Western Europe: the overthrow of oppressors, justice and economic freedom for all, and a dominant position in the State for the working classes.

Let it be agreed that those who engineered the revolution and those who sympathised with and supported them from outside

Russia were in many cases animated by the highest ideals. Let us remember also that even at that time most people outside Russia tended to contrast the Bolshevik régime with that of the Tsars, and to ignore the confused and incompetent, yet genuine and promising democracy which ruled from February to October, 1917, and which was the régime which the Bolsheviks actually overthrew.

Marxism, even in the early Leninist form, though committed to dictatorial methods, retained many of the traits of the radical egalitarian and internationalist conceptions of democracy out of which it had originally developed. But these ideas have been replaced by the use and the threat of force to impose progressively less democratic policies, except for brief periods of tactical retreat, ever since the Communist party secured control of the Russian State.

The predicted revolutions outside Russia did not take place, and what appeared at first to be a wonderful experiment, the forerunner of similar revolutions on a world-wide scale, became eventually a narrowly nationalistic movement. Nevertheless, out of the confusion of the times there has survived in the free world a body of opinion well disposed towards Russia, towards her revolution and towards those who were apparently trying to build a new social structure.

But the structure of the society which emerged in Russia is not new at all. The dictator surrounded by his bodyguard, the privileged few whose lives depend on their loyalty, the regimented masses, the aggressive foreign policy—this is a very ancient pattern.

One of the tragedies of to-day is that there still survive sincere and idealistic men and women who, in many countries, because they cling to an illusion which destroyed itself thirty years ago, look benevolently upon or actively support the state which is working for the destruction of all that they value.

The scientist who sets himself above the law because he thinks he is serving humanity when he is merely bolstering up the inhumanity of Russia; the economist who believes that there is a world of economics in which co-operation with Russia divorced from all political and human reality is possible; the pacifist who allows his love of peace to serve Soviet aggression; and, perhaps most tragic of all, the religious man who sacrifices his intellectual integrity lest it should lay bare to him his service to the cause of evil—all these men, because their judgment has been lost in an old illusion, are now dedicated to a cause which is fast destroying, in all the territories which it controls, all that the hope of true progress offers to humanity.

For example, in 1952 a man like Professor Day Lewis (Professor of Poetry at Oxford) wrote that he and his fellow signatories of the Authors' World Peace Appeal were convinced that " different political systems can live peaceably side by side ". This intelligent and well-meaning man appears to be capable of closing his eyes, ears and mind to the fact that the object of Communism is, by the nature of Communism, to destroy all other systems !

Mercifully the victims of this deception are few, but they are pathetic, for the spectacle of idealistic men innocently (for many of them are in the last analysis innocent, even if their ignorance is wilful) and eagerly working to destroy not themselves but the things they believe in, should excite no feelings of hatred or contempt, but only pity.

But, leaving aside all questions of ethics, it is clear that revolutionary motive, genuine or false, provided in the years after the First World War the perfect motive for aggression—regardless of whether that aggression was to be committed by a nation bent on destroying other nations or by a revolutionary force attacking established evils everywhere.

The organisers of the attempt at world revolution were able to invoke enthusiasm, idealism, instinct for change and human betterment, for service in a noble cause serving the interest of the many against the privileged few. Also, since it offered the prospect of one world in which artificial differences between nations ceased to exist, and since wars are fought between nations, it offered the prospect of universal peace.

Not only the aims but the methods to be employed could readily obtain approval and support from many persons outside the Soviet Union who accept the general validity of Marxian doctrine while others to whom revolutionary methods were abhorrent could perhaps be mollified by an appeal to the long-term aims and the larger idealism of the movement.

If, therefore, the Government which finally seized power in Russia after the October Revolution genuinely sought to help the proletariat of the world to set up its dictatorship all over the world, then it deserved the support of all who were prepared to accept dictatorship, with all that it implies, as their form of Government, and as a means to a desirable end.

And this support would still be available if the aims of the Soviet Government were later to become nationalist, imperialist and aggressive, provided that it succeeded in deceiving its foreign supporters into believing that they were still supporting some worthy and idealistic aim.

Whatever happened, however, it was obviously in the Soviet Communist interest to hold before the world the revolutionary ideal and all the ideas associated with it, either in a mood of crusading fervour or calculated cynicism. What is clear is that the first requirement for aggression without war—namely, a plausible motive—is present in the Russian case. The vast conspiracy can almost be called a holy vocation.

The second requirement for political aggression is an effective method to be conducted ostensibly by nationals of the potential victim. For this purpose the revolutionary ideas of world Communism have proved to be perfectly suited.

In recruiting traitors it is wise not to use the unpleasant word treachery; if what is required of them can be presented as service in the true interest of their country and the world, so much the better. Those who are actuated by genuine humanitarian and social ideals, provided that they know nothing of Communism in practice, make promising recruits. But there are many others as well; the idea of belonging to a revolutionary movement, often operating illegally in dangerous circumstances, appeals to schoolboy instincts which not everyone outgrows. The attack upon the existing fabric of society appeals to those who, often starting from genuinely idealistic viewpoints, for moral or other reasons find themselves misfits or outcasts from society. The respect for violence and calculated indifference to the elementary rules of humanity appeal to the bully, the sadist and the worshipper of force, who can as well become Fascist or Nazi as a member of the Communist Party, and the pseudo-scientific approach of Communism to everyday problems appeals to those scientists whose professional integrity is weaker than the particular set of motives which draw them personally towards Communism.

There are, therefore, many fields of recruitment for potential traitors to serve the operation.

III

In the devising of a workable procedure for the operation, the tactics advised and set out by Lenin are quite explicit, and valid either for world revolution or for imperialist aggression. The spearhead for the overthrow of the existing structure of society must be the Communist Party. This party must receive its instructions from Moscow, either as the capital of the aggressor Government or as the directing centre of the world revolution.

Its functions—to present Soviet policy in a favourable light, to infiltrate into positions of importance and responsibility, and to bring public opinion to take a favourable view of the Soviet Union—require much skill and ingenuity. For not only do most people reject the revolutionary aims and methods as described by the Soviet Government, but they also view with grave suspicion the policies of the Soviet Government as a State towards other States.

The tactics described by Lenin for meeting this difficulty are, briefly, that any method is permissible in order to achieve the desired end, the moral explanation given being that the end is so desirable that any means of achieving it are justifiable. His actual words were:—

> "We must be able to resort to all sorts of stratagems, manœuvres, illegal methods, evasions and subterfuges only so as to get into the trade unions, to remain in them, and to carry on Communist work within them at all costs." *

The policy laid down in these words, written in 1920, has been carried out with pertinacity and no little success, especially in France and Italy.

The Communist aim is that penetration of the trade unions should be followed by the unity of all workers in a single Communist controlled organisation. They attempt to achieve this by constant appeals to the workers to form alliances. For instance, the General Council of the Communist dominated World Federation of Trade Unions, at its meeting in Berlin in November, 1951, adopted a resolution which stressed the importance of united action and suggested that trade-union organisations should set up " united action committees " in factories as well as " trade union co-ordination committees ". At the same

---

* Lenin: *Collected Works*, Vol. 25, p. 198, 3rd Russian edition.

meeting it was made clear that in order to attain such unity of action it was necessary to win over workers of different affiliations; one way of achieving this was *not* to insist that they should adopt the entire W.F.T.U. programme if there were points with which they disagreed. The application of this technique can be traced in international and national trade-union organisations.

When the Germans left Eastern Europe the régimes installed by the Red Army were, to a large extent, controlled by local Communists, or Communists of local origin, who had been trained in Moscow. In the same way the Communists were able to take control of the trade unions, either at once or within a short period. Where complete control could not be established at once, or where the workers attempted to offer resistance to that control, it was forcibly imposed by police terror and these methods were made the more effective by barring the secret ballot in trade union elections, so that each worker who tried to vote anti-Communist could immediately be identified.

The rôle of the trade unions as a body for conveying Government instructions and requirements to the working classes is basic in Soviet doctrine. This doctrine is now obligatory in the satellite States. The Hungarian paper *Nepszava* on 25th February, 1949, announced measures " to create the organisational conditions ensuring the Party a leading rôle in every branch of trade union activity in the factories, alike in the general direction and in questions of detail ".

The rôle of the trade unions in the Communist States is no longer to protect their membership, but to carry into effect the decisions of the ruling party. The overriding points for a Communist trade union are: (i) output must be raised at all costs in the interests of the State Plan; and (ii) labour discipline must be tightened. All other considerations are subordinate to these. The Communist leaders have never disguised their intention of using the trade unions as a means of riveting the control of the Party on the mass of the workers.

It is abundantly clear that in the Communist-controlled countries the trades unions are merely the instruments of the Communist Party.

At this point it is proper to pay tribute to the zeal and attention which the Communist crusader pays to the business of his cause. It is notorious that—for example—in the British trade union movement the relatively small number of active Communists exercise an influence out of all proportion to their numbers. They do this because they are prepared to work to obtain key positions in the branches, and when other members go home or are too lazy to attend meetings, the hard working Communists capture the machine. It is also right to say that the Communist shop steward or unionist is often notable for his zeal in attending to the personal difficulties of his fellow-members. In the same way the Communists in France were often very active in the Resistance movement. A British officer who used to be parachuted into France during the war told the author that in a Resistance group he could always be sure that the Communists in it were waiting with a well thought out plan.

As with the trade unions, so, of course, with all other institutions in a free community, as the following quotations show:—

"Communism rejects parliamentarianism as the form of the future; it rejects it as a form of the Class Dictatorship of the Proletariat; it rejects the possibility of winning over the parliaments; its fixed aim is to destroy parliamentarianism.

"Therefore, there can be a question only of utilising bourgeois State institutions with the object of destroying them . . .

"The Communist Party enters such [bourgeois government] institutions not in order to do constructive work, but in order to direct the masses to destroy from within the whole bourgeois State machine and Parliament itself. *

"To a revolutionary, on the contrary, the main thing is revolutionary work and not reforms; to him reforms are by-products of the revolution. That is why, with revolutionary tactics under the bourgeois régime, reforms are naturally transformed into instruments for disintegrating this régime, into instruments for strengthening the revolution, into a base for the further development of the revolutionary movement.

"The revolutionary will accept a reform in order to use it as an aid in combining legal work with illegal work, to intensify, under its cover, the illegal work for the revolu-

* "The Communist Party and Parliamentarianism" (Theses adopted at Second Congress of Communist International). *Theses and Statutes of Communist International*, New York Central Committee of Communist Party of America, 1921.

tionary preparations of the masses for the overthrow of the bourgeoisie.

" *This* is what making revolutionary use of reforms and agreements under the conditions of imperialism means." *

The political history since 1945 in all the countries now beyond the Iron Curtain contains the familiar feature of the Communist Party first coalescing with the Socialists and others, usually with a Communist in the Cabinet in the key position of Minister of the Interior. From this internal position the Communists then extend their power until the day when their erstwhile colleagues find themselves on trial as traitors and enemies of the people.

In other words, a workable technique for damaging and overthrowing the State through an agency operated from Moscow was evolved through the employment of national Communist Parties. These facts are not disputed by the Communists, who merely differ in giving them the rather different description of " furthering the aims of world revolution ".

They cannot very well dispute the official statements of the Soviet Government, although they are for the most part obliged to deny, distort or explain them away for their own propaganda purposes. The real basis of their case is that the Soviet Government is acting throughout in the interests of world revolution.

This is both true and not true, depending upon how one interprets the phrase " world revolution ". If a " world revolution " is regarded as meaning a free, and rapid progression towards (say) world democratic government, the Communist claim is quite false. If it means an upheaval calculated to impose Stalinism on the world, then the Soviet Government is certainly serving the aims of such a world revolution. This is the kind of world revolution in which the Soviet leaders are interested.

It follows from this—and the fact has to be faced—that any member of a Communist Party of any country, whatever his motives and whatever his own interpretation of his actions, is in fact working on behalf of the Soviet Union for the overthrow of the existing structure of society. If he were simply aiming at introducing a better form of society in his own country, that would be an internal matter only, in which questions of treason would not arise. If, however, it can be shown that the new form

* Stalin: *Problems of Leninism,* Foreign Languages Publishing House, Moscow, 1941, p. 70.

of society he is seeking to establish in fact entails total subservience to the Soviet Union, difficult questions of the conscience of the individual and the security of the State at once arise.

If for some reason or other the citizen in question sincerely believes that it is in the interests of humanity to bring his democratic State under the domination of a totalitarian State he must be allowed to propagate his ideas. But it is important that he should be quite sure that he realises the true nature of the totalitarian State and that he should realise (for example) that when he has achieved his object it will be impossible for him to reverse his course should experience teach him that his new situation is not, as he hoped it would be, better than his old one. By submitting to the totalitarian State, the citizen in question has sacrificed the freedom which he enjoyed in the democratic State. The author once discussed this very difficult question with a British Home Secretary, in the following terms:

> Author. If a society was formed in Britain to abolish Parliament, what would be your constitutional duty if that Society secured so much support that it could promote enough abolitionist M.P.s to secure a majority for the abolition of Parliament?
>
> H.S. If in this hypothetical case it appeared that the society was becoming strong enough to overthrow Parliament, it should be suppressed.
>
> A. With respect, is that not a violation of democratic principles, and would not the supposed growth of the society demonstrate that a majority of the people had become indifferent to their liberties and their guardianship by Parliament?
>
> H.S. Do you mean there must be liberty to destroy liberty?
>
> A. I mean that, as you and I believe in Parliament, the only way to re-establish it in the esteem of the nation in the hypothetical case we have imagined would be to allow the people to find out by painful experience the iniquities of a dictatorship. But the true democratic procedure should surely be for those who believe in Parliamentary democracy to be careful by precept and action to ensure a healthy, liberty-loving public opinion in which the

Society for the abolition of Parliament would only be ridiculed.

H.S. We can agree on that.

It is one of the purposes of this book to set forth the evidence about the real nature of the Russian controlled Communist dictatorship, in the belief that if these facts are established it will be seen that Communist policy in fact is very different from what they pretend it to be, and that this deceit on the part of the Communists is inevitable if they are to seduce free men from their democratic beliefs.

The principles of the Soviet technique can be summarised as follows:—

First, the parties concerned—the aggressor and his victim—must not appear as individual sovereign States. This difficulty is overcome by the Soviet Government presenting itself not as the government of one nation, but as the servant of the world-wide revolution. Once this picture is accepted, neither Russia nor her victims are concerned with national frontiers.

Secondly, acts of aggression are justified by representing that they are not acts of aggression: this follows from the rejection of national frontiers, and is also explained by the doctrine that the ends justify the means. Naturally if some adventitious pretext or justification arises, so much the better.

Thirdly, human idealism is exploited partly by the original revolutionary ardour and partly by exploiting any emotional situation that may arise, such as a resistance movement in war, or resistance to the threat of tyranny (e.g. the Spanish Civil War). The Soviet Union thus identifies itself with "The Good Cause".

Fourthly, the weaknesses of democratic society are exploited and used. The Soviet Government employs its resources—political, economic and propagandist—to create economic distress, foment civil disturbances and in general create doubt as to whether the non-Communist world is worthy of preservation. Closely linked to number four in this broad catalogue of Soviet methods is a fifth activity: it consists of a world-wide and extensive use of propaganda to divide the democratic nations from each other and exacerbate "the class war" within each nation. This argument says that capitalist society cannot be reformed; it must be destroyed by revolution.

Sixthly, the true nature of the aggressor must be concealed.

The Soviet Government has dealt with this problem by presenting to the world a totally untrue picture of conditions in the Soviet Union.

In order to safeguard this false picture, free access to Russia has been forbidden whilst an elaborate technique has been evolved of inviting selected visitors to go and see selected places and to hear only those views which are favourable to the régime. They are then sent back to their countries to propagate a glowing account of life in a Communist State, which bears rather less relation to the truth than those enthusiastic accounts of life in Nazi Germany brought back by gullible travellers and Nazi agents during Hitler's régime.

Finally, sufficient force must be available. The Soviet Union's attitude to its own public opinion and its methods of controlling it are well known, as are the internal discipline and methods of enforcing it in the Communist Parties abroad.

The Soviet authorities have officially stated that the presence of the Soviet Army as a threat is a necessary condition of a successful revolution.

Chapter II ended with the question: Is the Soviet Government a totalitarian aggressor conforming to a standard pattern of what may be called " peaceful aggression "?

We submit that enough evidence has been set forth in Chapter III to justify the laying of the charge that the Soviet Union is such an aggressor. We shall see whether further evidence justifies a verdict of guilty or not guilty.

CHAPTER IV

DEMOCRATIC APATHY AND SOVIET MYTHOLOGY

WE have seen in Chapter I that States, whether totalitarian or democratic, are menaced by external and internal forces.

In Chapter II we have singled out an external danger to which democratic States are exposed, and this danger was described as " peaceful " aggression. Incidentally the introduction to the book—which is an essential part of this work—explains why the paradox of " peaceful " aggression is not perceived by many worthy people who have been brought up to believe that " aggression " means " war ", and that war only means physical combat.

In Chapter III we considered whether or not the policies of the Soviet Union, when set alongside the theoretical methods of " peaceful " aggression, appeared to conform to those methods.

In this fourth chapter we shall consider the two chief reasons why the " peaceful " aggression of the Soviet Union has made some progress during the past thirty years. It would be foolish to deny that the Communist conspiracy has achieved considerable results, and hazardous to assume that this conspiracy will fail unless the democratic States maintain, and indeed increase, their efforts to defend themselves; politically, economically and militarily.

For the success of an operation of political or peaceful aggression there must be a climate of public opinion in the victim State which is tolerant and indifferent to what is going on, and easy to deceive. It is ridiculous that a community which has both vitality and self-respect should allow such an operation to make any serious head-way.

Why, then, in a mature society such as Western Europe has Russian-controlled Communism made progress during the past thirty years? The main reasons are two in number.

There is first the fact that until about the beginning of the 20th century the free or democratic way of life, with its various institutions, such as freely elected Parliaments, a free Press, freedom of religion and so forth, was generally accepted as the morally right and practically correct method of human government. Seen in its most advanced—if still relatively undeveloped—form in the Western countries it was being transferred (notably by Great Britain) to overseas lands. Less advanced countries were toiling up the arduous road of parliamentary democracy, and Russia had its Duma. This parliamentary democracy had emerged sometimes through the flames of revolution, sometimes by evolution, sometimes through civil war, from the age of feudalism. The majority of Western men when Karl Marx was toiling in the British Museum Library never supposed that a rival creed would arise which would challenge democracy with as fierce a challenge and on an even wider front than that upon which Islam once challenged Christian Europe. It was forgotten that the price of liberty is continual vigilance. Democracy was taken for granted with the same comfortable assurance as was the inevitability of what the Victorians called progress. Democracy did not bestir itself in its own defence because there appeared to be nothing against which it needed to defend itself.

It was as recently as 1944 that a few people came together in London to found the Hansard Society,* a non-party educational body dedicated to the task of promoting interest in Parliamentary democracy all over the world. By 1952, notwithstanding its meagre financial resources, its work was described in a letter to *The Times* (May 29th, 1952), signed by the Prime Minister (Mr Churchill), Mr Attlee and Mr Clement Davies as being of " *exceptional importance at this time in our history* ". The Council of the Hansard Society, of which the author has the honour to be the chairman, includes Mr Mavalankar, Speaker of the Indian Parliament, and Mr Walter Lippman.

Moreover, the economic and social problems which confronted democracy, as a consequence of the extent to which man's

---

* It is extraordinary that this impoverished and strictly unofficial society, which started with a capital of £100 and had managed to get its income up to £4,000 p.a. by 1952, is *the only body* in the world devoted to doing for the cause of democratic Parliamentarianism, in all its many aspects, what the immensely powerful Cominform does for the cause of Communism. Every reader of this book is earnestly requested to send for *The Story of The Hansard Society*, obtainable, price 1s. 3d., post free, from Hansard House, 39 Millbank, S.W.1, so as to apprise themselves of what has been done, is being done and could be done in the shape of *positive action and education for the democratic cause.*

material achievements had outstripped his political thinking owing to the progress of applied science, were exceptional and complex.

Could democracy cope with them? Two world wars suggested that Western civilisation had yet to find the answer of how to avoid suicide. Democracy was therefore in a bad way when the baleful glare of Communism began to be seen above the horizon of time and in due course its sun rose in Russia. There was a lack of enthusiasm for democracy in the West, when Communism caught it half asleep in a nightmare of its self-created problems.

But, as Mr Churchill once said: " Democracy is the best of a number of unsatisfactory systems of government " (or words to that effect). It is only of recent years that the democratic peoples have begun to wake up to the fact that the inescapable choice before them is between a democracy which is capable of unlimited improvement and a tyranny which is absolute.

If the first reason for the success of Communism can be summarised as being due to a lack of belief within democracy in the values of this way of life and its capacity for dealing with modern problems, coupled with a false assumption that no alternative could challenge democracy, the second reason is the skill with which the Soviet Union has created the illusion that Communism in practice, as exemplified by the external and internal policies and achievements of the Russian State, has provided the material for a wonderful and golden-age chapter in human history. In summary this operation can be described as the creation and exploitation of the Soviet myths.

II

The catalogue of these myths is as follows:—

1. The World Revolution.
2. The Anti-Fascist Myth.
3. The Heroic Soviet Myth.
4. The Peace Myth.
5. The Paradise Myth.

We will examine these one by one.

Myth number one is that Russia is serving a glorious cause called " world revolution ". Its implications are that under the kindly paternal guidance and control of the Soviet Union the democracies will jump all the painful and tiresome stages of evolution, and very rapidly reach a perfect democracy; so perfect that even the State, in Lenin's words, " will wither away ". In short, those who feel that they are in the purgatory of a democracy open to much legitimate criticism are invited to make a short cut through Hell into Heaven.

Unfortunately, all the available evidence is remarkably conclusive that the Hell is an easily attained reality, whilst the Heaven remains eternally remote.

The second myth is that the Soviet Government occupied a pre-eminent position in the world-wide struggle against Fascism. Certainly Communists were active in the period before 1939 in agitating against totalitarian Governments and methods in Germany, Italy and Spain, and certainly the Governments of those countries found in opposition to Communism and Soviet policy a convenient rallying cry of the type dictators need.

Unfortunately, however, the very extensive services rendered by the Soviet Government to Hitler for nearly two years from August, 1939, to June, 1941 show that " anti-Fascism " was merely the exploitation of a healthy democratic instinct and the perversion of it to Communist ends. Indeed, it is still being used as a slogan in a world where Fascism's principal manifestations are to be found in the Soviet Union itself.

We now come to the heroic Soviet Myth. This is the myth that the performance of the Soviet Government and people in the Second World War proved the superior material strength and spiritual ardour of the Communist State. Certainly the Russian people fought with the utmost heroism from about six months after the German troops first crossed the frontier in June, 1941, and their powers of endurance and their courage in defence and attack aroused the admiration of the entire world.

Certainly also the Soviet Government displayed great courage, ability and resourcefulness in improvising their recovery and counter-offensive out of what appeared to be total defeat. These facts, however, with the rest of the evidence, prove nothing to the credit of the *Communist* structure of the State: rather the reverse, for it must never be forgotten that for the first six months of the German attack a large proportion of the population of the invaded areas welcomed the

German Armies as liberators, and units of the Soviet Army as large as entire divisions surrendered in their formations without offering any resistance.

It was only the incredible stupidity of the Germans, whose arrogant cruelty to all Russians roused the army and civilian population against them, that arrested this complete collapse of Soviet morale. What the Germans succeeded in doing was to release the old patriotic instincts of the Russians from beneath the thin veneer of twenty years of Communist ideology. The Russian Government was quick to take the hint, and from then onwards patriotism, and not Communist propaganda, became the driving force in the war effort.

The war was officially called the Great Patriotic War, and through the medium of the Press, films and radio every effort was made to link up the struggle with the Germans with the national achievements of the Russian people under Peter the Great, Catherine the Great and in the Napoleonic Wars.

Since the mass of the Russian people, or at all events the older ones, had remained sincerely attached to the Orthodox Church, notwithstanding the prolonged campaign against religion, officially described as the opiate of the people, and such measures as the setting up of the anti-religious museum at Leningrad, the rulers of the Soviet took steps to bring the Church into the war effort. The godless Museum was closed and the Patriarch of Moscow was enthroned with a ceremony broadcast all over Russia. All the great ecclesiastics of the Greek Orthodox Church, such as the Archimandrites of Alexandria and of Antioch, were invited to Russia. They departed—as the author observed when in Russia as one of an all party group of British M.P.s in 1945—laden with priceless ikons and other marks of favour.

In this connection an amusing incident occurred. We were present at a preview of a new film on Peter the Great, and noticed with interest that he was depicted as receiving his authority from the Church. A cynical Russian official sufficiently high up to enjoy some intellectual freedom admitted that in the original version of the film the Church had not been allowed to appear, but the new line of policy had made it necessary to re-shoot half the film.

In Moscow in 1945 M. Stalin expressed to the M.P.s his appreciation of the invaluable help Russia had received from

D

the British and Americans. He volunteered the information that the Russians then had a superiority of five to one in men and three to one in machinery over the Germans—" thanks to the supplies you have sent us "—and were meeting with practically no opposition in the air " because all the Luftwaffe is in the West ".

Whilst Mr Stalin was thus talking truthfully to British M.P.s in the Kremlin, the Russian State-controlled Press was full of complaints that Russia's allies were not fighting !

Very soon after the end of the war some of the grips which the Communist Party had thought prudent to relax on the life of the nation in order to release national patriotism were restored in full measure. The truth is that Russia survived not because of the Communist régime, but in spite of it. She survived because of the bravery of her people and the help of her allies. But the achievements of the Russian people under the stimulus of wartime patriotism still lead some people to suppose that it was all due to some special quality in Soviet Communism.

Other people explain that Communism must have some remarkable qualities and virtues because of the undoubted fact that in Russia there is to be found a genuine pride amongst the people in their achievement since the revolution. Either through ignorance or deliberate dishonesty, the apologists for the Soviet régime fail to point out several things. For example, this spirit is most readily discernible in the small privileged class who direct the affairs of the Soviet Union in the interests of the Communist oligarchy. Also, it should be remembered that similar pride, and similar achievements to justify it, can be found in any totalitarian régime among those who have a belief and a vested interest in its survival, notably during modern times in Fascist Italy, Nazi Germany, Imperial Japan and, perhaps, the Argentine. There is no doubt that among the Russian underdogs—that is to say, the majority of the population—there is a pathetic pride in achievements by no means remarkable in themselves, such as a tall building or a power-station. This is the direct result of the Soviet Government's policy of shutting out all knowledge of the far greater achievements of the non-Communist world.

Industrial development, slum clearance, the spread of education, hydro-electric schemes, progress in medicine and social services, are all to be found in a far greater degree in parliamentary democracies, such as Great Britain and the United States. There, however, the effort put into these achievements is so widely dispersed over the community, and such progress is taken so much for granted, that it attracts less attention.

In fact the Communist apologists do a curious disservice to the Soviet Government by allowing a sense of surprise and of wonderment to tinge their account of developments in the Soviet Union which in a free society are regarded as impressive but normal.

Next we come to the Peace Myth.

Priority has always been given by all Soviet agencies at home and abroad to spreading the illusion that the Soviet Government wants peace whilst Western Powers want war.

It has been a promising field to exploit, became the desire for peace is universal; therefore propaganda which sought to make use of this emotion might be expected to evoke a ready response. The apologists who visit the Soviet Union report as though it were something surprising that the Russian people want peace, overlooking the fact that nobody has ever suggested or thought it conceivable that the Russian people or any other people would want war under modern conditions.

This so-called " discovery " merely directs the minds of sensible people to certain facts, for instance that the alternative to war is not the single word " peace ". The alternative to war is peace upon alternative conditions: peace by free and equal discussion and negotiation, concession and the guarantee of a lasting settlement; or peace as an instrument of blackmail, enabling the potential aggressor to achieve his aims not by resorting to war but by making peace, or abstaining from war, conditional upon the granting of his demands.

Informed public opinion has been quick to observe that it is the latter alternative for which the Soviet Government has built up its elaborate façade of peace propaganda. Of course the Soviet people want peace; and of course the Soviet Government wants peace, provided that it is peace on Soviet terms. Equally, they will not resort to force and overthrow the peace if they know that the outcome will be disastrous for themselves. There is nothing new in this technique, except the scale of it, but, as something new and significant, that the Soviet Government want peace without considering what they mean by peace does not decrease the likelihood of war. The details of the Russian Peace Campaign are examined in Chapter X.

Last we come to that facet of Soviet Mythology which we have called the Paradise Myth. It is perhaps the foundation stone of the whole edifice of falsehood. Briefly, it is that Soviet man is superior to other men,* that Soviet society is superior to other forms of society, that the Soviet people are happier than other people, that the Soviet Union is, in brief, the people's paradise. All that can be said of this myth is that not one word of it is true. Its falsity will become manifest as the facts are revealed, but some short comments on it will be made here.

The savage restrictions on intercourse between the Soviet people and the free world are designed equally to prevent the truth about life in Russia leaking out and the truth about life in the free world filtering in. This makes it easy for the Soviet Government to pretend that the model factories, hospitals, rest homes, etc., displayed for the benefit of visitors are typical of the whole, and thus to present an inaccurate picture of the Soviet Union. The shutting out of knowledge of the free world makes it easy for the Soviet Government to convince the Russians that they are singularly blessed in their way of life, because they have no knowledge of an alternative way of living with which to compare their own.

Finally, it is a most astonishing " higher form of society " which has to be preserved against itself by *armed* security police numbering, on the best estimates, about 600,000 men. Since the facts that emerge from the Soviet Union, despite all the efforts of its Government, are markedly at variance with any known conception of human happiness, it is scarcely to be wondered at that the Soviet Government take drastic measures to preserve this basic piece of their mythology, and it makes it all the more necessary for the non-Russian world, whatever their political views and their attitude to the Soviet Union, to find out the facts. We shall come back to this aspect of the Mythology in Chapter XI.

* " Stalin the Superman " deserves a separate study all to himself.

III

If the arguments in this chapter and the evidence are correct, certain conclusions emerge. The first is that the democratic nations must examine their souls and realise that the liberties enjoyed by individuals in democratic States are not privileges which are obtained automatically, but are the results of duties performed. Democracy is a " way of life ", and not an easy way. There can be no question at all that the Communists not only *say* that they mean to extirpate this way of life; they have done it wherever they can, and intend to go on trying to do it. Nor is there any doubt that the realities of the alternative way of life imposed by Communism are quite different from what the Communists declare them to be. The myths are not truths, or even half-truths; they are lies.

If to apathy, the peoples of the democratic States add self-deception about what Communist life is like, the destruction of democracy is very probable, and the value of democracy will only be learnt through its absence.

The apathy of the democratic peoples, the lack of fire in their bellies, the international squabbling which takes place—as opposed to democratic discussion—in (say) the N.A.T.O. group, are profoundly disturbing. A year ago the ignorance amongst democratic peoples about the realities of Communist life was equally alarming. At the moment of writing there has been an improvement in that department, and some considerable effort is being made to unveil the facts about the Communist conspiracy, but much remains to be done. As recently as August, 1952, when a protest was sent to a popular newspaper in Britain because an article about life in Russia was published which it could be proved gave an absolutely false picture, the Editor replied: " We had our reserves about this, but much too much publicity has been given to the other side "—*i.e.* the facts about life under the Communists. In other words, this editor appeared to believe that if he published a column of truth on a subject, he was under a kind of moral obligation to publish a column of lies on the same subject.

CHAPTER V

SOVIET PROPAGANDA

SINCE Communism has an intellectual basis, and is in a sense a religion which seeks to capture the citadels of men's minds, the utmost importance is attached by Communists to what is called " Propaganda ". This is a respectable word which has become a prostitute through misuse by dictatorships, so that one hardly dares say, for example, that the Christian Church exists to propagate the Gospel of Christ. One of the problems which confronts anyone who attempts to assess what Russian controlled Communists are up to at this time in world history, is that of answering the question : " Where and how are Communism and Russian Imperialism related to each other? " In theory, Communism is an international movement whose headquarters may be anywhere. Again, in theory there is no such thing as a national Communist Party. There are Communists and non-Communists. But in practice the important fact at this time in history (1953) is that in 1917 the International Communist movement captured the body, if not the soul of the Russian Empire, and with two exceptions shortly to be mentioned, the policy of the International Communist movement and that of the Russian State have been indistinguishable one from the other.

The exceptions are : First, the Tito defection, which, unimportant in its domestic implications, has been of international significance by inventing " Titoism ", and is of strategical value to the free world. Secondly, the advent to power of Communism in China. This may, and in the opinion of this writer will, one day lead to a great schism in the Communist world, but that day may be far off, and for the moment Peking appears to be a powerful and faithful ally of Moscow. But an ally is not a satellite.

We are therefore justified in stating that the propaganda put out by the Communist Party in this conspiracy can also be regarded as propaganda by and on behalf of the Russian State. But, because of the nature of Communism, this propaganda, even though it often operates in a manner and style indistinguishable from what one would expect if it were merely Russian imperialistic propaganda, has certain basic characteristics which must be examined. This rather complex point can be illustrated by remarking that the British Council does propaganda for the British way of life, and because the British way of life is based on democratic principles, the British Council's propaganda is in fact propaganda for democracy.

If Soviet propaganda were irresponsibly opportunist it might, theoretically at any rate, be expected to exploit any grievance of any disappointed group or clique in any country. And it has at least a tendency to do so. But the Stalinists, though the social order in Russia has deviated considerably from that envisaged by Marx, and even from that set up by Lenin, are devoted to the forms of Marxism–Leninism; and their party, in spite of the fact that it constructed a completely new form of society without taking over any of the forms of its predecessors, has its own historical roots and background. The principles and techniques of Soviet propaganda, therefore, cannot be studied without reference to the historical bases of Stalinism and the associated questions of political tactics and organisation, since both the form of the propaganda and the choice of audience are to a large extent determined by them.

It is therefore necessary at this stage in our investigation to give the reader an outline of the philosophical spring-board from which Soviet propaganda endeavours to leap into men's minds.

According to the Marxist analysis, the key to the understanding of history is to be found in changes in production.* Such changes are the result of the contradiction, which finds its expression in the class struggle, between the class which is holding up the development of the productive forces because it is to its interest to maintain the existing economic order, and a new class whose interest lies in the further development of these forces which it is to the advantage of society as a whole to promote. In the present context these two classes are the *bourgeoisie* and the proletariat, by the latter being understood the industrial workers.

At the same time it is recognised that society also contains

---

* For a shorter account see: *What is Communism*, by John Plamenatz, and for a detailed analysis see *The Theory and Practice of Communism*, by Carew Hunt.

certain elements which cannot be assigned absolutely to either of these two main divisions. Thus the peasants are neither proletarians nor *bourgeois* and are in fact survivals of pre-capitalist society. The *petite bourgeoisie* are equally *declassé*, and in any proletarian revolution its members must be regarded as a vacillating and uncertain element.

How the proletariat was to conduct the class struggle so as to enable it eventually to seize political power was set out by Marx with special reference to the industrialised States of Western Europe. Lenin, however, made the discovery that capitalism had now entered upon its final " imperialist " phase, which was characterised by the acute competition of the capitalist Powers to obtain control over backward countries in order to get cheap raw materials. From this he concluded that it would be easier to foment revolutions in such countries than in those which were more highly developed, and that they constituted the weakest link in the capitalist chain.

Hence the strategy of world revolution may be summarised as follows:—

The working class, represented by the Socialist proletarian movement, must obtain political power. In some countries it may be able to do so peacefully, but in the majority of cases a struggle (that is, a revolution) is likely, since violent opposition from the capitalist class may be expected. In its struggle for State power the proletariat should seek to win over the *petite bourgeoisie* and the peasants by appealing to their particular interests—that is, the desire of the peasants for land and the fear of the small tradesman of being crushed out by big business interests.

According to classical Marxist theory, the revolution will take place in two stages. The first stage will be a *bourgeois*-democratic revolution, in which the proletariat will be in alliance with the liberal *bourgeoisie*, although it will be in the position of a junior partner only. The second stage will be the proletarian revolution, which will take place when the proletariat, together with its peasant and *petite bourgeoisie* allies, has become strong enough to break the alliance with the *bourgeoisie* and seize power for itself. This strategy assumed, however, that a section of the *bourgeoisie* was genuinely liberal-minded. But at the time of the 1905 revolution Lenin decided that no such section existed in Russia, and he therefore laid down that while the revolution should still proceed in two stages, the *bourgeois*-democratic stage should be carried out under the leadership of the proletariat—that is, the proletariat should be the senior partner, though it would not at this stage introduce Socialism.

The present doctrine is a modification of the above. Industrialised Western Countries are held to be ripe for proletarian revolutions, though these will not be of the peculiar Soviet type which constitutes the pattern and example of what the perfect revolution should be. In backward countries, however, there must first be a *bourgeois*-democratic revolution, albeit under proletarian leadership, which will possess a nationalist character, as its objective is the removal of foreign exploitation. When the revolution has gone through this nationalist phase the proletarian revolution will follow. Thus, the revolution in China is officially *bourgeois*-democratic, and not proletarian, though, as the Communists are in complete control, it matters little whether it is called the one or the other.

But Lenin's major revision of Marx's teaching, or at least of what western Marxists had come to suppose that teaching to have been, was his assertion that the workers, if left to themselves, would never make a revolution at all, because the correct revolutionary principles, without which no revolution could be successful, do not arise spontaneously in the working-class movement, but have to be brought into it from outside. The corollary of the above is that revolutions must be carried out by an *élite*, from which it is only a step to the conclusion that after they have taken place, the *élite* must continue in control. In the U.S.S.R. this *élite* was the Bolshevik Party, the title of which the recent XIXth Party Congress has changed to the Communist Party of the Soviet Union.

From the above analysis it follows that the tactical aims of Stalinist propaganda and agitation are:—

(i) absolute control of the working-class movement;

(ii) to secure the support of the peasantry by promising land reform, and

(iii) to enlist support on a much more temporary basis of any other group which may be suitable material at a given moment, and in particular, in the colonial and " semi-colonial " countries, of the " national " *bourgeoisie*.

But to be effective these tactics must be directed towards certain targets, and generally the fewer the better, because with the increase in the number of targets the harder it is for the propaganda not to contradict itself. For this reason Stalinist propaganda falls into two categories:

First, for militant workers. They are the key-men (and women): the well-informed, active, intelligent workers capable of influencing and leading their fellow workers, and such intellectuals as can be converted into professional revolutionaries. The aim is to turn these into fully reliable Stalinists and educate them to analyse all situations in terms of Marxist theory, and to think of the U.S.S.R. as a working-class State where Socialism has been realised.

Secondly, for the remainder: the working-class " masses ", the peasants, the ordinary intellectuals, the nationalist *bourgeoisie* of colonial-type countries and other intermediate *petit-bourgeois* groups.

These latter are to be led, rather than educated, and so are treated to propaganda on a general basis of the ideas likely to appeal to them and convince them that Soviet policy is in their interests. In short, the propaganda exploits their desires and grievances.

A few words are necessary about the types to whom the first kind of Soviet propaganda is directed.

The " militant " worker may be an old Communist or *Communisant* for whom the propaganda is a means of fortifying his ideas. A sort of nostalgic conservatism keeps such men disciples of Russia—they have worked all their lives for a Russia which now no longer exists—but how can they admit this? With others it is a feeling that Russia is strong and has a chance of winning; if only she is what she professes to be, they think, how much easier will be the attainment of our ideals. This is wishful thinking based on a lack of reliance on personal strength. All that such men require is that they be given adequate interpretations of each event to soothe their doubts and confirm their prejudices.

But the " militant " worker may also be an ordinary Socialist or Marxist in a backward country where Stalinist–Marxist propaganda gives a reasonable picture of local conditions, or an older man of the same type even in such countries as England, who thinks in terms of events twenty years ago, when his political views were formed. He thinks that since Soviet propaganda gives an accurate, or what seems to him an accurate, view of local conditions, it is probable that its other assumptions are also true.

As for the intellectuals, propaganda for their benefit is an especially important weapon when it is desired to form Communist parties where they have not hitherto existed. In these cases the first people to be influenced are intellectuals who will be capable of organising propaganda among the workers. Hence the efforts made among colonial students. For example, in Ceylon the origin of the Communist Party and the rival Trotskyite Party may be traced, it appears, to a group of Marxist students from Ceylon at English universities in the early thirties.

In the more advanced countries the Communist Party attaches importance to gaining the support of intellectuals because of their prestige value, the Continental notion of the importance of *Kulturtraeger*, and because a Soviet State (and indeed even a large Communist Party) requires its own technical and administrative intelligentsia, including people who can write propaganda.

Although as mentioned above an analysis of Stalinist propaganda indicates that the policy is to churn out a brand of butter and a brand of margarine, this is not an easy task. Propaganda for the *élite* can be kept to a large extent from the masses, but the reverse is not true. In principle, in the early days, Communist propaganda was a popularised and simplified version of the more indigestible Marxist interpretations offered to the *élite* and was based on the actual policies pursued. Since then, however, it has become increasingly obvious that Soviet policies are not always, to put no finer point on it, in accord with the principles of Marxism or Socialism, and that Soviet propaganda frequently accords *neither* with the Soviet policies *nor* with the principles of Marxist analysis.

This is obvious, and would be disturbing, to the *élite* targets of Communist propaganda if a mechanism of justification did not exist. But, when pressed, intelligent Communists defend reactionary acts and statements by the U.S.S.R. on the perfectly orthodox thesis that for a Communist the test of goodness is simply whether the revolution is assisted or not. Lenin stated this clearly thirty years ago.

The Communist argues that the teachings of Marx, confirmed by a generation of direct experiment, tell us that humanitarian sentiments are out of place and of no significance in the interpretation of history. The salvation of the human race can be assured only by accepting this fact and by accepting responsibility for unpleasant actions.

Apart from the general and basic theses which appeal to almost everyone, and which are dealt with later, the main special appeals to the non-*élite* section of the audience can be summarised as follows:

(i) *For the workers :* The U.S.S.R. is a State run by the workers, a Socialist State where complete social equality prevails except perhaps that the workers are in a better position than other groups. The Socialist and trade-union leaderships in non-Communist countries have betrayed the workers and have no real Socialist objectives; a larger share of the national wealth is immediately available to the workers if they undertake militant action, especially by strikes.

(ii) *For the peasants :* Communist policy is that the land should be given to the peasants; no other party will remove it from the landlord's hands; therefore militant action is necessary to secure it.

(iii) *For the colonial and " semi-colonial " nations* (and to an increasing extent in all countries outside the United States): The imperialist nations are exploiting their countries while they are regarded and treated as inferior races; there is no racial prejudice or oppression in the U.S.S.R.; militant action (especially rebellion or war) against the imperialists is necessary to secure liberation.

On the question of racial discrimination it is interesting that Sir Godfrey Huggins, in commending the White Paper on Federation to the South Rhodesian Legislative Assembly in June, 1952, said: " The real appeal of Communism is not to the African masses, but to the urban intelligentsia, and the appeal is not on account of its economic doctrines, not because of its world view, but because of one element in its philosophy—abolition of colour prejudice."

The main themes of Soviet propaganda are, wherever

possible, linked with certain general principles of " progressive-
ness ". In particular, at present, these are :—

> National Freedom.
> Social Equality.
> Peace.

The actual aims of Soviet policy are often absolutely opposed
to these principles. But at present Soviet propaganda is largely
made up of a continuous effort to induce as many supporters
of these three principles as possible to support Soviet policy.

The " national freedom " theme is largely used in the
colonial territories and in what are regarded as the " semi-
colonial " territories of the Middle and Far East.   Even India
still awaits national liberation, according to the Communists.*

The " social-equality " theme is a general background one
to the effect that the U.S.S.R. is an ideal society, and exploits
the ordinary day-to-day economic struggles of the working
class of the West.

The " peace " theme, however, is entirely general, and now
(1953) bears very much the main emphasis of the propaganda
campaign.

The methods by which the Soviet Union puts across the
notion that its militarist and aggressive policies are identical
with world peace (and its other propaganda points) are the
same as those of Hitler.   The " Big Lie " is told, on the old
theory that it is more likely to be believed than a small one, and
is then repeated insistently.   In all statements from the Soviet
side the assumption that the U.S.S.R. is working for peace,
and the various subsidiary assumptions, for example, that
Mr Attlee is a warmonger,† are taken for granted.

In the international field, as in internal politics, Soviet policy
is to concentrate as many allies as possible against its main
opponent.   The main opponent of the Soviet Union in 1941–
45 was Hitler's Germany, and Soviet propaganda and tactics
abroad were switched to support anything that would assist
the Allied war effort (even to the extent of supporting extreme

---

* One of the charges againt the Soviet economist Varga was that he
thought India had achieved independence [see Planned Economy No. 6,
Dec. 1948].

† Moscow radio on February 13th, 1951, accused Mr Attlee of having an
" appalling face " and being " an unleasher of the war in Korea ",

Right-wing candidates in British by-elections against independent Left-wing candidates).

At present, however, the main force capable of preventing unlimited Soviet expansion is obviously the United States. The whole force of Soviet tactics is therefore directed to assembling against the United States, and to an increasing extent the United Kingdom, and their supporters, as large and effective a coalition as possible of States, parties, social classes, races and other groups.

It is curious to see how an attack on the Marshall Plan as an American instrument for impoverishing Europe, which merely sounded ridiculous when it was first propounded, is gradually becoming by these techniques a part of the political debate, whether it is believed or not.

The XIXth Congress of the Communist Party provided plenty of evidence of the concentration against the U.S.A. The following extract from L. P. Beria's speech on 7th October, 1952, is typical:

> ". . . The American imperialists, who have grown fat on two world wars, intoxicated with the crazy idea of establishing world domination, are again pushing the peoples into the abyss of world war.
>
> The present masters of the United States of America, the Morgans, the Rockefellers, the Mellons, the Duponts and others, who control the American State and war machine, are energetically forming new world monopolies, such as the European Coal and Steel Community and the World Oil Cartel, with a view to taking over the economies of other States more quickly and subordinating them to their own interests. They want to establish their undivided rule in all parts of the world so that, by plundering and enslaving the peoples of other countries, they may ensure themselves super-profits. To achieve this, they need war. With the object of preparing war, American big capital in conjunction with the American military, are taking upon themselves all the functions of a fascist régime in order, within their country, to suppress the people's desire to preserve peace, and to suppress all opposition to their reckless policy. In pushing the country on to the path of war they also reckon that an armaments drive and a war situation will make it possible to avert an economic crisis, the United States of America having spread a net of military bases all over the world and vigorously knocking together

all kinds of aggressive military blocs, they are feverishly preparing war against the U.S.S.R. and other peace-loving States."

On the whole, the greatest Soviet successes are the mere exploitation of popular words like " peace " and " democracy " without further subtleties. But in certain cases considerable skill has been used to adapt them to the needs of Soviet policy. For example, the Stockholm appeal against the atomic bomb contrived to represent itself as fully answering the world's desire for peace, whereas in fact it merely asked, in general terms which had already proved impracticable in the United Nations debates, for the abolition of a particular weapon. This must be regarded as a considerable Soviet success, since to expose the pretensions of the appeal involved a certain presentation of facts and arguments, whereas the appeal started off with the advantage of merely presenting itself as a " peace appeal ", even in the minds of its opponents.

This part of the campaign is further discussed in Chapter IX.

Another aspect of Soviet propaganda is the extremely violent terms in which it is conducted. The effect of this probably varies from country to country. The tone of polemics in Russia has always been more violent than in most other countries, and it took on an added virulence in the bitter faction struggles of the twenties and early thirties. This tone has now imposed itself on all Communist propaganda language. In England, for example, it largely defeats its own aims, but in countries accustomed to a violent tone in political polemics it may be more effective.

Until 1952 the organisation of Stalinist propaganda was centralised in the Soviet *Politbureau*. At the XIXth Congress of the Soviet Communist Party in August 1952 (the XVIIIth was held in 1939) the *Politbureau* of thirteen members and the Orgbureau (administration) were abolished and replaced by a *Presidium* of thirty-six members, whilst the powers of the Secretariat were increased. The propaganda campaign, whose direction it is supposed is now being undertaken by the *Presidium*, operates through the Press, radio, books, etc., through the Cominform and a network of ancillary bodies, such as the World Peace Council. In practice, the popularising of Soviet propaganda themes outside Russia depends very largely on the

Communist Parties in the free world and, to a much lesser extent, on the international organisations dominated by Moscow.

These parties have been submitted to a discipline as rigid as that in force in the Soviet Union; they are treated as subservient and servile agents. The Stalinists, in their contempt for their followers abroad, think that any act, however absurd or disgraceful, which in their view strengthens the power of the Soviet Union, is worth taking, seemingly regardless of what might be expected to be its effect abroad.

The rôle of the Communist Parties abroad has been to provide Marxist cover-stories for Soviet acts, or in any case where Marxism cannot be stretched to cover them, to justify them anyhow. It is doubtless partly because of this that Communist propaganda has taken on the screamingly self-righteous tones usually associated with a guilty conscience.

Soviet propaganda has had its main successes in those countries where legitimate grievances on the part of the working and peasant classes have not been redressed. The working-class movement has shown itself more likely to fall under Communist control where the capitalist classes behave irresponsibly.

In China the military success of Communism was very largely due to the political collapse of its opponents, through their incapacity to effect much needed reforms. On the other hand, Communist propaganda has on the whole failed, for example, in England, the Low Countries and Scandinavia, where, under whatever government, all classes have shown a certain amount of responsibility, and as a rule, in those Asian countries where national grievances were removed by the early achievement of independence. This gives some idea of where we may expect Communist propaganda to have success in certain circumstances—in particular the Arab countries, Persia and the colonial territories of Africa—unless democracy provides an effective solution of legitimate grievances and distresses.

As a conclusion to this chapter a balance sheet showing the assets and liabilities of Soviet Propaganda is offered to the reader.

The assets are:—

    (i) The unsatisfactory character by true democratic standards of some of the groups and régimes most opposed to the U.S.S.R., such as Spain, Yugoslavia and the Argentine. It does not follow that because a régime is opposed to the U.S.S.R. it is automatically entitled to a clean bill of health.

(ii) The fact that the present régime in the U.S.S.R. emerged from one established by something described as a Socialist and proletarian revolution conducted by a Socialist party; a revolution which in its early stages produced a régime that showed some egalitarian and progressive features; and the remnants of a tradition to this effect in the Socialist movements in the West.

(iii) Exploitation by Communist parties of the prestige of the anti-Fascist liberation movements.

(iv) The remnants of the 1941–45 period of goodwill towards the U.S.S.R. when a vast amount of naïve pro-Soviet propaganda was put out by Russia's allies.

(v) The lack of direct racial prejudice among Communists—up to the present time.

(vi) The ineptitude and inaccuracy of much anti-Soviet propaganda, particularly in the early stages, which has prejudiced many people against anti-Soviet propaganda in general.

(vii) The security curtain which to a large extent prevents more than a general account of Soviet social shortcomings.

(viii) The centralised control and the unlimited budget available, together with the efficient and world-wide organisation of the Communist parties. This ensures that continuity and magnitude of effort which are essential to successful publicity campaigns.

(ix) A philosophy capable of satisfying demands for a rational yet dynamic interpretation of the world, and capable of presentation in forms both of sufficient sublety to attract the intellectuals and of sufficient crudity to appeal to popular public opinion.

(x) Its appeal to the tendency to worship power. Even its lies, crudities and injustices have positive effect in this respect. With this may be considered its strong appeal to intellectuals to sacrifice not merely their consciences but also their intellectual independence in the interests of " higher " ideals.

E

The liabilities of Soviet propaganda are:—

(i) That it tallies so ill with reality that some, at any rate, of its falseness leaks out almost everywhere.

(ii) It is conducted with a rigid centralism by men ignorant of many of the realities of the outer world.

(iii) The economic recovery of the West.

(iv) The non-imperialist nature of British and other colonial policies during recent years.

(v) Freedom of Press and speech, etc., still exists in most of the non-Communist world.

(vi) The memory, in many places, of unpleasant Stalinist tricks—from the Nazi–Soviet pact to the fraudulent conduct of trade union branch elections.

(vii) The effect in the outer world of chauvinist propaganda directed to an internal Soviet audience, *e.g.* the line " the Russians invented everything ".

(viii) The fact that, to a large extent, Western and other governments and organisations and newspapers have taken the Soviet measure, and that intelligent and well-organised counter-Soviet propaganda services are now (1953) beginning to take shape.

It would be a very grave, and probably damnable error to brush aside Communist propaganda as being of no importance. Just as it is not enough that justice be done but must be *seen* to be done, so Communist propaganda cannot merely be ignored. It must be exposed as false, but in doing so care must be taken not to fall into the error of smugly suggesting that there is nothing capable of improvement in our own arrangements!

Some of the developments which are helping in this exposure and promise in the end to defeat Communist propaganda, though they are not adequate and need to be persisted in and encouraged, are:—

(*a*) The real grievances which that propaganda exploits are progressively being redressed.

(*b*) The facts about the nature of Soviet society and Soviet policy are increasingly becoming available to the citizens of the free world.

(*c*) Educational advances in Western and colonial territories increasingly enable the population to think critically.

Nevertheless, it must never be forgotten that the price of liberty is continual vigilance, and vigilance is not a static occupation.

In conclusion it should be noted that an adequate counter-offensive to Soviet propaganda should include not only an exposure of the lies of this propaganda, but also a positive propaganda about the truths and achievements of democracy. In so far as the Western nations have taken steps to counter Soviet propaganda, the measures have chiefly been negative and defensive in character; almost apologetic on occasions.

There is needed a positive policy in the battle of ideas; a dynamic of democracy, even though by the very nature of democracy it can never aspire (and should never try) to imitate the self-righteous dogmatic doctrinal attitude of the Communist, for whom truth, the whole truth and nothing but the truth has been revealed once and for all to mankind by Lenin—subject, of course, to modern interpretation by " the father and mother of all wisdom ": J. V. Stalin.

CHAPTER VI

THE BASTION

A CONSPIRACY needs a headquarters and a base, and in the case of the vast conspiracy we are considering this has been provided by the Soviet Union. The need for concentrating upon the creation of this bastion, this " womb of revolution ", was always a policy firmly maintained by Lenin. Trotsky, on the other hand, believed in the need for a continuous policy of world revolution without which an independent development in Russia could not be sustained.

Though the Soviet régime has always been an open and ruthless dictatorship, in its earlier years it was able to justify itself in the eyes of many people by pointing, in certain spheres, to a number of developments based on egalitarian, Socialist and humanist principles. When in the twenties, however, it became clear that the revolution had no immediate prospect of spreading to other States, Communist theory increasingly treated the U.S.S.R. as the " bastion " of revolution, which must be strengthened and preserved at all costs, including the sacrifices of those principles.

This decision led to a whole series of changes in the internal structure and to some extent in the external diplomacy of the Soviet Union, and ultimately to the assassination in Mexico in 1940 of Trotsky as the logical conclusion of the great purges of the Trotskyites in 1937 and 1938.

In internal policy the whole aim of the State became more and more simply to organise its population into a thoroughly disciplined instrument of the rulers' will; and to organise its productive capacities in such a way as to build up its industry and its productive power in general to a level high enough to support a military power capable of defeating any attacker, and later to justify attacking on his home ground any presumed potential enemy of the revolution.

The measures taken in the Soviet Union to these ends altered its social and political structure out of recognition, so that it lost such characteristics as could in any way be considered those of a " workers' " or " progressive " régime. What this amounts to in practice is discussed in some detail in Chapter XI, but a summary of the actions taken is as follows:—

(i) *Great-Russian chauvinism was progressively encouraged.*

The military leaders of the Tsarist past, who in the early days of the revolution were treated as oppressors, were glorified (*e.g.*, Suvorov, Alexander Nevsky). Rebels who fought against Suvorov, or Caucasians who resisted Tsarist generals—all of whom were honoured in the early years of Soviet rule—were later denounced.

The claim that Russia is the source of all inventions and discoveries—a type of claim that was specifically derided by Lenin—has now become the rule: the radio was invented by Popov, the aeroplane by Mozhaisky, etc., etc.

The notion of Slav superiority inherited from the Pan-Slav movement, which was an instrument of Tsarist policy, has been revived for Soviet use.

The Cyrillic alphabet has been imposed on races who in Lenin's time were given a Latin one. It has become a dogma that the Russian people have a special talent and genius, especially in politics, which the world should follow. Even the Russian language has been glorified.

The following quotations illustrate this trend:—

> " The services of the Russian people are exceptionally great, not only to the peoples of the Soviet Union, but to all mankind. The Soviet Union inspires the workers of the entire world for the struggle against exploiters and ravishers. The history of the Russian people proves their political wisdom, their military valour, and their genius. These facts from the history of our heroic people must be skilfully presented to the pupils in order to awaken in them a feeling of just pride in everything progressive and revolutionary which has so enriched the history of our country." *
>
> " The future belongs to the Russian language as the language of Socialism. . . . The democratic people are learning the Russian language, the world language of internationalism." †

* Third Edition of text book entitled *Pedagogy*, by Yesipov and Goncharov, published in Moscow in 1946, and approved by the Ministry of Education of the R.S.F.S.R. for use in teachers' training-schools.

† *Moskovski Komsomolets (Moscow Young Communist)* 6th March, 1949.

" The Russian language is the first world language of internationalism. . . . No one can call himself a scholar in the full and general meaning of the word, if he does not know Russian, if he does not read the works of Russian thought in the original. . . . Russians unquestionably occupy first place in the social sciences. All future advances in this science have been determined by the works of genius of Lenin and Stalin." *

" I should like to drink to the health of our Soviet people, and first of all to the Russian people. I drink first of all to the health of the Russian people, because it is the most outstanding nation of all the nations forming a part of the Soviet Union." †

" The force cementing the friendship of the peoples of our country is the Russian people, the Russian nation, the most outstanding of all the nations making up the Soviet Union [*tumultuous applause*] . . . as Comrade Stalin has said, the clear mind, staunch character and patience that are inherent in the Russian people . . . by their heroism, courage and valour . . . they were the architects of our victory over Hitler's Germany and Imperialist Japan ".‡

(ii) *Militarism became rife*.

Vast military parades marked all the main holidays. And later there was an increase of Tank, Artillery, Navy, etc., days, each with its parades. The simple uniforms of the early days gave place to stylised glamour. Officers' epaulettes were restored. There was a glittering outbreak of new ribbons and orders.

Conscientious objection to military service, which had been permitted at first, was made illegal in 1939. Training for war, and propaganda for war, became general in schools.

The official Soviet textbook *Pedagogy* of 1946, quoted above, calls for " military-political preparation of the rising genera-tion " and for participation in marksmanship and similar activities. Infants in kindergartens are encouraged as follows : " Here children play Red Army soldiers : in their hands are little flags, on their uniforms and caps are insignia of infantry-

* Zaslavsky, " Great Language of our Epoch ", *Literary Gazette*, 1st January, 1949.
† Stalin, " Kremlin Banquet for Red Army Commanders ", *Pravda*, 25th May, 1945.
‡ L. P. Beria at XIXth Congress, 7th October, 1952.

men, tankmen, sailors and aviators. They march in formation to the tune of a martial song." In 1945 the author saw many examples of this militarism in the nursery schools attached to factories.

If it be argued that in 1945 Russia was at war, it should be noted that the same theme of red-hot militarism will be found in school-books published in 1950 and 1951. Thus in a general reader called *Rodnaya Rech* each volume in the series has a section devoted to the Red Army. The nine-year-olds learn that:—

> " And the long-range guns
> Thunder along the pavement
> For work, for a peaceful life
> They are ready to battle ".

See also Stalin's letter to Gorki quoted on page 108.

School children from the age of 14 are expected to join the military training societies, Dorsarm, Dosflot or Dosav, amalgamated in September, 1951, into a single organisation called DOSAAF, where they receive basic military instruction. Boys from the ages of 15 to 17 do an hour's military training a week and attend a twenty-day camp annually. Ordinary physical training is done on the basis of the award of a badge for which the qualifications include marksmanship, marching, etc.

(iii) *Control of minorities.*

The non-Russian nationalities in Russia, many of whom in the civil war had sided with the Communists, who promised them autonomy against the White Russians who stood for a revival of Tsarist centralism, were subjected to stricter and stricter control.

The Communists, having made use of the national aspirations of these peoples in the struggle for power, in accordance with Leninist tactical theory, took a very different line once power had been won. It was noticeable in the Second World War that the nations accused of disloyalty by Moscow were precisely those, like the Chechens, who had fought on the Red side twenty years before.*

(iv) *Labour discipline.*

Incentives of a sort always regarded as illegitimate by the Socialists were introduced on the one hand; on the other, labour discipline was tightened to an extreme degree.

* See p. 171.

Attempts to introduce workers' control in industry, as had been provided for by Marx, had broken down at an early stage, and the working class began to experience the status of industrial serfs.

The seven-hour working day, which had been introduced early on, was finally abolished in 1940 and replaced by the eight-hour day.

The trade unions lost their last remnants of independence in 1928 and became instruments for " the raising of labour discipline ". The Soviet worker, who operates under a discipline which condemns him to " six months' correctional labour " if he is twenty minutes late for work, and who is paid according to a system of piece-work which involves continually higher production from him if he is to keep the same wage, is now merely an instrument for increasing Soviet production, and is entirely without the right to protect his own standards against superior decisions.

(v) *Class distinction introduced.*

The notion that the administration of the workers' State should be in the hands of the workers, who were, after a period of administrative work, to return to their ordinary work, never materialised.

Its corollary, that administrators should not be paid more than ordinary workers, was the original principle of Soviet administration, but it was soon dropped, and to an increasing degree the Soviet régime has come to depend on the highly paid services of a bureaucratic intelligentsia whose interest is thus bound up with the survival of the régime.

The Soviet Inheritance Tax of 1926, which was the equivalent of the British death duties, has been abolished, and tax rates on high incomes are the lowest of any industrial State in the world. The main tax in the Soviet Union is the " turnover " tax, which in 1950 produced more than half of the State revenue. It is, in fact, a purchase tax, and is very heavy on foodstuffs. Because this tax applies to everyone alike and makes no distinction as to ability to pay, it bears heaviest on the poorest.*

The large class of party leaders, factory managers and so on

* Lenin said in 1918: " Indirect taxes are taxes on the poor " (*Collected Works*, Vol. 5, 3rd Edition, p. 295).

earn incomes which may be some eighty times as great, after paying tax, as a worker's pay.

On 2nd October, 1940, a decree was published introducing fees for tuition in higher education, further contributing to the consolidation of the ruling caste.

(vi) *Control of social life.*

The divorce and sexual laws introduced in the earliest days of the Soviet régime on the old rationalist-humanist basis that the State should interfere as little as possible in private life, were abolished and replaced by laws whose objects were to secure the interests of the State by tightening its control over the individual and increasing the birth rate.

(vii) *Party discipline was made severe.*

The earlier oppositions were bloodily purged and no later ones permitted to emerge. In every respect the Soviet Union has become increasingly centralised, and increasingly totalitarian. Every newspaper is simply a vehicle for the rulers' propaganda. Every work of art must satisfy the party line. Science, which developed comparatively freely until a few years ago, has come completely under party control, to the extent that the party's Central Committee was openly made the highest court in judging the famous biological controversy over the Lysenko theories.

The slightest criticism of the régime in private conversation may lead to arrest. The Communist Party, the trade unions and other mass organisations, the State organisations, collective farms, the industrial trusts, are purely instruments for conveying orders and propaganda from the Presidium to the masses.

The elimination of the egalitarianism of the early days of the Soviet régime produced a society bearing little resemblance to anything conceived by the authors of the October Revolution. It resembled more closely the social order in process of construction by the Nazis from 1933 to 1939, a hierarchical society which was neither capitalist nor Socialist, but which was divided into an exploited, disciplined mass and a well-off, bureaucratic caste headed by an infallible leadership and inspired with a violent nationalism.

The present internal structure of Soviet society is relevant to its imperialism. The Yugoslav Marxists—especially Djilas, the leading theoretician of the Yugoslav Communist Party—have pointed out that this form of society, State-capitalist in organisation and terrorist in administration, is precisely the logical development of the conception put forward by Lenin early in the century of the imperialist State which must seek for foreign areas to exploit: Djilas also points out the parallel with the developments in the fascist State.

Djilas' point of view differs from ours: but it is not difficult to agree that a totalitarian dictatorship uncontrolled by public opinion is more likely to be imperialist than is any other type of State, and that a militarist bureaucracy is not a peaceable sort of ruling caste.

CHAPTER VII

THE SOVIET UNION AND COMMUNIST PARTY

WE have described in the preceding chapter some of the chief measures taken by the Communist leaders for the purpose of harnessing to their will the physical and spiritual resources of the Russian people and making of Russia an impregnable bastion from which, in accordance with the fundamental tenets of Communism, a crusade could be launched to communise mankind within the framework of a Russian Empire. We have also described the tactics considered appropriate to the action (see Chapter III) and said something about the methods of propaganda. In this chapter a description will be given of the main instrument through whose activities the operation is continuously kept in motion.

It was in 1919 that the Communist International was created for the purpose of providing the world revolutionary movement with an organisation accepting the Leninist interpretation of Marxism and formed on the same basis of "democratic centralism" as the Russian Communist Party.

The *Large Soviet Encyclopædia* (Volume 33, published in Moscow, 1938) describes the Comintern as follows:—

> "The Communist International, Comintern, the Third International, is an international comradeship of workers—it is a united World Communist Party, the leader and organiser of the world revolutionary movement of the proletariat, the bearer of the principles and aims of Communism, it fights for the establishment of a world dictatorship of the proletariat and for the setting up of a World Union of Soviet Socialist Republics."

It assembled in the first place a heterogeneous collection of Socialist factions and sects, and its first period was devoted mainly to ridding these of dilettante elements and turning them into copies, in training, discipline and organisation, of the Russian Communist Party. At this time, in the early twenties, public discussion about the desirability of various policies about to be undertaken raged freely in the Russian

Communist Party, and this was, of course, reflected in the foreign parties.

The Comintern was, in theory, the highest organ of the international Communist movement. A vote of the world Congress of the Comintern was binding on the Communist Party of the Soviet Union. So that, theoretically, if a world revolution had come at this point, the Communist Parties in Russia and elsewhere would have been subject to the majority vote in the Comintern. Whatever form the World Union of Soviet Republics took it would have been one organised and fully controlled in the last resort by that majority vote.

In practice, of course, the Russians wielded such prestige and influence that, as things were, they had no great difficulty in putting their views through even without much pressure, except when they interfered directly in the immediate tactics of a local—and particularly of the German—Communist Party.

By the early thirties the Comintern had been changed in effect into a reliable instrument of the Soviet rulers. At the 7th Congress of the Comintern in 1935 all resolutions were passed with that unanimity which had already overtaken the Congress of the Communist Party of the Soviet Union.

The Comintern, whose head after 1934 was officially the Bulgarian Georgi Dimitrov, was controlled by the Russian Manuilsky. The dominating figures in it were no longer the known chiefs of the national Communist Parties, but unknown Soviet agents like the Hungarian Gerö. The German Communist Party had a number of leaders removed successively on Soviet orders. The Polish Communist Party was so unsatisfactory that at one time it was dissolved. Its leader Hempel died in a Soviet prison. Bela Kun, the well-known leader of Hungarian Communism, was shot by the N.K.V.D. The basic axiom of the Communist Parties of the world became:—

> " The U.S.S.R. has no interests which are at variance with the interests of world revolution, and the international proletariat naturally has no interests which are at variance with those of the Soviet Union." *

* Knorin, " Fascism, Social-Democracy and the Communists " : speech to 13th Plenum of the Executive Committee of the Comintern, December, 1933.

This theory resulted in the complete subservience of the movement to Soviet plans. The crucial point in practice was that the policies of the Soviet Union, and hence of the world revolution, were not even theoretically decided by the highest organ of the world revolutionary movement, the Executive Committee of the Comintern, but handed on to the Comintern leaders after decision had already been made in the Soviet Politburo. In the circumstances, even if the Comintern had retained, as it did not, some organisational independence, it was bound doctrinally to carry out policies of assistance to the State policies of the U.S.S.R., over which it had no control.

High-sounding phrases about the U.S.S.R., existing only in the interests of the world revolution, lost all pretence of sincerity when it became clear that they did not submit their plans for approval by the official leadership of the world revolution.

In 1943 the Comintern was dissolved, probably as a gesture to Russia's allies. According to A. Zhdanov:—

> " The Comintern was founded after the First World War, when the Communist Parties were still weak, when practically no ties existed between the working classes of the different countries, and when the Communist parties had not yet produced generally recognised leaders of the labour movement. The service performed by the Comintern was that it restored and strengthened the ties between the working people of the different countries, that it provided the answers to theoretical questions of the labour movement in the new post-war conditions of development, that it established general standards for propaganda of the idea of Communism, and that it helped to train leaders of the labour movement. . . . But once the young Communist parties had become mass labour parties, the direction of these parties from one centre became impossible and inexpedient. . . . The new stage in the development of the Communist parties demanded new forms of connection between the parties. It was these considerations that made it necessary to dissolve the Comintern and to devise new forms of connection between the parties." *

On 5th October, 1947, *Pravda* published a communique, a

* *The International Situation*, A. Zhdanov, Moscow, 1947, pp. 43–47.

declaration and a resolution concerning the establishment of a Communist Information Bureau.

The communique opened by recalling that at the end of September, 1947 an information conference had taken place in Poland of representatives of several national Communist parties, and continued:

> " The participants in the conference heard information reports on the activity of the Central Committees of the parties represented. . . . After exchanging views on these reports, the participants . . . decided to discuss the international situation and the question of exchanging experience and co-ordinating the activities of the Communist parties represented at the conference. . . . Having in mind the negative effects caused by the lack of contact between the parties represented at the conference, and taking into account the necessity of a mutual exchange of experience, the conference decided in this connexion to create an Information Bureau.
>
> " The Information Bureau will consist of representatives of the Central Committees of the above-mentioned parties. The tasks of the Information Bureau consist in organising the exchange of experience among the parties and, if the necessity arises, in co-ordinating their activity on the basis of mutual agreement."

The resolution read as follows :—

> " The conference puts on record that the absence of liaison among the Communist parties taking part . . . represents a serious shortcoming in the present circumstances. Experience has shown that such a lack of co-ordination among the Communist parties is incorrect and harmful. The necessity of exchange of experience and voluntary co-ordination of the activities of the various parties has become particularly acute at present under conditions of the complication of the post-war international situation, when the lack of co-ordination of the Communist parties may lead to losses for the working class.
>
> In view of this the participants in the conference have agreed on the following :—
>
> > (i) To set up an Information Bureau from the representatives of the Communist Party in Yugoslavia, the Bulgarian Workers' Party (Communist), the Communist Party of Rumania, the Hungarian Com-

munist Party, the Polish Workers' Party, the All-Union Communist Party (Bolsheviks), the Communist Party of France, the Communist Party of Czechoslovakia, and the Communist Party of Italy.

(ii) The information Bureau is to be entrusted with the tasks of organising the exchange of experience, and, should the necessity arise, with the task of co-ordinating the activities of the Communist parties on the basis of mutual agreement.

(iii) The Information Bureau is to be composed of representatives of the Central Committees of the Parties, two members from each; delegates to be appointed or replaced by the Central Committees.

(iv) The Information Bureau is to have a fort-nightly press organ and later on a weekly one. The press organ to be published in French and Russian, and, if possible, in other languages.

(v) The Information Bureau is to be located in Belgrade.*

With the dissolution of the Comintern in 1943, Communists abroad were deprived of the last pretence that they had any say in formulating the policy of the movement. Soviet policy nevertheless remained unconditionally binding on them, as may be seen from the following:—

" At present the only determining criterion of revolutionary proletarian internationalism is: are you for or against the U.S.S.R., the motherland of the world proletariat? An internationalist is not one who verbally recognises international solidarity or sympathises with it. A real internationalist is one who brings his sympathy and recognition up to the point of practical and maximum help to the U.S.S.R. in support and defence of the U.S.S.R. by every means and in every possible form. . . . The defence of the U.S.S.R. as of the Socialist motherland of the world proletariat, is the holy duty of every honest man everywhere and not only of the citizens of the U.S.S.R." †

In Soviet jargon a " patriot ", like an " internationalist ", is anyone who supports the U.S.S.R., whatever his country or nationality. Their opposites are the " nationalist ", who

* *Soviet Monitor*, 5th October, 1947.
† P. Vyshinsky, " Communism and the Motherland ", *Voprosy Filosofii* (*Questions of Philosophy*), No. 2, 1948.

favours his own nation first, and the " cosmopolitan ", who thinks in terms of international, rather than Soviet, culture.

When, during the Second World War, the Soviet Army entered the countries of Eastern Europe and assisted the Communist Parties of that area to power, a further aspect of Soviet policy became apparent.

The Communist Parties of these countries were required to obey Soviet orders, and to attribute all their successes to Soviet support. It even became dogma that a genuine revolution could not be carried out without the support of the Red Army. The following quotations illustrate this point:—

> " It is also necessary to emphasise that the services of the French and Italian Communist Parties to the revolution were not less great, but greater than those of Yugoslavia. Even though the French and Italian Communist Parties have so far achieved less success than the Communist Party of Yugoslavia, this is not due to any special qualities of the Communist Party of Yugoslavia, but mainly because . . . at a moment when the people's liberation movement in Yugoslavia was passing through a serious crisis, the Soviet Army came to the aid of the Yugoslav people . . . and in this way created the conditions which were necessary for the Communist Party of Yugoslavia to achieve power. Unfortunately the Soviet army did not and could not render such assistance to the French and Italian Communist Parties." *

J. Berman, the Polish Communist leader, writing in the *Cominform Journal* of 15th March, 1949, gave as one of the " prerequisites for setting up the people's power in Poland "—

> " the liberation of Poland by such a revolutionary force as the Soviet army, whose arrival greatly strengthened the forces of the proletariat and the working peasantry, and could only alarm the bourgeoisie and landlords ".

Anna Pauker, writing in the *Cominform Journal* in August, 1950, speaks of her party's success, " in the favourable conditions created by the presence in Roumania of Soviet troops ".

The official Czechoslovak *Daily Review of the Press* on 11th August, 1948, summarises part of an article in the semi-

---

* Letter of the Central Committee of the Communist Party of the Soviet Union to the Central Committee of the Communist Party of Yugoslavia, 4th May, 1948.

philosophical Communist weekly *Tvorba*, entitled, "Fundamental Mistakes of the Yugoslav Communist Party", as
follows :—

". . . Three conditions were necessary for the creation
of the People's Democracy :—

" 1. That the proletariat represented by the Communist Party was leading the nation in its fight against
fascism.
" 2. That the leading class unmasked themselves
as allies of fascism and enemies of the nation.
" 3. That the Soviet armies were directly participating in the liberating of the people.

" Experience had shown that the third, the participation
of the Red Army in the liberation was the decisive factor.
This can be seen from developments in France where the
first two factors existed, but where the third and the main
one was missing. . . . Not fully realising the rôle of the
Red Army must lead to a non-Marxist explanation of the
creation of the people's democracies, and the playing down
of the leading rôle of the Soviet Union in the democratic
camp, to theories about being able to build socialism
without the help of the U.S.S.R. and finally to the betrayal
of the democratic camp."

In general, uncritical loyalty to the U.S.S.R. has long since
been made the touchstone of a good Communist. The following quotation shows this in a particularly barefaced manner :—

" *A revolutionary* is he who without arguments, unconditionally, openly and honestly, without secret military
consultations is ready to protect and defend the U.S.S.R.,
since the U.S.S.R. is the first proletarian revolutionary
State in the world, that is building socialism. *An internationalist* is he who unreservedly, without hesitation,
without conditions, is prepared to defend the U.S.S.R.
because the U.S.S.R. is the base of the world revolutionary
movement, and to defend, to advance this movement is
impossible without defending the U.S.S.R. Since he
who thinks to defend the world revolutionary movement
apart from and against the U.S.S.R. is going against the
revolution and is necessarily slipping down into the camp
of the enemies of the revolution." *

* Stalin, *Works*, Moscow, 1949, Vol. 10, p. 51.

F

Numerous instances could be quoted of the ludicrous position in which those sections of the Communist Party which are not located beyond the Iron Curtain have found themselves, when a sudden change of policy in Moscow leaves the local Communist Party high and dry on a mass of activity and propaganda which has suddenly become heresy!

The dilemma of the British Communist Party, which had to change its views about World War II in twelve hours, is a classic example, and so was the grave error committed by the Czech government which in a momentary access of capitalism welcomed the proposals for Marshall aid until called to their senses by Moscow.

We have considered, in the group of chapters of which this is the third, the following aspects of the Communist conspiracy: the Propaganda; the Bastion of G.H.Q.; the international instrument, *i.e.* the Communist Party and its Comintern and Cominform. It will now be convenient to probe this affair from the point of view of the Russian national State, and in the next chapter we shall examine Russian Imperialism and its attitude towards nationalism.

CHAPTER VIII

RUSSIAN IMPERIALISM

THE Soviet attitude to nationalities, national movements and the independence of States is that the interests of the Soviet Union, as the incarnation of the interests of the world, should override local interests. National ideals should be encouraged when they prove of assistance to Soviet policy, and suppressed when they oppose Soviet interests. Meanwhile in the U.S.S.R. a system of unreal local autonomy gives such superficial satisfaction to national feelings as is compatible with the simultaneous existence of a rigid centralism.

Soviet foreign policy regards the great industrial States, especially the United States, as its main opponents. It attempts to exploit differences between them, and to use against them the colonial peoples and the " semi-colonial " nations of the Far and Near East and Latin America. It makes use of all forms of economic strife and racial friction, and of any movement which may be of assistance in fomenting trouble between or within the free States.

The world Communist movement is required to give unquestioning obedience to the Soviet leadership. The Soviet Union, as the G.H.Q. of world revolution, is to impose its will on the world by a combination of military force with the activities of these parties.

The prospect, in case of Soviet success, is of a world rigidly centralised on Moscow, and in which every detail of life everywhere would be organised purely with a view to strengthening and perpetuating that rule.

Most of the " imperialism " of the past differed from that at present practised by the Russians in two important respects. In the first place, the conscious design of Russian imperialism to absorb the entire world is almost unprecedented, and in the second place, it has hitherto been practically unknown for imperialist Powers to plan and practise the absolute subordination in every respect of the subject territories to the centre.

In modern times the United Kingdom amassed numerous imperial territories, but at no time was any desire expressed even in the most extreme political circles to dominate the whole world. The conquest of particular areas was often not the result of a plan of even local expansion. On the contrary, countries were frequently occupied in the course of frontier wars and abandoned once or even twice before local difficulties led reluctantly to their annexation. Moreover, it has always been the avowed principle of British rule that dependent territories should eventually be able to rule themselves. The existence of the Dominions and the self-governing Colonies moving towards Dominion status (and beyond it) is proof that the policy was real.*

Nor has the British Empire been centralised. Throughout its area there is and always has been a great deal of devolution, of allowance for local practices and of rule through indigenous social and political forms.

The present imperialism of the U.S.S.R. is of a different character demanding world control and absolute centralisation of all aspects of the life of the world's population under Moscow control. It is a *total* imperialism.

Although it has been very rare for States to aim at dominating the whole world, it has been usual for the holders of political or religious ideas to wish to see them adopted by the whole world. This is a legitimate and natural desire, since if it is held that a general idea is absolutely good in itself, it is presumably the duty of its holder to attempt to secure its universal acceptance. How other people judge his efforts depends on their view of the desirability of his doctrine.

Political and religious ideas can, however, be propagated by persuasion or by force, or, as in the case of mediæval Christianity, and Islam, by a combination of the two; but the advocates of pure persuasion are frequently put in a difficult position if they find that in a given area the opponents of their notions use force against them.

The early founders of the Socialist movement believed in general that they could achieve their aims through ordinary political methods. But Marx held that these methods must involve revolutionary methods and he held that the success of socialism depended upon a closely connected series of revolutions in the main industrial countries of Western Europe. In

* See Appendix C, pp. 116–131, of *Problems of Parliamentary Government in Colonies*, Hansard Society, 1953. 10s. 6d.

uch countries as England and Holland this revolution might ake place peacefully. But everywhere the bitter resistance of he previous ruling classes was to be reckoned with.

He did not fail to see that national sentiments existed, and he advocated the temporary secession of, for example, Ireland from England, as a preliminary to a free union or federation between hem. But he did not develop the nature of the relationships among the revolutionary States or between them and the surviving capitalist States, though his general approach was that of the internationalist radical of that time, in regarding feelings of national rivalry as a vulgar barbarity which would have no place in a Socialist world which would, it seems, be organised as a single State.

The notions of a world State, or the alternative of a loose federation of Socialist States each of which could be trusted to go its own way, were those commonly held by Marxists at that time and thereafter. Nor did they regard the national question as one which would be of any great importance after the revolution.

When Lenin was developing the theory of the tactics of the Bolshevik Party before the Russian revolution, he took the view that the main capitalist States had now become exploiters even of the capitalists of the colonial and semi-colonial countries, and his tactical method of assembling as broad an alliance as possible against the centres of world capitalism involved in this sphere an alliance between the proletariat of the advanced exploiting countries and the nationalist *bourgeoisie* of the exploited countries. In Russia the subject races of the Tsarist Empire in fact provided most useful support to the Bolsheviks during the revolution.

After October, 1917, Lenin expected the revolution to spread over Western Europe, in which event he considered that the centre of gravity of the revolution would move to Berlin or London. In fact he, and the Communists, showed no Russian chauvinism about the matter, but judged it on the more Marxist basis of economic and technological power.

When, after the First World War, the expected revolutions in the West failed to mature, the Soviet Republic remained as the sole stronghold or bastion of the Communists. In the early stages (and in theory to this day) its significance in the minds of its leaders was solely this: that it was a base for the world revolution, a centre from which an internationalist doctrine could be helped to world victory.

> " Lenin never regarded the Republic of the Soviets as an end in itself. To him it was always a link needed to strengthen the chain of the revolutionary movement in the countries of the West and East, a link needed to facilitate the victory of the proletariat of the whole world over capitalism." *

Stalin also makes it plain what strategic rôle, in general, the U.S.S.R. would play in the struggle for world Communism. He says:—

> " The victory of Socialism in one country is not a self-sufficient task. The revolution which has been victorious in one country must regard itself not as a self-sufficient entity but as an aid, *a means for hastening the victory of the proletariat in all countries*. For the victory of the revolution in one country, in the present case Russia . . . is the beginning of and the groundwork for the world revolution . . .
>
> " There can be no doubt that the development of the world revolution, the very process of the breaking away from imperialism of new countries will be quicker and more thorough, the more thoroughly Socialism fortifies itself in the first victorious country, the faster this country is transformed into a base for the further unfolding of the world revolution, into a lever for the further disintegration of imperialism . . .
>
> " This [assistance] should be expressed first, in the victorious country achieving the utmost possible in one country for the development, support and awakening of the revolution in all countries. Secondly, it should be expressed in that the victorious proletariat of one country, having expropriated the capitalists and organised its own Socialist production, would confront the rest of the capitalist world, attract to itself the oppressed classes of other countries, raise revolt among them against the capitalists, and, in the event of necessity, *come out even with armed force against the exploiting classes and their states* . . .
>
> " The free union of nations in Socialism is impossible without a more or less prolonged and stubborn struggle by the Socialist republics against the backward states." †

* Stalin, *Works*, Moscow, 1947, Vol. VI, pp. 50–51.
† Stalin, *Problems of Leninism*, Foreign Languages Publishing House, Moscow, 1941, p. 113. (Our italics.)

The *tactics* of the Communist movement in this struggle are also described by the same writer:—

> " Our revolution has already passed through two stages, and after the October revolution it has entered a third stage. Our strategy changed accordingly. . . .
>
> " Third stage: commenced after the October revolution. Objective: to consolidate the dictatorship of the proletariat in one country, using it as a base for the overthrow of imperialism in all countries. The revolution is spreading beyond the borders of one country; the epoch of world revolution has commenced. The main forces of the revolution: the dictatorship of the proletariat in one country, the revolutionary movement of the proletariat in all countries. Main reserves: the semi-proletarian and small-peasant masses in the developed countries, the liberation movement in the colonies and dependent countries. Direction of the main blow: isolation of the petty bourgeois democrats, isolation of the parties of the Second International, which are the main support of the policy of compromise with imperialism. Plan for the disposition of forces: alliance of the proletarian revolution with the liberation movement in the colonies and dependent countries." *

This definition has been included in each successive edition of *Problems of Leninism*, and in his " Letter to Comrade Ivanov ", published in *Pravda* on 12th February, 1938, Stalin emphatically repudiated the suggestion that his teachings in the *Problems of Leninism* were out of date.

On the twenty-fifth anniversary of the publication of Stalin's essay, *Foundations of Leninism*, from which the above and other passages are quoted, the Soviet newspapers *Izvestia* and the *Literary Gazette* maintained that this work was as applicable to-day as ever:

> " The book, *Foundations of Leninism*, has firmly taken its place in the ideological life of the Bolshevik Party, has become a vital revolutionary guide to action for the Soviet people building Communism, for all fraternal Communist parties abroad in their struggle against capitalist slavery, against imperialist reaction. . . . It has brilliantly withstood the test of time and is confirmed by enormous historical

* Stalin, *Problems of Leninism*, Moscow, 1941, pp. 59–60.

experience, and to-day still preserves all its mighty organisational and mobilizing power in the struggle for the victory of Communism." *

" J. V. Stalin's work of genius on Leninism stands out to-day as the shining, irresistible truth of our great epoch ... and now, after 25 years, it is our mighty ideological weapon, an irreplaceable, trusty and tried guide. It arms ideologically tens of millions of fighters for Communism throughout the world, and shows them the only correct path to liberation from the chains of capitalist slavery." †

At the XIXth Congress of the C.P. in his speech on Oct. 7th, 1952 from which some extracts have already been quoted, L. P. Beria brought the record up to date when he said that the " great service " rendered by Comrade Stalin was that he had " directed the spiritual and physical forces of all the peoples of our country to one great goal—the consolidation of the might of our motherland and the victory of Communism ".

Thus these pronouncements are not vague doctrinal vapourings, but are statements, in characteristically military phraseology, in which the present head of the Soviet Government has given his general analysis of the world situation and his strategic plan for the overthrow of all foreign Governments. The developments in Soviet foreign policy at present, such as for example the attempt now (1953) being made to drive a wedge between the U.S.A. and the other democratic powers, can only be properly understood if it is realised that they represent tactical manœuvres in the carrying out of this plan.

What the above statements teach may be summarised as follows:—

(i) The aim of the Soviet leaders is to extend their régime over the entire globe.

(ii) The special role of the U.S.S.R. is to serve as a base from which this operation can be carried out.

(iii) These plans can only be realised in a " stubborn struggle between the U.S.S.R. and the non-Soviet countries ".

(iv) The Soviet rulers will use as their main weapons the power of the U.S.S.R., and the revolutionary move-

* *Izvestia*, 26th April, 1949.
† *Literary Gazette*, 27th April, 1949.

ments in other countries. They will strengthen these by alliance with nationalist movements in dependent countries, and with peasant movements.

II

One of the differences which should *not* exist between the sincere Communist and the sincere democratic man is that the former accepts, and indeed insists, upon the view that: " The world and all men in it is my parish ", whilst the democratic peoples are only slowly beginning to realise, through painful experiences, that, in the phrase coined by the late Mr Willkie, there is only ONE WORLD, and that it should be as much their business by democratic methods to bring about a democratic world as the Communists make it their business by Communist methods to create a Communist world. If this latter event were realised it would, as things are at present, be a Russian-controlled Communist world.

In this modern world, for the possession of whose body and soul an epoch-making and historic struggle is now taking place, one of the strongest of political emotions which appeals to men is the idea of nationalism.

Its origin in Europe can be traced back to the Reformation, but it grew rapidly in importance during the 19th century, when many new national States came into existence. World War I, with which was linked President Wilson's " self-determination "-of-peoples doctrine, accelerated the process. The nationalism idea spread to the Asiatic peoples during the first half of the present century and is embryonic in Africa.

Although it would take us too far off our present course to go into the matter in detail, it is relevant at this point to draw attention to a fact which may be of enormous consequence to the world before the year A.D. 2000. This is the emergence since approximately A.D. 1900 of the nationalist idea in China, an idea foreign to the Chinese before it was brought to them by the West. Until then China had been a civilisation rather than a nation. The Chinese Communists will undoubtedly exploit the nationalist idea, and will do so having provided China for the first time for centuries with an effective central Government.*

Like most of the great ideas which have influenced human

* See also the author's book, *Western Civilization and the Far East* (Methuen, 1924).

history the conception of nationalism can be used for good and for evil purposes. In this modern mechanised world nationalism in its cultural and social aspects is most desirable, but in its political form, as represented by the sovereign national state (" My country right or wrong "), most democratic people would agree that nationalism is something which must be controlled by international agreements reflected in such organisations as U.N. or N.A.T.O.

However, to embark on a discussion of nationalism would be to stray outside the limits of this book. All we are concerned with in these pages is to note that the nationality or nationalism idea is a very powerful and widespread element in world political thought, and as such one might deduce *a priori* that it would be given much attention by the Russian-controlled Communists in order to see how it could be best exploited for their purpose of advancing the conspiracy. This deduction—as we shall see—is correct. It will be convenient to consider the Soviet Union's policy towards nationalism under three headings. First, in regard to the nationalists inside the Russian frontiers. Secondly, the policy towards the border and smaller neighbouring States now (1953) behind the Iron Curtain. Thirdly, policy towards the " Capitalist States ".

Stalin was the main theorist of the Bolshevik Party on the " national question ", even before the revolution. The thesis developed by him in his work *Marxism and the National Colonial Question* and elsewhere may be summarised as follows:—

(*a*) The Socialist movement should satisfy all national aspirations by liberal grants of autonomy and of minority rights.

(*b*) In a Socialist State national cultures should be " national in form, Socialist in content ".

(*c*) The proletarian party should remain united within a single State, even though the State be divided into federal units.

(*d*) The proletariat should in principle be in favour of the right of all nations to form independent States. But the recognition of this right did not imply that it was a duty. On the contrary, the proletariat in the nation concerned should work to settle the question in whatever way suited the interests of the world revolution as a whole.

This qualification is expressed by Stalin as follows:—

> "This does not mean that the proletariat must support every national movement, everywhere and always, in every single case. It means that support must be given to such national movements as tend to weaken, to overthrow imperialism, and not to strengthen and preserve it. There are cases when the national movements in certain oppressed countries come into conflict with the interests of the development of the proletarian movement. In such cases support is, of course, entirely out of the question. The question of the rights of nations is not an isolated, self-sufficient question: it is a part of the general problem of the proletarian revolution, subordinate to the whole, and must be considered from the point of view of the whole." *

And:—

> "It should be borne in mind that as well as the right of nations to self-determination there is also the right of the working class to consolidate its power, and to this latter right the right of self-determination is subordinate. There are occasions when the right of self-determination conflicts with the higher right, the right of a working class which has assumed power to consolidate that power. In such cases—this must be said bluntly—the right to self-determination cannot and must not serve as an obstacle to the exercise by the working class of its right to dictatorship." †

In 1918–20 a situation arose in which concrete illustrations of the question were frequent. Stalin wrote:—

> "When a life and death struggle is being waged, and is spreading between proletarian Russia and the imperialist *entente*, only two alternatives confront the border regions: either they join forces with Russia, and then the toiling masses of the border regions will be emancipated from imperialist oppression; or they join forces with the *entente*, and then the yoke of imperialism is inevitable. There is no third solution. The so-called independence of a so-called independent Georgia, Armenia, Poland, Finland, etc., is only an illusion, and conceals the utter dependence of those apologies for States on one group of imperialists or another.
>
> "Of course, the border regions of Russia, just as all other

---

* Stalin, *Problems of Leninism*, Moscow, 1941, p. 52.
† Stalin, Report to the 12th Congress of the Communist Party, 23rd April, 1923.

nations, possess the inalienable right to secede from Russia, and if any of these nations decided by a majority to secede from, as was the case with Finland in 1917, Russia, presumably, would be obliged to record the fact and sanction the secession.   But the question here is not that of the rights of nations, but of the interests of the masses of the people both in the centre and the border regions; it is a question of the character—determined by those interests—of the agitation which our party must carry on if it does not desire to repudiate itself and if it wishes to influence the will of the toiling masses of the nationalities in a definite direction. And the interests of the masses of the people render the demand for the secession of the border regions at the present stage of the revolution a profoundly counter-revolutionary one." *

At the very beginning of the Soviet régime, in accordance with the views he had always expressed, Lenin had announced the independence of Poland, Finland and other areas.   In Finland this did not, of course, mean that the Finnish Bolsheviks were restrained from attempting to set up a Bolshevik régime, and in Poland, where it was clear that nationalist feelings were far too strong even for any attempt at Bolshevisation by local Communists, the Red Army proceeded to " test Poland with bayonets ".

A group of Polish Communists was set up as the Government of Poland in the area occupied by the Red Army, and the attempt was considered as a part of the world revolutionary strategy in which the Russian Communists would put themselves on the German frontier in a position to assist the developing Communist effort in Germany.

The failure of the Polish campaign and the end of the Civil War in Russia left the Communists in control of four theoretically separate independent States : Russia, the Ukraine, Byelo-Russia and Transcaucasia which had just been overrun by the Red Army in rather the same way as had been planned for Poland.

There was now a practical demonstration of what the " independence " of the three States which had been allowed to secede from Russia amounted to.   Lenin wrote :—

> " The Ukraine is an independent republic.   That is all right.   But in party matters it sometimes—what is the

* Stalin, *Marxism and the Colonial Question*, International Publishers, New York, 1942, p. 77.

politest way of saying it?—takes a roundabout course, and we have to get at them somehow. For the people there are sly, and I will not say deceive the Central Committee, but somehow or other edge away from us." *

In fact the Communists achieved such amalgamation when the Soviet Union was formed in 1922.

III

A liberal grant of regional autonomy was supposed to satisfy the smaller nations. However, in each case the autonomous republic or regions remain under the control of the united Communist Party, which in effect means control by Moscow. The " national in form, Socialist in content " means in practice that peoples are allowed to use their own languages, be ruled apparently by Communists of their own race, and nothing more. In practice, development in the Soviet Union has been towards an increasing emphasis on the special value of the Russians, on the denigrating of national heroes who had opposed the Tsarist régime (in the early years of the revolution this opposition had been praised) because they had been anti-Russian.

In the absence of local Communists in many of the more backward parts of old Russia, Russian Communists originally played a great rôle in the party in these areas, but even now, when there has been plenty of time to train locals, there is normally a Russian in a controlling position on the secretariat of the Central Committees of the Communist Party in the Central Asian Republics. The same principle applies in the Governments of the republics, where Russians are frequently deputy chairmen of the Government, and of the ministries, while the Security Ministry is normally staffed by Russians, and the Procurators (chief prosecutors) are Russians. A beginning has been made to extend this system to the countries of Eastern Europe, with the export of Marshal Rokossovski to Poland.

Even the " Union " republics of large nations with, on paper, the right to secede, have had all serious power taken from them and given to the Government in Moscow by Article 14 of the Soviet Constitution, which reserves to the centre such matters as : war and peace, diplomatic relations (on paper the " republics "

* Lenin : " Political Report of the Central Committee of the Eleventh Congress ", 27th March, 1922, *Collected Works*, 3rd Russian Edition, Vol. XXVII, pp. 251–2, Leningrad, 1935.

are allowed to " enter into direct relations with foreign States "
(Article 18A). In practice this right has never yet been utilised
Even if it were, the Central Government would retain contro
under Article 14, which states that " the establishment of genera
procedure governing the relations of Union Republics witl
foreign States " comes under the jurisdiction of the Centra
Government. So do defence, foreign trade, security, changes o
republics' mutual frontiers, economic planning, credit and
currency, education, criminal and civil codes and many othe
matters. Thus even formally the local autonomy of even th
" freest " of the republics amounts to almost nothing, while ir
practice the admitted total centralisation of the local Communis
Parties reduces it to absolutely nothing. This bogus autonomy
has been useful to the Kremlin. It has used it to secure
admission to the United Nations of the so-called independen
nations of the Ukraine and Byelo-Russia. These represent
atives invariably vote and speak as the agents of Moscow.

That the complicated apparatus of " autonomy " was no
welcome to the local populations was apparent from the start
Not only were there continual revolts in the early twenties ir
such areas as Bashkiria, but in the Communist Parties of the
national republics a whole series of purges removed leaders whc
tended to put their own republic's interests before those of the
party as a whole.

That Soviet national policy had, at most, only a propaganda
success *outside* the Soviet Union, and had not impressed the
minority nations of the Soviet Union was clearly shown during
the Second World War. Of the smaller nations whose territories were reached by the German armies, almost all have since
been deported to Siberia for anti-Soviet activities " in col-
laboration with the Nazis ". Autonomous republics and regions
abolished include the Chechen-Ingush Republic, the Crimean
Republic, the Kalmyk Republic, the Volga-German Republic
and the autonomous region set up for the Karacha.

In addition, a decree of the Supreme Soviet abolishing the
Kabardino-Balkar Autonomous Republic was promulgated in
June, 1945. In its place the Kabardin Republic was set up.
The Balkars were deported in 1944, and no longer constitute
either an administrative or geographical unit. The order
deporting the Chechens and Crimean Tatars was published in
Izvestia on 26th June, 1946. It says that many of these people

assisted the Germans in the armed struggle while " the main mass of the population . . . took no counter action ", and therefore orders their deportation to " other regions ".

These republics have not reappeared on the map, and it is known that the inhabitants were deported to Central Asia and Siberia in conditions which give little hope of their survival as nations. This is the most striking example of the Soviet attitude to small races, and shows the worthlessness of the autonomy system, and of Soviet propaganda which before their deportation had spoken, for example, of the Volga Germans' " limitless devotion to Communism ".*

The notion that Russian Imperialism, whose heavy yoke has fallen on these alien peoples, has a sacred mission in pursuing its conquests is centuries old, and the notion of Moscow as " the Third Rome " and of its ruler as a sort of holy God-King, though no longer expressed in that fashion, has been taken over unchanged by the present régime.

We have already quoted instances of the subservience to Moscow expected of foreign Communists. The following is typical of the extent to which they are expected to look up to the Russians as such:—

> " The Russian working class, the Russian people helped the backward peoples of our country develop their own national State, economy, culture. . . . By its self-confident struggle against the fascist pillagers, the Great Russian people in brotherly co-operation with all peoples of the U.S.S.R. saved the world from fascist enslavement . . . that is why the peoples of our country rally around the great Russian people. That is why the Russian people enjoy special respect and sympathy of all advanced mankind. . . . That is why the relationship to the Russian people is now the truest criterion for an evaluation of the real nature of the relations of one or another person to democracy, internationalism and Communism." †

There is also much to show that the Soviet citizen as such is regarded as a superior being to the foreigner.

Just as the Soviet Union has lost all those characteristics which in the early stages may have been held to have made it " a workers' State ", except for the covering of jargon and

---

* *Large Soviet Encyclopædia*, Vol. 41, p. 596, 1939.
† *Moskovski Bolshevik*, 16th April, 1949.

propaganda, so it is interesting to see in the Politburo's attitude to foreign nations how chauvinistic *a priori* reasoning has entirely replaced evidence.

In the dispute with the Yugoslav Communist Party, one of the Soviet letters mentions that Djilas, of the Yugoslav Communist Party, had complained to the Soviet Commander that the behaviour of his troops in Belgrade was worse than that of the British, and goes on to denounce this as a gross and undeserved insult, *because* the Soviet Army has a liberating role, while the British is imperialist.

A curious example of the way in which extreme nationalism is encouraged is the fact that Soviet papers ran a campaign just after the war for the " return " of a large part of Northern Turkey to the U.S.S.R. on the grounds that it had once been part of the mediæval Georgian Empire!

To summarise:—

(i) Soviet teaching holds that national rights should be respected insofar as they do not conflict with Communist interests.

(ii) National aspirations that may be directed against non-Soviet régimes are encouraged and exploited.

(iii) The national autonomy actually granted in the U.S.S.R. is a mere formality. Absolute control rests in Moscow.

(iv) Even this façade is destroyed and whole nations condemned to virtual extermination when Moscow thinks fit.

(v) A considerable specifically Russian chauvinism has been encouraged in recent years. The Russian nation and culture are held to be superior to all others.

(vi) Hence, to judge from what has happened to the minorities in Russia and the satellites, the outlook for a world ruled by the Soviet leaders would be at best one of submission to a highly centralised Russian rule under a cloak of local institutions, and with the Russians treated as a superior race.

We will now consider the policy of the Soviet Union towards the smaller States which have had the misfortune to be Russian neighbours.

IV

In the twenties and thirties the Soviet régime posed in the international sphere as the only great Power with respect for small States, denounced the Tsarist agreements which gave Russia special privileges in certain Asiatic countries and concluded a series of treaties of peace, friendship and non-aggression with almost all her neighbours.

It is as well to remember that this was preceded by a period in which a series of Soviet attempts to overthrow the governments of its small neighbours by force had been made, successfully in Transcaucasia, Central Asia and the Ukraine, and fruitlessly in the Baltic countries and Poland. The peaceable treatment of the small States was limited to the period from about 1920 to 1939, when the U.S.S.R. was on the defensive and no other policy was feasible. Much propaganda use was made of this necessity, but as soon as the situation changed and the Soviet leaders saw advantages in more unscrupulous behaviour, their aggressions were renewed.

In 1939–40 the U.S.S.R. invaded Poland and Finland, annexed the Baltic States and obtained considerable territory from Rumania by ultimatum. The Soviet attitude to the smaller States, together with its behaviour with regard to treaties, is illustrated by the experience of Lithuania, Latvia, and Esthonia.

The U.S.S.R., which had already " renounced all rights of sovereignty for ever " over Lithuania by a treaty of 12th July, 1920, signed with her on 22nd September, 1926, a non-aggression pact (renewed in 1931 and 1934 and remaining in force to this day) in which she guaranteed to respect the sovereignty of Lithuania and its territorial integrity in all circumstances. It was strengthened in 1933 by a convention defining aggression, which stated that " no considerations of a political, military, economic or any other nature shall serve as an excuse or justification for aggression ".

When, on 10th October, 1939, Lithuania signed, under heavy pressure, a Mutual Assistance Pact, under which the Soviet forces set up bases on Lithuanian soil, Article 7, nevertheless, guaranteed that it would " not in any way affect the sovereign rights of the contracting parties, in particular, their State organisation, economic and social systems, military measures,

G

and, in general, the principle of non-intervention in internal affairs ". This guarantee lasted for nine months, for on 14th June, 1940, Lithuania received a Soviet ultimatum demanding the resignation of the Government, the arrest of the Chief of Police and the Minister of the Interior, and the free entry of Soviet forces. The Red Army occupied the whole country, and held, on 14th July, under a new and unconstitutional electoral law, " elections " for an Assembly which on 21st July voted for the incorporation of the country into the U.S.S.R., though such an incorporation had not figured even in the electoral programme of the single body presenting candidates.

On 3rd August, 1940, Lithuania was declared part of the Soviet Union. Yet Lenin had said:—

> " If any nation whatsoever is detained by force within the boundaries of a certain State, and if (that nation) contrary to its expressed desire . . . is not given the right to determine the form of its State life by free voting and completely free from the presence of troops of the annexing or stronger State and without any pressure, then the incorporation of that nation by the stronger State is annexation, i.e., seizure by force and violence." *

The experiences of Esthonia and Latvia were practically identical.

In recent years, particularly since Hitler showed the way, Soviet foreign policy has been conducted in a more and more openly imperialist fashion. In Soviet relations with Germany before 1941, territories were exchanged, " spheres of influence " discussed, and so on, without the least pretence of consulting the interests of the inhabitants of the territories concerned.

Originally an obligation existed for the U.S.S.R. to cede a section of Lithuanian territory to Germany. This was not disputed by the Russians, who eventually agreed with the Germans to purchase their rights for a large sum in dollars.

Molotov stated in his conversation with Hitler in Berlin on 12th November, 1940, that by the exchange of Lublin for Lithuania, all possible friction between Russia and Germany had been avoided.

During the Berlin conversations with Hitler and Ribbentrop there was a considerable amount of discussion about the division of the world into spheres of influence, to which Molotov assented

* *Collected Works*, 3rd Russian Edition, Vol. XXII, p. 14.

while stating that Stalin's opinion must be asked about specific proposals. On 26th November, 1940, the Soviet Government informed the German Ambassador in Moscow that it was prepared to accept the Four-Power Pact proposed by Ribbentrop on certain conditions, one of which was the establishment of Soviet land and naval bases " within reach of the Bosphorus and the Dardanelles ", and another that " the direction of the Persian Gulf " be recognised as a Soviet sphere.*

In post-war years the Soviet attitude, frequently expressed, has been that the great Powers' wishes should automatically be binding on the smaller Powers. In the international conferences, and in all Soviet proposals for the settlement of world tension, it has been the consistent Soviet line that extra powers of vote or veto should be given to the larger Powers, and agreement between them should short-circuit the United Nations Organisation.

The Soviet Union's relations with smaller *Communist* States are in some ways even more striking.

The Soviet views, already described, that the interests of world revolution must override local or national ones, and that the rulers of the Soviet Union are the supreme directors of the world revolution, determined the U.S.S.R.'s attitude to the Communist States formed since 1944. The intolerance and rigidity with which those theories were interpreted in practice provide admirable examples of the absolute subservience required.

In 1948 the revolt of the Yugoslav Communist Party occurred. Correspondence between the Soviet and the Yugoslav Communist Parties started with the withdrawal on 18th March of that year by the U.S.S.R. of its civil and military experts from Yugoslavia, on the grounds that they had met an unfriendly atmosphere, were watched by Yugoslav security authorities and that information had been withheld from them. The Yugoslavs counter-charged that the Russians were attempting to bring the Yugoslav Communist Party under the control of the M.V.D. Although later a number of charges on grounds of theory were made against the Yugoslavs, it is reasonably clear that the quarrel really took place because the Russians insisted on, and the Yugoslavs resisted, Soviet domination of Yugoslav economy

* *Nazi–Soviet Relations*, German Secret Documents, published by the State Department.

and direct control of the state through secret agents of the Yugoslav Communist Party.

In recent years all the Communist Parties of Eastern Europe have suffered purges of many of their leading members. The most striking case was that of Bulgaria, where the original accusations against Kostov were of attempting to bargain in economic matters with the U.S.S.R., and where purges involved most of the leading Communists in two spheres—the secret police and military intelligence and the economic ministries. These purges are still going on, and no book can be published quickly enough to keep up to date.* It appears that the " life " of the head of the secret police in a satellite state is about twelve months.

The political aspect is clear enough: the Russian leaders wish to reduce the local Communist Governments to mere instruments of their own Policy, without any shade of autonomy being left them. An interesting example of the way in which Russians treat local Communists as inferior beings may be seen in the Yugoslav–Soviet correspondence, where the Soviet leaders, when there was a disputed account of a conversation between a member of their embassy and a Yugoslav official, said that they must accept the former's version since he was a Soviet citizen.

The economic aspect is also important, for it is clear that many of these Communists were forced for the first time into an anti-Soviet position by the fact that the Russians were subjecting their countries to economic exploitation. In Rumania and Hungary especially the most important centres of industry are operated by " joint " companies under Soviet control, which dominate the entire economy, and whose profits, tax free, go to the Soviet Union.

In their trade relations all these countries also have to accept Soviet terms, which are normally most unfair to them. One of the charges against the Bulgarian Communist Kostov at his trial was that in negotiating the trading agreement with the U.S.S.R. " he argued every point: the exchange rate of the rouble; the question of German assets; setting a high price for Bulgarian tobacco and a low price for Soviet goods; refusing after the Russians devalued the rouble in 1948 to accept any devaluation of Bulgarian credits accumulated in 1940 ".†

* That is why the Prague trials of November 1952 only get this footnote!
† Evidence of Boris Hristov from the official report of the Kostov trial.

It may also be noted that the uranium round Jachymov in Czechoslovakia and at Buchovo in Bulgaria is mined under direct Soviet control, with the areas concerned under Soviet political and military rule. In addition, the Communists of Hungary, Poland and Czechoslovakia, who at first welcomed the Marshall Plan, which would have assisted the economies of their countries were forced to change their minds on Soviet orders.

The theoretical basis of the Soviet attitude to the world Communist movement has been mentioned earlier. The developments of it described here in relation to allegedly sovereign and independent Communist States have a special interest, in that they give a further illustration of the conditions envisaged for a world under Stalinist rule.

It is clear that the Soviet leaders regard small States in general as pawns whose fate should be decided by their larger fellows; their independence may be extinguished at will and an alien ideology imposed on them by force; and when they become Communist they must submit to complete Soviet political control and economic exploitation. Finally we come to the attitude of the Soviet Union towards the " Capitalist " States.

V

The Soviet Union, by its nature, regards the centres of world capitalism as its main opponents. In the present circumstances this means the United States, and perhaps to a lesser extent, (at this time 1953) Britain. The aim of Soviet policy is to concentrate against them their own working class and the colonial and " semi-colonial " countries of Asia, Africa and South America, together with any other States that can be induced to oppose them. The Soviet Union also exploits all rifts which occur among the " imperialists ". And the special hatred of the Stalinists for Social Democrats (who, in their view, confuse the working class by hypocritical anti-capitalism, and deflect it from its true revolutionary course) is carried into the sphere of international politics.

Communists regard a war or a series of wars between the Soviet Union and " imperialist " States, which can only be resolved by the destruction of " imperialism " and the successful world revolution, as inevitable. As Lenin says in a well-known passage:—

> " We are living not merely in a State, but in a system of States, and the existence of the Soviet Republic side by side with imperialist States for a long time is unthinkable. One or the other must triumph in the end. And before that end supervenes a series of frightful collisions between the Soviet Republic and the bourgeois States will be inevitable. That means that if the ruling class, the proletariat, wants to hold sway, it must prove its capacity to do so by military organisation also." *

But Communist theory recognises periods of retreat and recession in the revolutionary movement and adapts itself to them. As Lenin said:—

> " To carry on a war for the overthrow of the international bourgeoisie, a war which is a hundred times more difficult prolonged and complicated than the most stubborn of ordinary wars between States and to refuse beforehand to manœuvre, to utilise the conflict of interests (even though temporary) among one's enemies, to refuse to temporise and to compromise with possible (even though transient, unstable, vacillating and conditional) allies—is not this ridiculous in the extreme? Is it not as though, in the difficult ascent of an unexplored and hitherto inaccessible mountain, we were to renounce beforehand the idea that sometimes we might have to zig-zag, sometimes retracing our steps, sometimes giving up the course once selected and trying various others? " †

In international politics, in the same way, it admits the temporary co-existence of the imperialist and Soviet States. It is a not uncommon trick of Soviet propaganda for Stalin to give set-piece interviews to foreign statesmen or journalists and to emphasise the possibility of the " peaceful co-existence " of the two systems. These statements are always given great prominence by Soviet publicity as evidence of peaceful intentions. They are not so much inconsistent with Stalin's basic principles as misleading, in that they do not specify for how long and on what terms the " peaceful co-existence " is admissible. Fortun-

* Lenin, *Selected Works*, International Publishers, New York, 1943, Vol. III, p. 33, quoted by Stalin in *Problems of Leninism*, Moscow, 1940, p. 156.
† Lenin, *Selected Works*, Vol. X, p. 111, quoted by Stalin in *Problems of Leninism*, Moscow, 1941, pp. 69–70.

ately he has made this clear in less ephemeral form in his published works:—

> "I think that the existence of two opposite systems, the capitalist system and the Socialist system, does not exclude the possibility of . . . agreements . . .
> "The limits to these agreements? The limits are set by the opposite characters of the two systems between which there is rivalry and conflict. Within the limits allowed by these two systems, *but only within these limits*, agreement is quite possible."*

Moreover Stalin prefaced his remarks with the following words:—

> "We are, evidently, speaking of *temporary* agreements with the capitalist governments in the sphere of industry, trade, and *perhaps*, in the sphere of diplomatic relations." †

It has already been made clear that the " rivalry and conflict " are expected to go on until the victory of world Communism. The main weapons of Soviet international policy have been summarised by Stalin as follows:—

> "The tasks of the Party in foreign policy are: One, to utilise every contradiction and conflict among the surrounding capitalist groups and governments for the purpose of disintegrating imperialism: Two, to spare no pains or means to assist the proletarian revolutions in the west: Three, to take all necessary measures to strengthen the national liberation movement in the east, and Four, to strengthen the Red Army." ‡

These points speak for themselves, but it is convenient to deal here with the Soviet attitude to war, which arises from point four above.

We have already seen that war is regarded as inevitable. In addition the Soviet leaders have done their utmost to create a militant atmosphere in the U.S.S.R., and to prevent the

---

* Stalin's " Interview with the First American Labour Delegation in Russia ", 9th September, 1927, quoted in Stalin's *Works*, Russian Edition, Vol. 10, p. 123, Moscow, 1949.
† My italics, op. cit., p. 122.
‡ Stalin, " The Party Before and After the Seizure of Power ", *Works*, Moscow, 1947, Vol. V, p. 111.

population having access to any literature decrying war as such. Condemning such literature Stalin writes:—

> "But we support a liberating anti-imperialist revolutionary war despite the fact that such a war, as is well known, is not only not devoid of ' horrors of bloodshed ', but even abounds in such horrors ".*

The fact that the Soviet Union is the most highly militarised State in the world, not merely in its armaments, but even more so in its propaganda atmosphere and in its educational system, is not accidental. Occasional Soviet statements that their aims are purely defensive are propaganda. Soviet doctrine teaches not only that war is inevitable, and that war waged by the Soviet Union or States, or movements supported by it is justified, but also that, if judged necessary, *aggression* is legitimate. The following quotations give the Communist attitude clearly:—

> "The Social Democrats (i.e., Bolsheviks) may even find themselves in the position of having to demand aggressive wars.
> "In 1848 Marx and Engels considered a war on the part of Germany against Russia to be necessary. Later they tried to influence public opinion in England to induce England to go to war on Russia.
> "Obviously in this question (as also in views on patriotism) it is not the offensive or defensive character of the war, but the interests of the class struggle of the proletariat, or rather the interests of the international movements of the proletariat, that represent the only possible point of view from which the question of the attitude of Social-Democracy towards a given phenomenon in international relations can be considered and solved." †
> "If war is waged by the exploiting class with the object of strengthening its class rule, then it is a criminal war, and ' defensism ' (*i.e.*, the view that one must defend one's own country) in such a war is a base betrayal of Socialism. If war is waged by the proletariat after it has conquered the bourgeoisie in its own country and is waged with the object

---

* Extract from Stalin's letter to Gorki (17th January, 1930) published for the first time in 1949, pp. 175–176 of Vol. 12 of Stalin's *Works*, Moscow, 1949. See also page 108.
† Lenin, *Collected Works*, 3rd Russian Edition, 1935, Vol. 12, p. 317.

of strengthening and extending Socialism, such a war is legitimate and ' holy '." *

" We Marxists have always stood, and do stand, for a *revolutionary* war against *counter-revolutionary* peoples. For example, if Socialism were to be victorious in America or in Europe in 1920 while, let us say, Japan or China were advancing *their* Bismarcks against us—even if it were at first only diplomatically—then we certainly would be for an aggressive revolutionary war against them." †

" The character of the war (whether reactionary or revolutionary) is not determined by who the aggressor was, or whose land ' the enemy ' has occupied. It is determined by the class which is waging the war and the politics of which this war is the continuation." ‡

Thus the Soviet rulers consider in their relations with the capitalist world, that violent clashes are inevitable, and that wars—and even aggressive wars—which serve Soviet interests are justified.

It is always very hazardous to forecast what the next tactical expression of Soviet-controlled Communism may be, but at the moment of writing (Jan. 1953) for reasons set forth on page 197 we are disposed to think that the Kremlin may realise that the policy of " peaceful aggression " in Europe has been exploited to the full. It has produced great results but it has also produced N.A.T.O. Peaceful co-existence—in Europe—may now become the slogan. Only the most wishful thinkers will be deceived; the long term strategical objection must remain the same for so long as Communism is what it is.

VI

The practical results of the theories mentioned above have been remarkable, as can be seen from the following summary of the expansion of the Soviet Union or Red Empire since 1939. Since that date the Soviet Union has acquired 265,172 square miles of new territory—an area larger than France, Belgium,

* Lenin, *Left-wing Childishness and Petit-bourgeois Mentality*, Russian Edition Vol. 22, p. 510.
† Lenin, *Collected Works*, 3rd Russian Edition, Vol. 18, p. 250.
‡ Lenin, ibid., Vol. 23, p. 380.

the Netherlands and Denmark—and an additional population of 22,733,780. The details are as follows:—

PARTICULARS OF TERRITORIES ACQUIRED

	Area sq. miles	Population
EUROPE		
Eastern Poland	69,000	11,000,000
BALTIC STATES		
Esthonia	18,353	1,117,000
Latvia	25,402	1,950,000
Lithuania	22,959	2,880,000
RUMANIAN PROVINCES		
Bessarabia . . .	17,000	3,000,000
Northern Bukovina . . .	4,031	500,000
CZECHOSLOVAKIA		
Ruthenia	4,921	725,000
FINLAND		
Petsamo Territory . . .	3,130	2,000
Area adjoining Petsamo . .	176	—
Porkkala (lease) . . .	114	—
Karelian Isthmus . . .	10,570	486,365
4 Islands Gulf of Finland . .	19	2,935
Salla sector . . .	3,010	5,550
Fishermen's Peninsula . .	143	930
East Prussia	4,500	300,000
FAR EAST		
Tannu Tuva	64,000	70,000
Kuriles	3,944	18,000
South Sakhalin . . .	13,900	415,000
Port Arthur (lease)	—	29,000
Dairen (lease)	—	232,000
	265,172	22,733,780

The above table does not take into account the enormous *de facto* increase of area and population represented by Poland, Rumania, Albania, Bulgaria, Hungary, and Czechoslovakia, quite apart from the East German Zone.

CHAPTER IX

THE SOVIET UNION AND PEACE

IN Chapter VIII it was mentioned that one of the powerful political ideas now current in the world is called nationalism, and it was explained how the Soviet Union exploits this fact as part of its world-wide campaign. Another big idea of universal interest and concern is expressed by the word *Peace*.

Most men and women have always strongly desired peace, but the modern totality of war, coupled with the circumstance of two world wars in the life-time of one generation, have caused humanity to develop a very lively and passionate interest in this subject.

In the introduction to this book we have set down some observations on the subject of *peace* and *war*, together with the meanings, correct and incorrect, which should be assigned to these words. However, the subject is of such vital importance that the argument will be restated in different words.

There is a school of thought, to which the author has adhered for many years which believes that much confusion has been brought into the question of the discussion of peace and war because of the association of the word " war " with military operations, *but with no other form of non-harmonious relationship between nations.*

These observations are made to explain why in the passages which follow we are using the terms *peace* and *war* not as they ought to be used * IF it were properly understood that peace in practice and in theory should mean much more than a state of non-military operations.

We are concerned here not with how the words *peace* and *war* ought to be understood and used, but how they *are* used. Therefore we say that the opposite of peace is war; that war is the rupture of all normal intercourse between nations and the use (as distinct from the threat—a vital difference) of armed

* And invariably are used in *National News-Letter* which dismisses as nonsense the conception that we are not *at war* and therefore are at peace with Russia.

force by each nation. *That, and only that is war, according t*
current fallacious ideas.

Similarly, every other relationship is peace, according to
generally accepted ideas. That is to say, any relationship
(even a conflict) between two nations, whatever its result
that does not involve the use of armed force, is compatible with
peace. Thus peace describes the relationship that exists, say
between Great Britain and France, or Italy and the United
States; it also describes the relationship between Germany and
Czechoslovakia before and after March, 1939, and between
Soviet Russia and Czechoslovakia before and after February
1948. It describes the relationship between the North Atlantic
Treaty Powers, and between these Powers and Soviet Russia.

Peace thus describes every international relationship, from
harmonious co-operation to the imposition of one nation's
will upon another by means of the threat (as distinct from the
use) of armed force, and a consequent state of subjection as
complete as if the conquest had been the result of a victorious
war. All this is called peace!

This word peace can even be twisted to describe the relations
between the U.S.A. and British Governments (especially the
British Government) and the Communist Government of
China, although the troops of these nations are fighting each
other in Korea.

Of course it is not peace in any strict or real sense. But
technically it is peace; and anyone can support, justify or
work for any of these international relationships by invoking
the name of peace. Conversely, anyone who says he is working
for peace may, consciously or unconsciously, be working for
anything from mutual understanding and international co-
operation to national aggression by all means short of war.
All this follows from the fact that peace has many aspects;
and the consequences are considerable.

Since peace has so many meanings, it is not to be wondered
at that the ideal of peace should have been put to many uses.
In unscrupulous hands it can be, and often is, employed as a
mask for deception and blackmail—and the two are often used
together.

A weak Government may appeal to peace to justify action
which would otherwise be unacceptable to its own people.
All Governments that feel called upon to explain their policy

to their own public or to world opinion tend (with or without good reason) to use the ideal of peace as their justification.

These are old-established practices. They start from the simple premise that people prefer peace to war. Therefore, a Government, when dealing with an equal or a weaker Power, would be foolish to *use* force if the *threat* of force will provide the government with what it wants; if it decides to use force, then it must claim that it is to forestall the enemy's use of force, or that the use of force is unavoidable, just and not greatly harmful to the State; and if a Government yields, without fighting, to superior force, it justifies itself by the desire to preserve peace and save needless destruction and loss of life.

Thus the love of peace innate in most people has always been both a real and desirable inspiration to Governments and a sentiment admirably adapted for exploitation for wrong purposes.

Under modern conditions, when science and technology have made the greatest gulf in history between what peace could be and what war would be, the emotional opportunities offered to the unscrupulous to exploit the love of peace and the fear of war are greater than ever.

Science has offered the prospect, if another war came, of unspeakable horrors of which the recent war gave a foretaste. Science has made it possible, if sanity prevails, to raise the whole world's material standards of prosperity to unknown heights. The contrast is without parallel. Stalin put his finger on the opportunities that this modern contrast gave for exploiting war-weariness when he referred to " the circumstance that the October Revolution began during the imperialist war, at a time when the labouring masses, weary of war and thirsty for peace, were by the very logic of events led up to the proletarian revolution as the only way out of the war. This fact was supremely important for the October Revolution, for it put into its hands the mighty weapon of peace, furnished the opportunity of relating the Soviet revolution to the ending of the hated war, and thus creating mass sympathy for it."

Peace can be invoked, sincerely, mistakenly, cynically, cunningly, to justify Government policy. The reluctance to contemplate war that puts so proper a restraint upon the actions of a Government can be exploited as an instrument of aggressive policy, if the horror of war can be used to influence the population of a potential victim.

If, through the use of modern communications or through the help of supporters inside the country concerned, a potential victim's will to resist can be diminished, and its fear of war increased, then its love of peace can be exploited and inflated to justify non-resistance to aggression. Obviously, peace propaganda addressed to a potential enemy need spare no horror in denouncing war, and need not cease to emphasise the peace-loving aims of the potential aggressor. For no Government, however aggressive, will elect to gain by war what it can gain by peaceful means.

It is far better, therefore, to dress up aggressive aims in the robes of peace, and simultaneously to whip up fear of war as a reminder of what might happen if peaceful means of aggression, such as intimidation and subversion, should be met by force or otherwise frustrated.

If two Governments organised an anti-war party in the territory of the other, and each was responsive to its own public opinion, then the prospect of war between them would be to that extent diminished. Under modern conditions, however, the Governments least responsive to public opinion are those most likely to start a war; and dictatorships would in no circumstances tolerate any group in their midst which advocated weakening their military preparedness. Further, they take drastic steps to ensure that only the views they approve and their own assortment of facts ever reach their people. Consequently the exploitation of the fear of war in the population of another country is a weapon especially useful to dictators; and its use has often proved to be evidence of aggressive intentions.

Modern history provides one striking example of the exploitation of the love of peace by totalitarian Governments to achieve aggressive aims and consolidate gains already achieved. The technique is worth examining in detail.

From 1933 onwards, Hitler pursued a consistent programme of remilitarisation and territorial gains at the expense of neighbouring States. Each successive step was nicely calculated to take account of public opinion in those countries which might possibly obstruct German designs; each was accompanied by protestations of Hitler's love of peace, such as :—

" National Socialist Germany wants peace because of its fundamental convictions. It wants peace also owing to the realisation of the simple primitive fact that no war would be likely essentially to alter the distress in Europe. It would probably increase it. Present-day Germany is engaged in the tremendous work of making good the damage done to it internally. None of our projects of a practical nature will be completed before a period of from 10 to 20 years. None of our tasks of an ideal kind can be completed before 50 or perhaps 100 years have passed. . . . What then could I wish more than peace and tranquillity . . . ? Germany needs peace and desires peace."

When Germany repudiated the Locarno Treaty, Ribbentrop's speech to the League of Nations announcing the repudiation (19th March, 1936) contained the following passage:—

" This German people now has but one sincere wish, to live in peace and friendship with its neighbours and from now on to co-operate to the best of its ability in building up a true European solidarity. . . ."

On 18th March, 1938, directly after the incorporation of Austria in the German Reich, Hitler paid tribute to Mussolini's help, and continued:—

" And thus on this occasion, too, the Axis which binds our two countries together has rendered the greatest service to world peace. For Germany only desires peace. Germany wants to do no harm to other nations."

Finally, in a speech at Wilhelmshaven on 1st April, 1939, referring to his entry into Prague and the rape of Czechoslovakia ten days previously, Hitler said:—

" The early prosperity of the town rose together with the rise of the Reich after its struggles for unity. This Germany was a Germany of peace. While the so-called peace-loving, virtuous nations were waging a whole series of wars, the Germany of that day knew only one aim—to preserve the peace, to work in peace, to raise the prosperity of her people, and thus to contribute to human civilisation and culture.

" This Germany of peace-time with infinite industry, with creative genius, and with persistence had sought to build up her life at home and, through participation in the peaceful competition of peoples, had sought abroad to secure for herself the place in the sun which was her due.

" Despite the fact that for decades this Germany was the surest guarantee of peace and devoted herself only to her peaceful activities, this did not prevent other peoples and in particular their statesmen, from following up this rise of Germany with envy and hatred and to it their final answer was war.

" We know to-day from historical documents how at that time a policy of encirclement was systematically pursued by England. . . .

" I have thus, I believe, done a great service to the cause of peace, for I have betimes made worthless an instrument which was destined to be effective in war against Germany. When folk now say that this is the signal proving that Germany now wishes to attack the whole world I do not believe that anyone seriously means this : that could be only the expression of an extremely bad conscience. Perhaps it is anger at the failure of a far-reaching plan, or is it perhaps that thereby it is hoped to create the tactical condition necessary for the new encirclement policy ? However that may be, I am convinced that in acting thus I have done a great service to the cause of peace.

" And arising from this conviction three weeks ago I decided to give to the coming Party Rally the name ' The Party Rally of Peace.' For Germany does not think of attacking other nations." *

The Nuremburg Peace Rally, due to be held in September, 1939, was never held, for by that time Hitler had decided that his preparations were complete, and his political arrangements satisfactory, and had launched his attack on Poland. The political preparations had been rounded off by the act which made war certain, the Nazi–Soviet pact of 22nd August, 1939. This pact included a secret agreement between Stalin and Hitler to carve up Poland and absorb it in their respective empires.

Britain and France, in accordance with their treaty obligations, went to the aid of Poland as soon as Hitler's attack had begun. But long before their intervention could have any effect, Soviet troops had also invaded Poland. The Nazi and the Russian armies met, and Poland disappeared. I

* In June, 1939, the author met in Berlin an old friend who had been violently anti-Nazi. He astonished me by saying that he had now become convinced that Hitler's protective seizure of Czechoslovakia had proved the Fuehrer's peaceful intentions.

was then in the interests of Hitler to end the war while he prepared his next act of aggression. Accordingly, on 28th
September, 1939, a joint communiqué was issued over the
signatures of Molotov and von Ribbentrop, which read as
follows:—

"After the Government of the German Reich and the
Government of the U.S.S.R. have, by means of the treaty
signed to-day, definitely settled the problems arising from
the collapse of the Polish State and have thereby caused a
sure foundation for a lasting peace in Eastern Europe,
they mutually express their conviction that it would serve
the true interest of all peoples to put an end to the state of
war existing at present between Germany on the one side
and England and France on the other. . . .

"Should, however, the efforts of the two Governments
remain fruitless, this would demonstrate the fact that
England and France are responsible for the continuation
of the war, whereupon, in case of the continuation of the
war, the Governments of Germany and of the U.S.S.R.
shall engage in mutual consultations with regard to
necessary measures."

What happened next can best be shown by quoting from
statements made at the time. *Izvestia* was the first to take up
the "peace" theme, on 9th October, 1939:—

". . . a termination of hostilities would be in the
interests of the people of all nations. In the speech
which Hitler . . . delivered in the Reichstag on 6th
October he put forward the German proposals intended to
regulate the question of Poland and to end the war.

"Hitler's proposals can be accepted, rejected, or
subjected to certain amendments, but it must be admitted
that they can in any case serve as a genuine and practical
basis for negotiations directed towards a speedy conclusion
of peace.

"In view of this, it might be supposed that the governments of Britain and France, who in their declarations
show their desire for peace, would bring a serious and
business-like attitude to bear on this chance of ending the
war quickly."

Izvestia again, on the same date, said:—

"War or Peace—that is the question. The supporters
of the slogan 'War to its victorious conclusion' stand for

H

the further prosecution of the war, stand for war against peace."

At the same time the authoritative Communist Party line was made clearer in the official Soviet journal *Bolshevik* (Issue 19):—

> " The British Government makes full use of its emergency powers and smothers free thought and every protest against the unjust Imperialist war . . . (i.e. the decision to fight on after the fall of Poland until Hitler was defeated).
> " Alarmed and bewildered, the working classes in Britain and France ask ' What next? In whose interest must we go into the trenches? ' "

This gave the line for all Communist propagandists in Britain and France to hinder the war effort and agitate for peace with Hitler. The British and French Governments were to be branded as aggressors against the peace-loving Hitler (for had not he and Stalin just made a peace offer?) and the fear and dislike of war were to be fully exploited for this purpose.

Stalin personally endorsed this version of war and peace in an interview given to *Pravda* on 30th November, 1939. He said:—

> " (i) It is not Germany who has attacked England and France, but England and France who have attacked Germany.
> " (ii) After the opening of military operations, Germany made overtures to the British and French Governments, proposing to them to make peace. The U.S.S.R. supported this peace offer.
> " (iii) The British and French Governments rudely rejected these German offers and the efforts of the U.S.S.R."

Thereafter " peace " became the order of the day for all Communist parties. Meetings were held in favour of " peace ", the morale of the fighting forces was to be weakened, war factories were to be sabotaged. The British and French Governments were the aggressors, but the people (and Hitler and Stalin) wanted peace. The British Communist Party's *Daily Worker*, in an editorial entitled " Hitler Speaks ", published on 1st February, 1940, said:—

> " Hitler repeated once again his claim that the war was thrust upon him by Britain. Against this historical

fact there is no reply. Britain declared war, not Germany. Attempts were made to end the war, but the Soviet-German peace overtures were rejected by Britain."

The climax of the British Communist Party's " peace " campaign, criticising every possible Government measure and encouraging strikes in factories, resistance to Government air-raid measures, discontent in the Army, etc., was the People's Convention on 1st January, 1941, which never so much as mentioned resistance to Hitler in its demands.

It is clear that once the Nazi–Soviet alliance had annexed Poland, it was in their interest to end the war at the earliest moment to consolidate their gains. When their peace offer, which was of course peace based on acceptance of a *fait accompli*, was rejected, then it was to both their interests to weaken the war effort of the British and French Governments.

This was done through Nazi agents and through the Communist parties, the tactics being to try to split the people from the Governments by playing on the love of peace, and portraying the Governments as prosecuting a useless and horrible war.

Thus from September, 1939, to June, 1941, through Dunkirk and the fall of France, the Battle of Britain and the Blitz, peace meetings were being held; campaigns for signature of peace petitions were being organised; the love of peace was being exploited by all possible means, to undermine the strength of the nation and its will to resist, and to preserve the domination of Hitler and Stalin over the mainland of Europe while the invasion of Britain was being prepared.

From the differing points of view of both the Nazi and Soviet Governments such a plan was sound. Its execution was poor, at any rate in Great Britain. The Communist Party was of no importance, and its influence negligible. It could not live down its deviation from the party line when it supported the British declaration of war against Stalin's ally, and its subsequent *volte face* was not only squalid but ludicrous; and to the vast majority of people the general principles of peace which the campaign was exploiting were obviously inapplicable to the situation in which Britain found herself.

Nevertheless, the campaign as a whole is important because it demonstrates the truth of a proposition already stated—

namely, that peace can be exploited as an instrument o aggressive policy.

The example of the " peace " campaign of 1939–41, con ducted as it was by a successful aggressor (Germany) and a associate (Russia) which had got what it wanted withou fighting, shows clearly how and why such an operation i conducted. The object is to weaken the opponent's will t fight or resist, by creating in the public mind a fear of war enlarging on the joys and general desirability of peace, an creating suspicion or hatred of the Government which i prepared to embark on or continue a war.

While some impact may be made by broadcasting, the mai conduct of the campaign must rest with agents, preferabl concealed or disguised, for example, as patriots, pacifists o defeatists. These have a free hand to exploit peace for an ends which will assist the policy of the Government they ar in fact serving. It may be Hitler's peace offer, agitating t end the war, weakening national morale, sabotage and strike when possible, etc. All this was done in the name of peace.

Enough has been written to show that the tearing up o treaties, territorial expansion, the destruction of nations, con solidation of conquests, intimidation, subversion and treachery all can be explained and justified as service to the cause o peace. But, armaments, conscription and treaties of allianc can be sincerely supported by nations desirous of maintainin peace. Then what policies is the lover of peace to support What principles are to guide him?

An answer is to be found in the nature of peaceful men Peace, is a relationship between States, and in the world as a present constituted, man, whether peace-loving or otherwise is a citizen of one State or another. But man has a very compli cated set of loyalties—he has a duty to his family, to the State, t humanity as a whole and to certain non-material and impersona values whose existence he regards as good. These loyalties ar often in conflict with each other, and the threat of war, and of th death and destruction which war brings, heighten that conflict

Moreover, no situation in international politics is simple o sudden. War is the outcome of a complex chain of events each of which may have required difficult decisions, although th pattern of events may be simple once the fundamental aims an motives of the protagonists have become clear.

In these difficult situations, the primary duty of the man of peace may well be to examine, not only peace, but also his own beliefs. Is there any situation or relationship, for himself, his family, his country or his creed, so terrible that the alternative of war and possibly death is preferable? What will be the consequences, moral and material, of resisting aggression with force? What will be the moral and material consequences of not resisting aggression? If peace is threatened, who is it threatened by? What are his motives, and to what extent are they a reaction against the threats of others? Is there a consistent pattern in the policy of a nation, and are its deeds consistent with its words about peace? To what extent can a peaceful man influence the policy of his or other Governments? Where does his duty lie?

In matters of peace and war a man's judgment of right and wrong is not solely his private affair. He presumably hopes that a majority of people will share his own beliefs and that his Government will do what he himself deems to be right.

Anyone who pronounces judgment on matters of peace and war therefore takes upon himself a very heavy responsibility. There is too much at stake for it to be disposed of without the most careful deliberation.

Good and sincere men have often thought deeply on these questions, and in any situation they may have reached a diversity of conclusions, based on their own personal convictions. It is not the aim of this book to pronounce judgment upon these various viewpoints. But, as the preceding pages have shown, professions of the love of peace can be expected not only from the sincere pacifist, the conscientious objector and the believer in neutrality, but also from the rabid dictator bent on aggression.

The currency of peace has been debased, and many counterfeit coins are in circulation. War has now become total, and terrible; it embraces in its toils the whole nation and men yearning for peace have become an object of exploitation by potential aggressors, since they can be used as a focus of resistance to defence in time of war or to defence preparations before war has broken out.

These modern developments can in effect drive the pacifist and the neutralist into a position, not of peace or neutrality, but into an unneutral, unpeaceful position of actively supporting

the enemy, unless he fully comprehends the rôle into which
the enemy has forced him. This is certainly the case if all
genuine and conscientious striving for peace is only allowed
expression in one camp.

He has therefore to know what is the attitude to pacifism
and neutralism, to peace and war, of a potential enemy State,
and then to determine for himself whether his own attitude is
contributing to any disparity in national strength which, if
the would-be aggressor thought it large enough to justify the
risk, might lead to war.

In this chapter there are posed many more questions than it
could hope to answer. They can, however, be distilled into
some simpler questions which can be answered with some
degree of certainty. The starting point is the fact, which is not
anywhere in dispute, that the present tension in the world is
between the Communist group of States led by the Soviet
Union and the non-Communist world.

We must therefore ask ourselves the following questions:—

> What does the Soviet Government mean by " peaceful
> co-existence "?
> Has the Soviet Government rejected war as an instru-
> ment of national policy?
> What is the attitude of the Soviet Government on matters
> of conscience—pacifism and neutralism?
> Is the Soviet Government deliberately exploiting the
> love of peace in the free world?*
> If so, is this exploitation specifically related to the aims
> of Soviet policy?

The answers to all these questions are fundamental to the
issues of war and peace. Fortunately they have all been
explicitly stated by Soviet Russian authorities and reliable
spokesmen elsewhere.

We will start with peaceful co-existence.

It is the aim of normal nations to live in peace with one
another. They may be rivals in trade or have conflicting
political and diplomatic interests and their friendships may
have their ups and downs. But within western democratic
international society the past 50 years have witnessed a striking

* See Chap. X.

change in the attitude of sovereign states towards the use of force as a means of settling disputes between them.

Their differences are resolved by formal machinery or informal arrangements; in either case the outcome is the result of an agreement upon mutually acceptable terms, based on tolerance and understanding of other points of view. This is the essence of peaceful co-existence between nations.

Nobody talks about peaceful co-existence between, say, the nations of Western Europe, or between the members of the British Commonwealth. This is because their relationships are regarded as normal and obvious, and not worthy of receiving a special, self-conscious title such as " peaceful co-existence ". This term is reserved for relationships in which the peace, or the co-existence, is an object of surprise and suspicion, if not downright cynicism.

Although Hitler may not have used the precise phrase, his speeches between 1933 and 1940 are full of the idea of peaceful co-existence between Germany and the rest of the world. His speech to the Nuremburg party rally in September, 1934, is a good example, with some interesting features:—

> " In the sphere of foreign policy we have in the most solemn form declared before the entire world the principles on which the German nation without hatred or desire for vengeance against others, seeks peace and friendship with those who 15 years ago still faced us as foes. In the profound recognition of the unavoidable consequences of a new war in Europe which could but lead to Communistic chaos, we have done everything in our power to improve and to free from venom our relations with those nations which formerly faced us in enmity. If our ceaseless appeals so often remained without any answer, yet we know that it is not the peoples who wish for conflict and war but rather small cliques of international agitators whose interest it is to make war, to profit from wars, but never to fight in war."

This was a very cunning line of propaganda. Hitler appears as the champion of peace, desiring peaceful co-existence with his former enemies. His desire is shared by the peoples of other nations, but their wishes are frustrated by a small group of international warmongers—not here specified as other Governments, although he made this clear at other times.

The implication was obvious: if the peoples of other nations would support the peace policy of Hitler—the re-occupation of the Rhineland, conscription, the repudiation of the Locarno Treaty, the withdrawal from the League of Nations, the union with Austria, the rape of Czechoslovakia, the attack on Poland —and if the peoples would turn against their own war-mongering Governments, then there would be peace.

Hitler also introduces the blackmail element—a reminder of the horrors of war and of the Communism which would follow, with the suggestion that they *will* follow if Germany's peaceful policy is frustrated.

But the phrase " peaceful co-existence " is mainly used to-day in discussions about the relationship between the Soviet Union and the free world. The reason is not far to seek. The nations of the free world, being democracies, have for long been willing to apply to Soviet Russia the rules that govern their relationships with each other. They have believed that the world could contain differing economic and social systems, that the internal affairs of other nations were not their concern, and that " live and let live " was a very sound rule for Governments to follow.

These are, of course, very foolish beliefs in certain circumstances, and are true only if " other nations " accept the fundamental principles of democracy. The point can be illustrated by a homely parable.

If a number of citizens are living in a community and each has some method of space-heating in his house, it is not the business of citizen A if citizen B has an electric fire and Mr C a coal fire, whilst Mr D prefers central heating, although, be it noted, it may be desirable for reasons of national economy to endeavour *to persuade* Mr C to use an economical grate and in the last resort, after due Parliamentary discussion, to compel him not to waste coal. Even in this case Mr C is still at liberty to form a society for the defence of open fires and campaign to have the law repealed. But if in this community there exists a Mr S, whose business in life is arson, then it is very much the business of Messrs A, B and C to concern themselves with what Mr S does with fire.

It is therefore immensely foolish and highly dangerous for democracies to assume that " live and let live " applies to the relationship between democracies and dictatorships, especially dictatorships such as the Soviet Union, whose *raison d'être* is the attainment of purposes which must involve the destruction of liberal democracy elsewhere. " Live and let murder " would be a better way of describing this appalling fallacy whose harvest (in the examples of Mussolini and Hitler) was reaped with blood, sweat and tears from 1939 to 1945.

The rulers of the Soviet Union have a totally different theory about the relationship between Communist and non-Communist states. It is—and we welcome this opportunity of paying them a well-deserved compliment—the correct theory. Moreover, they have always been frank, open and explicit about this theory, for they have never attempted to conceal their belief that the enmity between the Communist and non-Communist systems was complete and irreconcilable, and that in the end the one would destroy the other. They also believe, and have based their domestic and foreign policy upon the belief, that it was the Communist system that would win, and that it was their business to ensure that the Communist system was the victor.

Thus Lenin:—

> " We are living not merely in a State, but in a system of States, and the existence of the Soviet Republic side-by-side with imperialist States for a long time is unthinkable. One or the other must triumph in the end. And before that end supervenes a series of frightful collisions between the Soviet Republic and the bourgeois States will be inevitable. This means that, if the ruling class, the proletariat, wants to hold sway, it must prove its capacity to do so by its military organisation. . . ." *

And Stalin:

> ". . . in the further progress of development of the international revolution two world centres will be formed : the Socialist centre, attracting to itself all the countries gravitating towards Socialism, and the capitalist centre, attracting to itself all the countries gravitating towards capitalism. The fight between these two centres for the conquest of world economy will decide the fate of capitalism and Communism throughout the whole world, for the

* Lenin's report to the 8th Congress of the Russian Communist Party in the name of the Central Committee, 12th March, 1919.

final defeat of world capitalism means the victory of Socialism in the arena of world economy.*

" The draft programme [of the Communist International] bases itself on the uneven development of world capitalism and deduces therefrom the possibility of the victory of Socialism in separate countries, thence leading to the prospect of the creation of two parallel centres of gravity—a world centre of capitalism and a world centre of Socialism—struggling between them for the conquest of the world." †

The Second World War produced a temporary and tactical suspension of Communist hostility to the free world, which was soon corrected when the danger to Russia had passed.   Thus:—

" The fact that the Soviet Union and the highly developed capitalist countries showed themselves to be in the camp of powers, ranged against the fascist aggressors, showed that the struggle of two systems within the democratic camp was temporarily alleviated, suspended, but this, of course, did not mean the end of the struggle." ‡

Again, in 1948, the important Soviet periodical *Questions of Philosophy*, No. 6, wrote in its editorial:

" The fundamental concept of our epoch consists of the struggle between two camps—the imperialist one, headed by the U.S.A., and the anti-imperialist, headed by the Soviet Union.   The democratic, anti-imperialist camp, embodies and expresses the interests of the international proletariat and of strata of the working masses led by it in their struggle against capitalism and imperialism, for a better social order, for Communism.   This is a class struggle on a world scale."

The doctrines here enumerated were, and are, the official policy of the Soviet Government, and will remain so as long as the present political system survives in Russia.   But it was obvious to the Soviet leaders that the non-Communist world could not collapse or be overthrown in a day.   There had to be a long period in which both systems, Communist and non-Communist, existed side by side.

During this period, according to Communist theory, the

* In an interview with an American Labour delegation in 1927.
† Speech to the Central Committee in 1928.
‡ Varga, in the Soviet periodical *World and Politics*, No. 6, June, 1946.

non-Communist world would approach collapse, while the Communist Party was to hasten the process. Peaceful co-existence, therefore, was to be a temporary expedient whose duration would be determined by Communist theory and tactics and by developments in the non-Communist world. Stalin made this quite clear :—

"We cannot forget the saying of Lenin to the effect that a great deal in the matter of our construction depends on whether we succeed in delaying the war with the capitalist countries, which is inevitable, but which may be delayed either until proletarian revolution ripens in Europe or until colonial revolutions come fully to a head or finally, until the capitalists fight among themselves over the division of the colonies. Therefore, the maintenance of peaceful relations with capitalist countries is an obligatory task for us. The basis of our relations with capitalist countries consists in admitting the co-existence of two opposed systems." *

"The object of the Party is to exploit all and any con-flicting interests among the surrounding capitalist groups and governments with the view to the disintegration of capitalism." †

In the following extract from his *Problems of Leninism*, Stalin also describes the phase of Soviet foreign policy which began with the 1917 revolution and continues to-day.

"Objective: to consolidate the dictatorship of the proletariat in one country, using it as a base for the over-throw of imperialism in all countries. The revolution is spreading beyond the confines of one country; the period of world revolution has commenced. The main forces of the revolution: the dictatorship of the proletariat in one country, the revolutionary movement of the proletariat in all countries. Main reserves: the semi-proletarian and small-peasant masses in the developed countries, the liberation movement in the colonies and dependent countries. Direction of the main blow: isolation of the parties of the Second International, which constitute the main support of the policy of compromise with imperialism.

* Speech to the 15th Congress of C.P.S.U.(b), 2nd December, 1927.
† "The Party Before and After the Seizure of Power", *Pravda*, 28th August, 1921 ; *Works*, Vol. 5, p. 111.

Plan for the disposition of forces: alliances of the proletarian revolution with the liberation movement in the colonies and the dependent countries."

This is the background of Soviet foreign policy against which, and as part of which, Russian spokesmen are now propounding the theory of " peaceful co-existence ". Their statements of the theory run on fairly stereotyped lines. A Moscow *Pravda* article of 12th September, 1951, by N. Elizarov, entitled " On the Peaceful Co-existence of the Two Systems ", is a typical example. This starts on a somewhat unexpected note, which we italicise, in an article on peace. It begins:—

" The enemies of the Soviet Union, *opponents of friendly co-operation among peoples*, deny the possibility of the peaceful co-existence of the Socialist and capitalist systems. *The inspirers and instigators of new wars* spread, in various versions, the ill-intentioned legend that the Communists supposedly consider impossible the peaceful competition of the country of Socialism with capitalist States.

" The representatives of American and British reactionary Right-wing circles, writing in the Press and speaking from the rostrum of the United Nations, time and again have tried to attribute to the leading figures of the Soviet State statements which reject the possibility of the peaceful co-existence of the two systems.

" These slanderous speeches of the political businessmen from the camp of imperialism are designed to distort the essence and aims of the foreign policy of the Soviet State, to present the U.S.S.R. as the opponent of international co-operation, *to justify the policy of aggression and preparations for a new world war which the imperialist circles of the U.S.A. and Britain are openly conducting.*

" Irrefutable facts of history expose the evil intention and the slanderous character of these speeches by the enemies of peace, democracy and Socialism."

It continues by emphasising the peace-loving nature of Soviet policy, in a phrase which sounds strange coming from the Government which has created the Iron Curtain:—

" It is well known to the whole world that the Soviet State, from the first day of its existence, has conducted, consistently and steadfastly, a policy of peace and friendly co-operation among peoples. . . ."

The writer then restates the Communist doctrines already quoted above :—

> " The idea of the inevitability of the prolonged co-existence of the Socialist and capitalist systems flows from the theory of V. I. Lenin on the possibility of the victory of Socialism originally in one country, taken separately, and the impossibility of the simultaneous victory of Socialism in all countries.
>
> " Lenin proved that the simultaneous victory of Socialism in all countries is impossible under the conditions of imperialism, because of the unevenness of the economic and political development of the capitalist States. Social-ism will be victorious originally in one or a few countries. The remaining States will remain bourgeois for some time. Hence it follows that, in the course of this or that period, the co-existence of the country of victorious Socialism with the capitalist States which surround it is inevitable.
>
> " The Great October Socialist Revolution was the classic realisation of this brilliant theory of V. I. Lenin. An enormous country, occupying one-sixth of the earth, broke away from the imperialist camp. The world was split into two systems : the system of Socialism and the system of capitalism.
>
> " A peace-loving policy corresponds in full measure to the social nature and the vital interests of the Socialist State. Therefore, the Soviet Government from the very first days of the October Revolution, developed an active struggle for peace. The Soviet régime proposed to the governments of all the belligerent countries that negotia-tions for a just democratic peace should be begun immedi-ately."

And then he quotes Stalin's views :—

> " The great leader of the peoples, Comrade J. V. Stalin, in interviews with public figures of the U.S.A. and Britain, in answer to the questions of foreign Press representatives, has repeatedly emphasised the possibility and desirability of the peaceful co-existence of the two systems, and has pointed out on what foundations the friendly co-operation of the Soviet State with the capitalist countries can be based. . . .
>
> " Not for the reason that it fears war does the Soviet people stand for the peaceful co-existence of the Socialist and capitalist systems. As the experience of history

teaches, it is not the Soviet Union but the imperialist aggressors who should fear a new world war. The Soviet people considers the path of peaceful co-operation and competition with the capitalist States the most acceptable and expedient path. It is profoundly convinced of the fact that the victory of Socialism over capitalism will be ensured in the peaceful competition of the two systems."

Then back to the opening theme:—

" The bosses of the capitalist world, industrial kings, financial big-shots and their political business-men, fear peaceful competition with Socialism. They do not have faith in the internal strength and the vitality of the capitalist system. Military adventures present themselves to them as the only means of being delivered from the glaring defects and ulcers which eat away at bourgeois society. . . ."

Finally, the point to which the writer is leading up: peace can be preserved if the peoples of the world will join in the " peace " movement (described in a later passage of this work) against the warmongers:—

" In the present international situation a new world war is not unavoidable and inevitable. War can be averted by the energetic acts of the partisans of peace. The plans of the warmongers can be frustrated if the peoples display the greatest vigilance and firm resoluteness to fight with all their strength for a lasting democratic peace. The camp of peace, democracy and Socialism is capable of removing the threat of a new world war which is hanging over mankind. . . .

" The brilliant instructions of V. I. Lenin and J. V. Stalin on the possibility of the peaceful co-existence of the two systems—Socialism and capitalism—form the basis of the mighty movement of the peoples for the conclusion of a Peace Pact. The five great Powers bear the main responsibility for the preservation of peace and the guarantee of the security of the peoples. The experience of the Second World War showed that, in spite of differences in social-economic systems, in spite of various forms of government, these five countries can co-operate fruitfully in the interests of peace. . . ."

This article contains a simple and logical argument. Stalin appears as the champion of peace, desiring peaceful co-existence with the capitalist adversaries and rivals of Com-

nunist Russia. His desire is shared by the peoples of other
nations, but their wishes are frustrated by a small group of
capitalist warmongers. If the peoples of other nations will
support the peace policy of Stalin—that is, the current aims of
Soviet policy—and if the peoples will turn against their own
warmongering Governments, then there will be peace. There
remains the suggestion that war *will* follow if Stalin's peaceful
policy is frustrated. " The plans of the warmongers can be
frustrated if . . ." " The camp of peace, socialism and
democracy [i.e. the Soviet bloc plus supporters] is *capable* of
removing the threat of a new world war. . . ."

The Soviet theory of peaceful co-existence, according to the
versions given by Communist sources and illustrated above,
is that it describes a temporary relationship during the period
of the destruction of the capitalist world.

According to Soviet doctrine, the capitalist world will destroy
itself anyway; but equally according to Soviet doctrine, it is
the duty of the Soviet Government, and all Communists everywhere, to accelerate the process. Force may be used for this
purpose if its use appears expedient; but normally the emphasis
is on the destruction of the non-Communist world by all means
short of war.

Now, all situations short of war are classed as peace; it
follows, therefore, among other things, that if a pacifist or other
peaceful man thought the avoidance of war more important
than the preservation of free nations and institutions, he could
accept, without affront to his conscience, any methods employed by Communists to attain their ends.

Of course, before deciding to accept a peaceful co-existence in
which this destruction was continuing by " peaceful " means, he
would have to satisfy himself that the result of this destruction
would be the introduction of a political system which would
have less evil consequences than those of a war.

This raises very large questions which are outside the scope
of the present book. But the Communist attitude to the
particular moral issues of war, pacifism, neutralism and
aggression is of the highest importance to peaceful people, both
because of their intrinsic significance and for other reasons
which will be made plain later on. Of these issues, the most
important and illuminating is raised by the question: What is
the Communist attitude towards war?

The answer to this question, as consistently given through the years by Lenin and Stalin, is the true foundation of the whole Soviet treatment of peace and war. And the answer is, briefly, that it depends on the war. As we showed by a quotation which will be found on page 85, Lenin held the view that a war is not only legitimate but holy, provided always that it is waged by the proletariat and has for its purpose the strengthening and extending of socialism. This means the Soviet regime.

Stalin said in 1930, in his letter to Gorki (published in 1949) :—

> "As far as war stories are concerned, they must be published only after careful selection. There is a mass of stories on the book market which depict the 'horrors' of war and which instil hatred towards *every* kind of war (not only towards *imperialist* war, but towards *every* other as well). These are bourgeois-pacifist tales, not worth much. We need stories which will lead readers' minds away from the horrors of *imperialist* governments, which organise such wars. Moreover, we are not, after all, opposed to *every* war. We are *against* imperialist war because it is counter-revolutionary war.

Stalin went on to explain a passage already quoted on page 84 that he favoured a liberating, anti-imperialist war notwithstanding the fact that it must be expected to abound in the horrors of bloodshed.

Now, it must be recalled that the Russian Communists had predicted a series of revolutions in other countries after the Russian revolution; and when this prophecy was not fulfilled, a new doctrine was introduced, in which Soviet Russia figured as the base or springboard for further revolutions in other countries. These are variously described as imperialist, capitalist, backward or aggressor nations.

Stalin set forth his theories on this subject in the passage which has already been quoted on page 66, and it will be useful to summarise them again in the part of this book which examines the attitude of the Soviet Union to peace.

Stalin led off with the basic theory that Communists must be careful to remember that the revolution in one country, which happened to be Russia, was not an end in itself. Its ultimate purpose must be to "hasten the victory of the proletariat in all countries". He then emphasised that the more thoroughly and solidly Socialism establishes itself in the first country the faster this first country (i.e. Russia) will be "transformed into a base" from which world revolution can be fomented and used to disintegrate Imperialism. Socialism means in this context the preliminary period of dictatorship which for an indefinite length of time is to precede the full flowering of the Communist state. At the 19th Congress of the Communist Party in Moscow in 1952 the four essays by Stalin which set the tone of the conference appeared to indicate that this length of time would be very considerable.

The fomentation of revolution in other countries is to be regarded as taking place by two methods. First there is to be propaganda and agitation. This is what Stalin seems to mean by the words "support and awakening of the revolution in all countries". Secondly, "the victorious proletariat of one country" having organised itself and got rid of its own capitalists is to raise revolts amongst the oppressed classes of other countries and "in the event of necessity come out even with armed force against the exploiting classes and their States".*

The final sentence of this last quotation is particularly interesting. The subject of the sentence is "the victorious proletariat of one country". That is, the Soviet Union would come out "even with armed force" against non-Communist States. For such a war is, by the Russian definition, legitimate and holy.

This type of war must be glorified; and as the Soviet leaders identify Russian foreign policy with the aim of extending the revolution, it follows that any military operations in which the Soviet Union is directly or indirectly engaged are legitimate and holy. Those must be prepared and trained for; whereas any other war is imperialist and wicked, to be denounced and its horrors exploited to the full. This explains how the imperialist war waged by the warmongers against a peace-loving Nazi Germany from 1939 to 1941 became overnight the great patriotic war of liberation which continued from June, 1941, until August, 1945.

Thus the question, "What is the Communist attitude to-

* Stalin, Preface to *The Road to October*, 1924.

I

wards war?" is answered by the Communist leader
thus :—

> "We view with favour any war which is designed to
> serve the aims of Russian policy; other types of war we
> interpret as caused by the structure of the non-Com
> munist world, and we use the horrors of war as a means o
> prejudicing people against it."

This statement largely answers the next question: What i
the Soviet attitude towards pacifism and non-violence? Bu
here again the Soviet leaders have obliged us by being clear and
explicit. Lenin said :—

> "We are not pacifists. We are opposed to imperialis
> wars for the division of spoils among the capitalists, but we
> have always declared it to be absurd for the revolutionary
> proletariat to forswear revolutionary wars." *

Stalin dealt with pacifism in non-Communist States in these
words :—

> "Imperialist pacifism is an instrument for the prepara
> tion of war and for the masking of these preparations by
> pharisaical talk about peace." †

Lenin also said :—

> "To talk about ' violence ' in general, without examinin
> the conditions which distinguish reactionary from revolu
> tionary violence, means being a petty bourgeois who re
> nounces revolution, or else it means simply deceivin
> oneself and others by sophistry. The same holds true o
> violence against nations, but that does not prevent Socialist
> from being in favour of a revolutionary war. The clas
> character of the war—that is the fundamental questio
> which confronts a Socialist (if he is not a *renegade*)." * ‡

As with war, then, so with pacifism. It depends upon th
war; there is one kind of war, and one kind of pacifism, fo
the Soviet Union, and another kind for the non-Communis
world.

Precisely the same distinction is to be found in the Sovie

* Lenin, *Selected Works*.
† Speech to the Central Committee of the Communist Party, July, 192
‡ Socialists in the Western sense, Social Democrats and members of th
Western Labour parties, came under the heading of "renegades".

attitude towards neutrality and non-aggression pacts. Here the main source is the *Large Soviet Encyclopædia* (Vol. 41, published in 1939). Non-aggression pacts between non-Communist Powers are attacked :—

> " The position of neutrality in the contemporary imperialist system is, under all conditions, not only a dangerous illusion which does not to any extent really prevent the neutral State from being drawn into war but is indeed a condonation of aggression and a factor aiding the unleashing of war."

The argument here is that imperialist (*i.e.* non-Communist) Powers used non-aggression pacts as political and strategic weapons for use in their aggressive aims. Of Soviet non-aggression pacts, the *Encyclopædia* says :—

> " In our foreign policy, neutrality, particularly our neutrality agreements, is quite a different concept in principle and accords with the basic lines of Soviet foreign policy and the consistent struggle of the U.S.S.R. for peace. The U.S.S.R. has concluded such agreements with Turkey (17.XI.1925 prolonged to 7.XI.1945), with Persia (1.X.1927), with Afghanistan (24.VI.1931), with Lithuania (28.IX.1926 prolonged to 31.XII.45), with Germany (24.IV.1926 prolonged on 24.IV.1931 indefinitely), with Finland (21.I.1932 prolonged to 31.XII.1945), with Latvia (5.II.1932 prolonged to 31.XII.1945), with Esthonia (4.V.1932 prolonged to 31.XII.1945), with Poland (25.VII.1932 prolonged to 31.XII.1945), with France (29.XI.1932), with Italy (2.IX.1933), and with China (21.VIII.1937). . . .
>
> " In our agreements the neutrality obligations are subordinated to the obligation of non-aggression supplementing and developing this obligation. Furthermore, our agreements do not make a fictitious distinction between war and intervention, but extend neutrality obligations to all cases of military action in general (' if one of the contracting parties is exposed to aggression '). Besides this, our agreements confirm the obligations of non-participation in an economic and financial boycott directed against the other country. Thereby our agreements are a weapon in the struggle for the destruction of the front of imperialist States against the U.S.S.R.
>
> " At the same time our agreements, aimed at paralysing the unleashing of war, establish mutual neutrality

obligations only in the case of one of the parties being the victim of aggression. All the agreements have a special stipulation reserving the right to each party of being free from obligations under the treaty without warning in the case of the commission of aggression by the other party against any third State. Thus our agreements on neutrality in no way limit our obligations to participate in the organisation of collective security and not only do not contradict them, but on the contrary supplement them as a constituent element in our struggle for general peace.

" Our agreements, in distinction from the agreements customary in the imperialist system, which in fact have the aim of establishing combinations against other States, are peace agreements in the full meaning of the word. Our agreements with the countries of the East, enslaved by imperialism, have special significance.

" In accordance with the general line of our policy in relation to these countries, our neutrality agreements are directed to the task of helping these countries and strengthening their independence in respect of the imperialist Powers. This was shown particularly in our agreement with China, concluded on 21st August, 1937, at the moment of the outbreak of Japanese aggression in China.

" While stressing the significance of our neutrality agreements, as acts of the peaceful policy of the U.S.S.R., it is, nevertheless, necessary to take into account that, under conditions of the evidently approaching aggression of the fascist countries, our neutrality agreements have only a subordinate significance in ensuring the defence of general peace. The main task is the organisation of collective security, and the strengthening of the defensive power of our country."

The caveat in the last sentence is important in the light of the subsequent fate of Lithuania, Latvia, Esthonia, Finland and Poland. As late as 31st October, 1939, Mr. Molotov was saying:—

" The special character of these pacts of mutual assistance in no way implies any interference on the part of the Soviet Union in the affairs of Esthonia, Latvia and Lithuania, as some foreign newspapers are trying to make out. On the contrary, these pacts of mutual assistance strictly stipulate the inviolability of the sovereign of the signatory States and the principle of non-interference in each other's affairs. . . . We stand for the scrupulous and punctilious observance of the pacts on the basis of complete reciprocity, and we declare that all the spreading of nonsense about Sovietising the Baltic countries is only to the advantage of our common enemies, and of all Soviet provocateurs."

Almost simultaneously the non-aggression pact with Poland had ended in this:—

" The Governments of the U.S.S.R. and Germany have undertaken the task of establishing peace and order on the territory of the former Polish State. . . . The extraordinarily rapid disintegration of the State apparatus of Poland is irrefutable proof of its artificiality and removes the reasons for a prolongation of the war in Eastern Europe. Even the blind can now see that the Polish State cannot be resurrected in its past form or on its former territory." *

But the misfortunes of Poland had their advantages elsewhere:—

". . . As you have seen, the capitalist world has recently been obliged to retrench and retreat somewhat, while the Soviet Union, as a result of the inclusion of the Western Ukraine, and Western Belorussia within her frontiers has increased its territory, as well as its population, by about 13 million people. We can, therefore, congratulate the peoples of the Soviet Union on the fact that our Soviet family has grown from 170 million to 183 million." †

In other words, the general conception in the non-Communist interpretation of neutrality is that the neutral State does not participate in war, as Sweden and Switzerland did not take part in the Second World War; the Soviet interpretation is that a nation signing a pact of neutrality and non-aggression with the Soviet Union can remain neutral only as long as the defence requirements of the Soviet Union permit.

The distinction is of some importance to those to whom a neutral, middle position commends itself in the present world situation. On the personal level, where the individual attitude to the basic issues of conscience has to be thrashed out, a

* *Izvestia*, 9th October, 1939.
† Molotov, speech on 6th November, 1939.

valuable comment is given by a prominent non-Russian spokesman for the Soviet viewpoint upon peace, Signor Nenni.

He gives a clear statement of the attitude of the Soviet-controlled world " peace " movement towards personal neutralism, in a statement about the further policy of this organisation.   He says:—

> " The Executive Bureau of the organisation acquainted itself with the scope of the movement for neutrality in France, Italy and in general in those countries which in the event of war are called upon to be nothing but a strategic base and a protective barrier for British–American imperialism. We now have broad possibilities for co-operation with all these movements to the extent that they do not constitute (like, for example, some movements for neutrality) some deviation from the decision of concrete problems of the defence of peace and from the obligation to wage a struggle against the warmongers." *

The Communist attitude to personal neutrality is stated even more clearly in a *Pravda* article broadcast by Moscow on 3rd October, 1951. In a section on the work of the Council and its subordinate National Peace Committees discussing the exploitation of neutralism, the author, M. Pierre Cot, said:—

> " In these conditions national peace committees have a double task. They must make the best use of the contradictions among the various elements in the war camp, impede accord between them and so paralyse the aggressive war machine. At the same time they must help the anxious peoples to find the right way out of the present situation and thus turn a vague anxiety into active resistance against war and militarism. This double task demands an estimating of the ways in which the various countries differ economically and politically. The same methods of struggle cannot be waged in the U.S.A., for instance, as in People's China.
>
> " In certain Western countries, or rather in certain circles in these countries, resistance to war preparations takes a mainly passive form—neutralism: the ' without us ' movement in Germany; religious pacifism.
>
> " The same can be said of India and the Arab countries. Such partial forms of resistance to war are too weak-kneed to merit recommendation by the World Peace Council.

* World Peace Council meeting in Berlin, February, 1951.

If they become widespread they could atrophy the entire peace struggle. No one has the right to neutrality between peace and war, between enslavement and liberty.

" Nevertheless, the practical value of such tendencies in the movement must not be ignored. For instance, if the countries of Western Europe were to change their policies to-morrow and to begin basing them on neutralism, and if such changes brought about the abandonment of the Atlantic Treaty, then the new world war coalition would be broken up and the U.N. restored to its proper function.

" The World Peace Council must constantly strive to turn passive resistance into active resistance; but nothing prevents it from taking joint action at the same time, with those whose work in defence of peace is in itself too slight to merit endorsement on its own account. No one, I fancy, will condemn those who refuse to carry arms for religious reasons, or those neutralists who would join us in demanding the prohibition of weapons of mass destruction, the ending of the Korean war or a Five-Power Peace Pact.

" Joint campaigns are a splendid means of widening the movement. We must let no opportunity slip of acquainting the masses with our ideas. Our national committees claim no monopoly of the struggle for peace, though they should be in the forefront of the peace struggle."

In other words, neutralism is to be a useful ally and a stepping stone towards militant co-operation against the defence preparations and the policy of the non-Communist world.

Finally, what of peace?

There is nothing to suggest in Communist doctrine that what the Soviet leaders mean by peace is in any way different from what the non-Communist world means. In every Communist statement in which the word " peace " occurs, *it appears to mean* " any relationship other than war ". Where the difference lies is in the idea of " war ". For just as the Soviet leaders distinguish between unjust, imperialist war, and holy wars which serve Soviet aims, so they distinguish between peace as an absence of *any* war and peace as an absence of an unjust, unholy war not serving Russian aims.

This important distinction makes it clear that certain curious and apparently inconsistent statements about war and peace are in fact quite logical and coherent, provided that the sense in which words are being used is kept in mind.

Further, as the earlier passages of this chapter have tried to make clear, what the peaceful man has to consider is not the notion of peace itself, but the terms and conditions upon which it is to be attained and preserved. Communist authorities, like the Nazis and Fascists, have written a very great deal about peace. It is hard to reconcile it with many observed facts in the world to-day, unless two cardinal definitions are remembered.

Peace in Communist parlance means the maintenance of any relationship short of war upon the conditions demanded by the Soviet Union—*i.e.* peace on Soviet terms. *War*, if spoken of with favour, means war as an instrument of Soviet policy; if with disfavour, it means war between non-Communist States or war redounding to the disadvantage of the Soviet Union. The United Nations campaign in Korea as a counter to Soviet inspired aggression is a wicked imperialist war by Soviet definition although, at the same time it serves Soviet policy to keep a conflict in being in which the Russian losses are nil.

Some observations from the *Moscow Literary Gazette* of 21st June, 1951, provide us with a characteristic example of the Soviet attitude to war and peace.

> "We are conducting a stubborn struggle for peace, but we are not pacifists who, concealing themselves behind lying phrases about rejecting all kinds of war, in fact assist the imperialists, the perpetrators of bloody slaughter.
> "What grandeur, beauty and nobility distinguish the just, liberating people's war. The highest, most noble qualities of the people's spirit are revealed in the bloody trials of battle, in the soldier's arduous task. And how joyous it is to recognise that Soviet literature, having delineated these beautiful traits of the visage of Soviet man, has done an immense job for the education, for the spiritual tempering of the entire people."

This accumulation of evidence from Soviet sources is important because of its undoubted authenticity. The fact that part of it is some years old does not affect its value.

In a country where the Government has exclusive control of publishing, as well as Press and broadcasting, it is easy to ascertain whether any statement or complete published work is still the official viewpoint of the Government; for if it is not it either disappears or is rewritten to conform to the new line.

As M. Pierre Cot said in the passage quoted on page 115, "No one has the right to neutrality between peace and war, between enslavement and liberty". The true democrat accepts on behalf of his faith this challenge, since in this all-embracing struggle, in which there is no place for observers or bystanders, the alternative to standing for democracy is to desert it.

CHAPTER X

PROSTITUTING PEACE

HAVING shown that a desire for peace can be exploited as an instrument for an aggressive policy, we are now in a position to examine how in practice the Soviet Union exploits the peace theme as part of the Communist Conspiracy.

Soviet Russia is, so its leaders state, working for the destruction of the non-Communist world as we know it. In place of the existing democracies there is to appear a series of " people's democracies " in which the revolution has been achieved by the establishment of the dictatorship of the proletariat. They describe the régimes of Czechoslovakia, Poland and the other East European States as one type of the dictatorship of the proletariat, and the process of extending this political system to other nations is to continue indefinitely, as opportunity offers. These revolutions are to be achieved through the agency of the local Communist parties, aided by the use or threat of force from the Soviet Army.

Meantime, the normal instruments of diplomacy and international intercourse between Governments are employed to further this revolutionary end, to break up and defeat any organised political opposition by other nations to Soviet policy.

From which it follows that, from the Soviet point of view, it is impossible for anyone to serve the cause of peace, or of the well-being and progress of humanity, unless he bases his views and his actions upon Soviet policy.

It is fairly clear that the Soviet Government decided to embark on a major offensive to exploit the love of peace at the same time as it decided, in the summer of 1947, that Russia had nothing more to gain from the wartime policy of co-operation with the Western Powers, and resumed its normal policy after the temporary tactical diversion from 1941 to 1945.

In September, 1947, the Communist Information Bureau, or Cominform, was set up, and was virtually announced as an instrument of political aggression against the non-Communist world.* In the announcement of the establishment of the

* See p. 58.

Cominform there is a statement to the effect that the world is divided into two camps: one imperialist and anti-democratic, and the other—the Russian camp—anti-imperialist and democratic. Though the former was aggressive and desired to unleash a war, the peoples of the world did not want war and could prevent it. The report of A. Zhdanov, the Soviet representative at the inaugural meeting of the Cominform, contains the following:—

> "The Soviet Socialist State is profoundly alien to any aggressive exploiting motives and is interested in establishing the most favourable conditions for the accomplishment of a Communist society. External peace is one of such conditions. As the bearer of a new and higher social system, the Soviet Union in its foreign policy reflects the hopes of all progressive mankind which strives for a lasting peace and cannot be interested in a new war, which is a product of capitalism."

This hypothesis, which is a standard Communist propaganda thesis, is the foundation of the entire "peace" campaign, and it will be seen how it accords precisely with the Soviet attitude towards peace and war, and with the declared aims of Soviet policy.

Anyone who co-operates in the "peace" campaign is, of course, giving effect to this policy and, whether he realises it or not, is wittingly or unwittingly accepting the hypothesis on which it is based. Since the organisers of the campaign have always hoped that as many non-Communists as possible would take part in it, their problem was obviously to concentrate upon exploiting the emotional aspects of peace and the fear of war, to keep quiet about the obvious links with Soviet policy, and to hope to build up a big enough façade of non-Communist peace-lovers to conceal and at the same time further its true aims.

The first overt move was taken at a "World Congress of Intellectuals" held in Poland at the end of August, 1948. Many of the delegates were neither Communists nor Communist sympathisers, but a number of these were soon put off by the way the procedure of the conference was manipulated by the Communists. At the Congress it was agreed that National Peace Committees of intellectuals should be set up, and an "international liaison committee of intellectuals" established.

In April, 1949, a Peace Congress was held in Paris and

Prague, called jointly by the International Liaison Committee of Intellectuals, and the Women's International Democratic Federation (a Communist-controlled organisation). The Paris Congress set up a permanent "World Committee of the Partisans of Peace ", later known as the " World Peace Committee ", and later still as the " World Peace Council ". The World Peace Committee then set up a small permanent bureau (of about twelve), and this bureau, now known as the Executive Bureau of the World Peace Council, directs the operations of the World Peace Movement on strict Communist lines.

The World Peace Movement is not by any means the only international organisation controlled by the Soviet Government for political warfare purposes.

A number of these international bodies was created during the war and shortly afterwards, the main ones being:—

> The World Federation of Trade Unions.
> The World Federation of Democratic Youth.
> The International Union of Students.
> The Women's International Democratic Federation.
> The World Federation of Democratic Lawyers.
> The International Organisation of Journalists.
> The World Federation of Scientific Workers.

At first many non-Communists took part in these organisations in the sincere hope that they could form a meeting-place for mutual co-operation between East and West. However, the procedure of their meetings, and the resolutions to be adopted, came more and more to be arranged by the Executive Bureau, which was always under Communist control, and the organisations themselves became instruments of Soviet policy and merely propaganda. They are now generally recognised as merely a useful means of propagating any policy or line desired by the Soviet Government.

The ostensible purpose of each organisation is to serve the interests of a particular group, such as lawyers, women and trade unionists. One feature which they all have in common is that the policy, procedure and general direction are in the hands of a small Executive Bureau, in which the key positions, and if possible the majority of the seats, are occupied by Communists or trusted collaborators. This ensures that the organisation does nothing unfavourable to the interests of the Soviet Union and can devote its energies, quite regardless of the ostensible aims of the movement, to serving Russian political ends.

The " peace " movement was organised in a precisely similar manner. When the permanent Executive Bureau was set up, seven of the twelve members were known to be Communists, and four others, whether they called themselves Communists or not, were indistinguishable from them in everything they said and did. The permanent Committee numbered 138, containing fifty-eight non-Communists, thirty representatives of Soviet Russia and the satellite States, thirty-six Communist sympathisers and fourteen of uncertain political views. The link with the other Communist-controlled international organisations was ensured by including representatives of the principal ones on the Executive Bureau.

The first plenary meeting of the World Peace Committee took place in October, 1949, in Rome, and its proceedings were illuminating. Yugoslavia was formally expelled from the World Peace Committee for deviation from the Cominform path, and Communist China substituted. The Soviet delegates said that the object of the " peace " campaign was not to exhort, but to take positive action; this action was supplemented by a Kremlin directive issued through the Cominform, which stated :—

> " The struggle for a stable and lasting peace, for the organisation and consolidation of the forces of peace against the forces of war, should now become the pivot of the entire activity of the Communist parties and democratic organisations." *

This order is of high importance. Since that date all Communist propaganda, all Soviet-controlled subversive activities in the free world, all hate propaganda in the Communist empire, has somehow been linked to the theme of peace. Further, the " democratic organisations "—that is, the Communist international bodies such as the World Federation of Trade Unions, as well as the national Communist parties—were instructed by this directive to focus their activities on working for the " peace " campaign. From this point the Soviet Government made no secret of the fact that the World Peace Committee was part of its world-wide machinery for influencing public opinion in a direction favourable to whatever its policy demanded, and for

* Directive to all Communist parties of the world ; published 29th November, 1949.

subversion and sabotage.   For example, in the autumn of 1949
the World Peace Movement took an active and open part in the
series of strikes and acts of sabotage which, especially in France
and Italy, were organised to prevent the arrival from the United
States of supplies and raw materials needed for the defence and
economic recovery of Western Europe.

Further, peace offered the perfect umbrella for any organising
or propaganda work required by the Communist machine to
give effect to the tactics illustrated by Lenin's dictum on how
trade unions are to be penetrated: quoted on page 18, but
worth repeating.

> " We must be able to resort to all sorts of stratagems
> manœuvres, illegal methods, to evasions and subterfuges
> only so as to get into the Trade Unions, to remain in them
> and to carry on Communist work within them at all costs.''

We now find a string of instructions issued by the Kremlin
through the Cominform, and on a lower level by the directing
bodies of the Communist international organisations and by the
Executive Bureau of the " peace " movement itself, on how the
campaign was to be conducted.   The following are the most
important since 1949, together with some comments by authori
tative Communist and " peace " campaign sources.   They
illustrate its evolution and purpose:—

In July, 1949, the World Federation of Trade Unions, meeting
in Milan, ordered its supporters " to take a most active part in
the organisation, propaganda and public activities " of the
World Peace Committee.

.   .   .   .   .

In November, 1949, Malenkov, a member of the Politburo
reported to the Moscow Soviet on the great importance of the in
ternational Communist organisations in the " peace " campaign
and he mentioned particularly the youth, students', women's
and trade union organisations.   This was followed immediately
by the directive quoted above, instructing all Communist bodie
to give absolute priority to " peace " campaign requirements.

.   .   .   .   .

Another directive issued through the Cominform in Novem
ber, 1949, reads:—

> " Particular attention should be devoted to bringing
> together into the movement of the supporters of peace the

trade unions, women's, youth, co-operative, sports, cultural and educational, religious and other organisations, as well as scientists, writers, journalists, workers in the cultural field, parliamentary leaders who are in favour of peace and against war."

This is a direct application of the Leninist principles of infiltration, and is the authority for the organisation or exploitation by the World Peace Council, or the national peace committees and Communist parties, of the peace appeals by scientists, authors, musicians, teachers, etc., which have since appeared.

. . . . .

At the Stockholm meeting of the World Peace Committee which issued the notorious "Stockholm Peace Appeal" in March, 1950, the general secretary of the organisation, a well-known Communist organiser and propagandist called Lafitte, claimed that fifty-two national peace committees were affiliated to the World Peace Committee. At the same meeting, a new note appeared when Signor Nenni, a prominent "peace" campaigner, stated openly that in a number of countries [in Western Europe] the "peace" movement had started to take direct action and would do more and more to prevent the manufacture and transport of weapons.

. . . . .

Also at the Stockholm meeting, Saillant, the Communist General Secretary of the World Federation of Trade Unions, who is also a member of the Executive Bureau of the World Peace Committee, said:—

"We find ourselves in a period in which propaganda and direct action can no longer be separated. It even seems that now is the time for direct action by the masses against the preparation of a new world war.

"We should state that one of the essential duties of the Defenders of Peace is the refusal to work on and produce war material in all capitalist countries. The working class is in the forefront of this activity."

He also said at Stockholm:—

"One way to root the movement deep in the hearts of the people is to organise committees for the defence of peace at the place where men and women carry out their daily work.

" The place of work must be the rallying place of the present and future forces of our world peace movement."

. . . . .

Two months later, at a meeting of the Executive Bureau of the World Federation of Trade Unions in Budapest, where the organising of " Peace Committees " was defined as one of its main tasks, Saillant said :—

" Greater and more widespread efforts will be made to set up peace committees at the place of work. It is by leading all the workers to unite at their place of work, to undertake concrete actions for the defence of peace . . . that the peace committees will have the opportunity of support ing among the rank and file all the efforts of the defender of peace. The rank and file struggle for peace must include concrete action to reduce or limit armament manufacture."*

. . . . .

On 22nd September, 1950, there was a directive via the Cominform to the " peace " movement ; a lengthy document of which the following is a summary :—

(i) Open American aggression poses before the Peace Movement new, great and militant tasks.

(ii) The consolidation of the peace struggle must go hand in hand with an all-round struggle against the armaments drive.

(iii) That is why the demand for the banning of atomic weapons has been supplemented with the demand for a general reduction of armaments.

(iv) This second demand includes the destruction of the existing stocks of all means of mass annihilation.

(v) These demands have been and will be supported by the following means :—

(a) Working class rallies in United States and Britain.

(b) Direct action of the working class of France, Italy, Belgium and Holland.

(c) Evasion of the military service by the youth of the United States, Britain, France, Belgium and Yugoslavia.

* From official report of the World Federation of Trade Unions session.

(vi) The peace struggle must be " activised " in the United States, Britain, Canada and Scandinavia.

(vii) To fulfil these demands it is essential to extend the peace movement among peasants, women and youth. Peasants form the basis of armies; women suffer from war.

(viii) The second World Peace Congress will help to solve these " new militant " tasks.

. . . . . .

On 18th September, 1950, the World Federation of Trade Unions stated openly that the purpose of the Peace Committees was to paralyse Western defences. An appeal of the administrative council of its transport department stated, according to the *Soviet Monitor* :—

" Expand the network of Peace Committees, intensify the campaign, the aim of which is to paralyse the transport of war material in countries preparing a third world war."

. . . . .

Statements by Joliot-Curie and Nenni, the former the President and the latter a member of the Executive Bureau of the World Peace Movement during the Warsaw Peace Congress, October, 1950.

Joliot-Curie said :—

" We must consider supporting those international organisations which take efficient initiatives in the safe-guarding of peace. I shall mention, for instance, the initiative taken by the International Red Cross, the Society of Friends, the Council for Peace inspired by Lord Boyd Orr, and the supporters of a world government. I am convinced that these organisations, if they have a sincere desire for peace, will find ways for an agreement with our movement. . . ."

Nenni said :—

" We know that on the principles of our programme even people who are still under the influence of the campaign of calumnies and lies which has been conducted against our movement are in agreement with us. That is why there exists for us a problem of fraternal meetings and discussions with other peace movements, whether it be the International Red Cross, religious movements against war, the British Peace Council, the movement for world government whose

K

President is Professor Einstein, the United Nations Associations. In the World Peace Council which is to be elected at our Congress a place should be reserved for the representative of those pacifist movements which are willing to establish with us a constructive basis for discussion in the interests of peace and of freedom."

. . . . .

Directive for giving effect to the resolutions of the Warsaw Congress, issued in *Cominform Journal* on 24th November, 1950:—

" . . . There now exist national Peace Committees and Councils in 75 countries, more than 150,000 Peace Committees function in the town and countryside, at the factories and offices in almost all countries . . . the Congress declared that the World Peace Movement must display extensive initiative both from below among the masses and in relation to Parliaments, Governments, and the United Nations. . . .

" This straightforward decision of the Peace Partisans helps openly to denounce the war-mongers who incidentally reject peace proposals and prepare a new sanguinary catastrophe for mankind. . . .

" The decisions of the Second World Peace Congress constitute a powerful weapon in the hands of the active fighters for peace, a programme for the militant mobilisation of the broad masses to frustrate the criminal schemes of the war-mongers. . . . They add to its (the peace movement's) intensive power in the cause of peace . . . the duty of the Communist Parties of all honest democracies is to ensure that the Congress decisions are brought to the knowledge of all people. . . ."

. . . . .

Directive to the Communist Press and agencies in all countries issued in the *Cominform Journal* on 8th December, 1950:—

It will " give ' special attention ' to the activities of the various Peace Committees, publicising and supporting their work."

It will " ruthlessly expose the warmongers, the aggressive foreign policy and reactionary home policy of the United States, the criminal war waged by the United States against Korea, and its aggressive adventures against the Chinese People's Republic."

It will " expose the policy of transforming the United Nations into a tool for carrying out the aggressive plans of American imperialism."

It will depict " the strengthening of the democratic anti-imperialist camp headed by the Soviet Union and the consistent and tenacious struggle of this camp in defence of peace."

It will " expose the imperialist propaganda of chauvinism, race hatred and national enmity, isolate the imperialist warmongers and fight for friendship between the peoples of their countries and the peoples of the Soviet Union and the people's democracies."

It will " devote more attention to the growth of the National Liberation Movement in Colonial and dependent countries."

It will realise that " *all these activities are indissolubly linked with stepping up propaganda of Marxism, Leninism and the tireless struggle against reactionary ideology.*"

The concluding sentence of this directive deserves special attention and reflection, as it reveals a further aim of the " peace " campaign. Through a genuine love of peace, through support for the " peace " campaign, through acceptance of the Soviet version of world affairs, peaceful men are to be drawn gradually down the scale until they end up as Communist converts. If they see the red light whilst fellow travelling and try to return to freedom they are ripe for blackmail.

· · · · ·

World Federation of Trade Unions directive of 9th December, 1950:—

" To acquaint all working people with the decisions of the Second World Peace Congress.

" To organise ever more resolute action of the working people against the transport and production of armaments.

" To draw up and put into effect a plan for a powerful unity movement to hinder the rearmament programme.

" To link closely the struggle for peace with the struggle to satisfy the urgent and vital demands of the working people.

" To extend and strengthen the peace committees and enterprises, to make them more active and to establish them where they do not exist."

· · · · ·

Then came the resolutions presented by the Executive Bureau to the World Peace Council, and adopted unanimously, at

their meeting in Berlin in February, 1951. These read as
follows:—

" (i) The World Peace Council, at its session in February,
1951, in Berlin, having examined with satisfaction the work
accomplished in pursuance of the decisions of the Second
World Peace Congress, has recognised the need for developing this activity on a still broader scale.

" The World Peace Council recommends all national
committees to spread with greater energy and to popularise
on a broad scale the Address to the United Nations, which
should penetrate everywhere and should reach the conscience of every man and woman. The World Peace
Council appeals to all to display initiative in this question
on a national and international scale.

" (ii) The World Peace Council notes with satisfaction
the adoption of laws against war propaganda in a number
of countries. It urges the [national committees to take
measures for drafting Bills for defence of peace and against
war propaganda which should be submitted to the Parliaments of the different countries.

" National committees should inform public opinion
about this in order to obtain broad popular support for
these measures.

" (iii) It urges the national committees to mobilise public
opinion for exposing and boycotting all sorts of publications,
written statements, speeches, films, radio broadcasts, etc.,
containing appeals for war.

" It recommends the national committees to carry on an
extensive educational campaign with the participation
of thousands of people of goodwill who in each country will
tirelessly expose lies serving the preparation of war.

" It instructs the Bureau to take measures for setting up
an information bureau at the Secretariat to issue objective
information and exact data exposing mendacious and
distorted reports aimed at keeping up war psychosis.

" (iv) The World Peace Council notes with satisfaction
that the contact established in pursuance of the decisions
of the Second World Peace Congress with numerous
associations and collectives has made it possible to develop
and expand still more the movement for peace.

" The Council adopts the following decisions:—

    1. To continue negotiations with the movement of
    mondialists in different countries in order to ascertain
    on what questions agreement could be reached and

joint actions carried out encouraging mutual participation in conferences and congresses.

2. It is desirable to organise on party lines the meeting proposed to the Quakers on the basis of documents and resolutions with the object of finding terms for joint actions.

3. It is important to acquaint Churches with the resolutions adopted at the present session of the Council and to ask them to support these resolutions. On behalf of the Bureau, the chairman, Joliot-Curie, has sent a letter to the World Peace Congress on disarmament. Several of the replies received to the letter are evidence of the interest aroused by this information.

4. It is necessary to develop contact with the movements in favour of neutrality existing in different countries in order that they should actually serve for the preservation of peace.

5. To find ways for co-operation with the Pacifist movements and all other groupings in so far as this contact and co-operation will serve the cause of peace.

" (v) The World Peace Council notes with satisfaction the initiative and proposals concerning the organisation of international conferences which will enable authoritative representatives of the public in different countries to exchange views and to settle jointly some problems in the interests of world peace. Such conferences will make it possible to attain new contact and a further expansion of the movement of peace supporters.

" In this respect the Peace Council :—

1. Approves the convocation in Paris or Brussels in the shortest possible time, by the Franco-Belgian Committee against the Remilitarisation of Germany, of a conference of the peoples of European countries whose Governments have signed the Atlantic Pact, with the participation of the German people in the conference. The object of this conference is to examine questions concerning the struggle against the remilitarisation of Germany and concerning a peaceful settlement of the German problem.

2. Approves the proposal for the organisation of a conference of the countries of Asia and the Pacific with the object of discussing chiefly questions of the struggle against the rearming of Japan and questions of the peaceful settlement of the conflicts now taking place, as

well as holding popular polls in the Asian and Pacifi
countries concerned regarding the remilitarisation c
Japan and the conclusion of a peace treaty with her i
the current year.

3. Instructs the Bureau to support the organisatio
of regional conferences: (a) of countries of the Nea
East and Northern Africa, (b) of the Scandinavia
countries.

" Recommends the Secretariat to examine the questio
of organising such conferences: (a) for countries of Blac
Africa, (b) for countries of North America and Lati
America (this conference can be held in Mexico in August.

" The World Peace Council urges national committee
of the countries concerned to apply the utmost efforts fo
the greatest success of these conferences.

" The World Peace Council decides to convene in th
Soviet Union in the summer of 1951, an internationa
economic conference—of economists, technicians, in
dustrialists, businessmen and trade union leaders of al
countries—for restoring economic relations and raising th
living standard of the peoples.

" The Conference agenda will consist of: (a) possibilitie
for improving the living conditions of the peoples in th
middle of the 20th century provided peace is preserved
(b) possibilities for improving economic relations amon
countries.

" In pursuance of the decisions of the Second Worl
Peace Congress concerning cultural relations, the Worl
Peace Council instructs the Bureau to render every suppor
in organising a conference of medical men proposed b
well-known medical men of France and Italy. Thi
conference will be held in Italy in the current year and wil
be devoted to the problem of struggle against the perniciou
influence of war preparations on the protection of the healt
of the popular masses.

" To instruct the Secretariat to study and assist in holdin
international conferences to discuss problems of the develop
ment of national culture and international cultural co
operation provided peace is preserved; writers and artists
scientists, workers of the cinema.

" To hold in 1951 a conference of writers and workers i
art.

" The World Peace Council instructs the Secretariat to
support the idea of convening in the future conferences o
teachers, journalists, sportsmen, etc.

" It proposes to consider the form of support which could be rendered to the initiative of youth, and student organisations in holding a big world festival in defence of peace in Berlin from 5th August to 19th August, 1951.

" (vi) The World Peace Council decides to set up at the Council an international cultural relations commission which will meet periodically. It recommends the setting up without delay at each national committee of a cultural relations commission, which should promote trips, if possible mutual, with the object of strengthening the cause of peace, as well as exchange of periodical publications and cultural exhibitions.

" It instructs the Bureau to study the question of establishing a cinema centre with the task of stimulating and co-ordinating the production and distribution of films in defence of peace, exposing in every way possible the use of the cinema for war propaganda.

" (vii) The Council recommends the Secretariat to do everything necessary in order that all peace-loving scientists should propose the inclusion in the charters of the international and national scientific organisations of which they are members of a demand that their scientific discoveries be used solely for peaceful purposes.

" (viii) The Council appeals to all national committees to pay most serious attention to the collection of funds for a world peace fund. The success of this campaign will be a new proof of the devotion of the peoples to the cause of peace. This will enable our movement to carry out its mission still more effectively.

" The fulfilment of all these measures will positively promote the extension of our movement, which should be conducted on the basis of the decisions defining our attitude with regard to the problem of peace and with the help of a broad educational campaign among all sections of the population in each country, a campaign which should create the foundations for free and honest discussion as well as for joint actions in defence of peace."

.   .   .   .   .   .

Resolution of the Bureau of the World Peace Council at their Copenhagen meeting, 5th–7th May, 1951 :—

" The Bureau exhorts all existing peace organisations, all social, religious and cultural organisations, actively to give their support to the world campaign for the peace demand, in such a way that each organisation chooses the form which it considers most expedient to the individual case."

Resolution of the Executive Committee of the World Federation of Trade Unions (Vienna, 3rd–6th July, 1951):—

> " Resolution on the struggle for Peace.
> " All trade union directives are directed to:—
>> " (a) Activise the struggle for peace and draw into it all men and women industrial and factory workers, intellectuals and all other sections of the population.
>> " (b) Consider as a primary task the struggle against production, loading, unloading and transport of arms on the basis of the widest possible working-class unity.
>> " (c) Take an active part in collecting signatures for the Five-Power Peace Pact appeal."

.   .   .   .   .

The political aims of this closely knit movement cover the Communist States as well as the free world, and are consistent throughout. In Russia and the satellites it is an official propaganda agency designed to strengthen popular support for nationalist or militant aims.

Thus in China on 4th July, 1951, the Peace Committee called on the Chinese people to intensify their efforts:—

> " To raise production and expand the donation campaign, which had already provided 1,970 aircraft as well as guns and tanks."

and

> " to mobilise students to enrol in military cadre schools."

A neat and concise comment on the World Peace Movement unexpectedly turned up from an official Communist source. The Czech trade union journal *Prace* on 28th March, 1952, said:—

> " . . . a strike in a capitalist country is a very effective way of fighting for peace, since it aims at paralysing war production and the transport of arms. But here it is a question of building up the greatest possible strength in the shortest possible time. . . . To put the arms of outstanding quality which we produce into the hands of the defenders of peace, into the hands of our People's Army, that is an act of peace."

In the free world the World Peace Movement is designed to support the day-to-day needs of Soviet policy and propaganda; to carry out a consistent policy of dividing and weakening the resistance of the free world to Soviet aggression. Thus it has agitated at different times, in concert with all the other Communist-controlled agencies, against:—

(a) United Nations' action in Korea;
(b) German rearmament and inclusion in the E.D.C.;
(c) the transport and manufacture of arms in the Western countries;
(d) the North Atlantic Treaty Organisation;
(e) the Japanese Peace Treaty;

and, above all, to foster hatred of the United States and British Governments. This reached a climax when, in March, 1952, at Oslo, the World Peace Council threw in all its resources to support the Communist charges made against the United Nations' Command of using bacterial warfare in Korea.

The World Peace Movement itself forms a coherent whole operating in the Communist Empire as well as in the free world. The difference is that in the free world it is composed of a few Communists, fellow-travellers and vague sympathisers, almost all of them being without credit or standing in the community: whereas in a Communist State they are in effect agencies of the Government. But the policy of the movement throughout the world is completely consistent. In the free world it seeks to weaken all sources of military strength and political unity: in the Communist world it is designed to build up the political and military strength of the State. In China, for instance, we find that a year after the Peace appeal already quoted:

" The Chinese Peace Committee gave final figures of the arms donation campaign as over 5,565 billion People's dollars, equivalent to the cost of 3,710 planes. This sum has been handed over to the headquarters of the Chinese volunteers in Korea." *

So there it is or was, at the moment of writing. Like a cancer cell, it grows and grows. The last few pages have not been easy reading, but it was desirable to record the facts in some detail about this vast enterprise on behalf of the Soviet Union, to capture the minds of men by invading them, not

* *New China* News Agency—June 25th, 1952.

in the belly of a Trojan horse but on the wings of a Picasso dove
coo-ing the word PEACE.

Now, whether we admire or disapprove of the building up of
this " peace " organisation, it is impossible to ignore the
evidence that it exists. It will also be observed that there
are two distinct but interwoven strands running through these
instructions. The first is the reference to the activities of national
and local peace committees, with heavy emphasis on the rôle
that they have to play wherever possible in fomenting industrial
unrest and sabotage in the defence industries and transport,
among their other " peaceful " activities. The second is the
insistence on committing scientists, teachers and cultural and
religious bodies to co-operating in the " peace " campaign on
conditions laid down by the organisation itself.

The organisation, direction, policy and detailed operations
of the world " peace " movement are in the hands of the
Executive Bureau. This Bureau is answerable to nobody but
the Soviet Government, conformity with the requirements of
Russian policy being ensured by the fact that the chairman, four
of the vice-chairmen, the secretary-general and many of the
members are Communists, and the remainder are reliable
supporters of the Russian viewpoint, and representatives of the
Central Committee of the Communist Party of the Soviet Union
are serving on the Bureau.

Close co-ordination with the other Soviet-controlled international organisations is ensured by the fact that the chairman
is also president of the World Federation of Scientific Workers;
two of the vice-chairmen are, respectively, president of the
Women's International Democratic Federation and vice-
chairman of the World Federation of Scientific Workers; the
President of the World Federation of Democratic Youth is a
member of the Bureau, and the Council of the World Federation
of Democratic Lawyers is also represented. Another member
of the Bureau is the general secretary of the World Federation of
Trade Unions. This is interlocking worthy of an international
cartel!

This Executive Bureau, originally twelve strong and now
forty-four, issues the directives under which the campaign is
conducted, and the so-called " draft resolutions " which are
adopted unanimously by the World Peace Council. This body
some 255 strong, is again composed of Soviet and satellite

representatives, Communists and reliable supporters of the Soviet viewpoint.

Unanimity in this body in support of the Executive Bureau's decision is virtually assured, since the Communists know their duty is to support Soviet policy, and the other representatives would not have been appointed if there was any danger of their deviating from the line. If they did they would be dismissed.

Below this body, on the national level, are a series of committees such as the British Peace Committee. The duty of these committees is to carry out the instructions they receive from above, their effectiveness depending upon the strength of the local Communist Party and the ignorance and gullibility of the public among whom they operate. Though the active nucleus of these committees is usually composed of Communists, and their sole ally is the local Communist Party, the more non-Communists who can be induced to serve the better pleased are the organisers.

These Committees have their directives handed down to them either straight from the Executive Bureau of the World Peace Council, or through the *Cominform Journal*. The local Communist parties receive parallel instructions to take supporting action in aid of the Peace Committees and to publicise their work. (See, for example, the directive on page 126).

National Peace Committees have four main functions: to obtain what publicity they can for the Soviet " peace " and other propaganda themes; to organise signature campaigns, petitions, etc., in accordance with the current requirements of Soviet policy; to organise local " peace " committees in towns, factories, etc., to perform similar tasks to those described above. The organisers claim to have set up over 300 such committees in Great Britain alone, and one can safely assume that by far the greater part of the non-Communist members of these committees have not the faintest idea how they are being used to serve Soviet policy. Finally, they have to give effect, in co-operation with the local Communist parties, to the directive dealing with the organising of peace appeals by scientists, authors, musicians, teachers, etc., demonstrations by ex-Servicemen " for peace ", and so on.

The method employed is as follows. A few Communist scientists, authors, etc., canvass some likely fellow scientists, etc., to join in a " peace appeal " containing blameless generalities about peace, which can be applied to any situation. An organisation is then started to give effect to these principles, and the utmost publicity is sought for the adherence of any notable non-Communist supporters.

From then onwards, depending upon the success of the organisers and the political innocence of the rest, the publicity and activities of the organisation are progressively angled to show that Soviet policy accords with the principles thus laid down, and that of the Western Powers does not; and any demands or resolutions put forward invariably demand changes in Western policy to comply with that of the Soviet Union. If the organisers fail, no harm is done to Russia or the " peace " campaign.

In so far as they succeed, the " peace " campaign has made some more converts, a section of the Western public has been weakened in its support for the defence and foreign policy of its Government, the evidence of converts to the Soviet viewpoint is trumpeted by the Russian propaganda machine throughout the Middle East, South-East Asia and Eastern Europe, and the myth of Soviet infallibility has had its life prolonged.

The one unfailing criterion of these arranged " peace " activities is that they never contain a single word of criticism of Soviet policy or propaganda, or a single note of dissent from the Soviet view of current events. A classic product of this technique has recently been circulating in the teaching profession, and is quoted and discussed in Appendix III.

It is not necessary for the organisers of these manœuvres to be Communists, provided they obey the directives of the world " peace " movement; but their complete subservience to Soviet policy raises the interesting question whether peaceful men who do not approve of Soviet policy can influence the policy of the world " peace " movement. The answer to this is emphatically " No ". The policy of the movement, as has been shown, is handed down from above, and not resolved democratically from below.

A very good example of this occurred in the summer of 1950, when the " peace " movement was collecting signatures for the so-called " Stockholm Peace Appeal " for the prohibition of the atomic bomb. Several hundred million signatures were obtained from this by peace committees and Communist Party organisations, most of them in Communist-governed countries,

nd most of them from people who had no idea of the implica-
ions of the appeal.

A few weeks later the Executive Bureau suddenly produced a
much more far-reaching series of demands, embodying all the
main objectives of Soviet foreign policy, which were dutifully
adopted by the Warsaw Peace Congress in the name of hundreds
of millions of peace lovers throughout the world, *i.e.* those who
had signed the Stockholm Appeal but had had no hand in the
ormulation of those demands.

On the national level, conformity with the rulings handed
down from above is demanded in an illuminating passage at the
nd of the eighth resolution quoted on page 131. The relevant
ection reads:—

> "The fulfilment of all these measures [ordered by the
> Bureau] will positively promote the extension of the peace
> movement, *which should be conducted on the basis of the decisions
> defining our attitude with regard to the problem of peace* and with
> the help of a broad educational campaign among all sections
> of the population in each country, a campaign which should
> create the foundations for free and honest discussion as well
> as for joint actions in the defence of peace."

The key to this resolution is in the words italicised. The
peace committees must attract all and sundry, but the resulting
activities, resolutions and petitions must conform to the directives
of the Executive Bureau. The policy of the Bureau will not
be influenced by the views of those non-Communists and non-
'peace" campaign participants if they differ from the line
handed down from above.

Anyone who conforms is encouraged to become more deeply
nvolved in the "peace" campaign. If a project does not go
according to plan or its members deviate from the prescribed
ine, it is quietly abandoned and disowned. It is impossible for anyone who disapproves of Soviet policy to get
his criticism adopted by the "peace" movement. As in all
other Communist-controlled organisations, including the Soviet
Union itself, criticism and free discussion are confined to ways
and means of carrying out directives handed down from above;
he orders themselves are sacrosanct.

Whatever else is disapproved of by the "peace" campaign—
British foreign policy, the decision of the West to defend itself,
he struggle to end banditry in Malaya—it will never find fault

in any aims or any methods of Soviet domestic or foreign
policy.

The final point to emphasise about the world " peace "
movement is its consistency. In any country where there are
Communists there is a branch of the " peace " movement
including Russia, the satellites, China and the Communist
controlled areas of Indo-China.

The demands and objectives of the movement are identical
throughout the world, and nothing that it says and does in
Western Europe is in the slightest degree inconsistent with what
it says and does in Communist-controlled countries. There
is nothing surprising in this. The aims of the movement are to
maintain peace upon Soviet terms, to aid and strengthen Soviet
policy, justify Communist aggression and weaken the resistance of
the non-Communist world to the aggressive aspects of that policy.

The musician, scientist or pacifist in Western Europe who is
persuaded to co-operate with the world " peace " movement is
working hand in hand with his companions in the movement in
Bulgaria, Russia, China or Vietminh. Their objective is the same
and their enemy is the same—the Governments, and the policy
and the existing fabric of society in the non-Communist world.

Conditions and the tactics to meet them, are obviously
different in countries under a Communist Government. For
here the objective of strengthening Soviet policy is attained by
whipping up support for the régime, warning of imaginary
attacks by imaginary warmongers, agitating for increased output and production and stirring up war hysteria and hatred
against the non-Communist world.

Thus it is that while the members of the world " peace "
movement in France and Britain are complaining of unfriendly
publicity about the Soviet Union, and calling it " war
mongering " and " war propaganda ", one of their colleagues in
the world " peace " movement in Bulgaria is saying:—

> " Mothers are to instil into their children a deep hatred
> of the imperialist war-mongers, the murderers of Korean
> women and children, and a firm loyalty and devotion to
> their liberators, the Soviet Union and the great Stalin."

While *Pravda* says (29th August, 1951):—

> " The collection of signatures for the appeal (for the
> Soviet Five-Power Pact) will promote the all-round

mobilisation of the working people of our country for the further strengthening of the might of the Soviet State, the bastion of universal peace."

The main difference between the " peace " campaign in the Communist world and in the free world is that in the former the population is obliged to co-operate with it, sign its petitions, take part in its demonstrations, and so on. It is part of the Government machine; woe betide anyone who publicly refuses to join the other 95 per cent. and sign in favour of the Stockholm Peace Appeal, and the Soviet Five-Power Pact, and join in its other activities.

In Communist East Germany there is a " peace law ", Article V of which reads:—

> " Anyone who, to aid the war-mongers, disparages the peace movement or stirs up public opinion against peace partisans on account of their activities or allows them to be persecuted will be punished by imprisonment and in serious cases by penal servitude."

This is the sort of society, and the sort of legislation, that the world " peace " movement seeks to extend into the free world. As this fact becomes generally recognised, it is scarcely surprising that in a free society it is only Communists and their consistent supporters who consciously work for the world " peace " movement. The remainder are a small and insignificant group acting from ignorance of the organisation which is exploiting them, or the ends which they are serving, or the consequences for the free world of achieving those ends. The majority of their fellows—pacifists, teachers, musicians, scientists—view them with indifference, pity, or contempt.

In fact, the principal consequence of the exploitation of peace through the world " peace " movement, and one which suits Soviet policy very well, is that an occasional genuine worker for peace may be bewildered and frustrated, and turn to the movement for want of an alternative. He may deliberately blind himself to the facts which his reason tells him are true, and allow his emotions to persuade him that " anything working for peace must be good ", and that " co-operation with the Communists must ease world tension ".

That this is nonsense, and dangerous nonsense at that, should be evident to any student of the facts; we have given the facts,

as stated by the Soviet Government and the organisers of the
" peace " campaign itself, about the structure and purpose of
the movement.   The case appears to be established that there
is no middle position between saying, on the one hand: " I
accept the Communist thesis and I desire to see the Soviet
system extended over the whole of Europe, Britain and the free
world; therefore I support the world ' peace ' movement," or,
on the other: " Whatever the deficiencies and inconveniences of
life in a free society, I will undertake any sacrifice to prevent it
succumbing, by force or by subversion, to Soviet Russia; I
recognise the world ' peace ' movement as an instrument of
Soviet policy designed to weaken the resistance of the free world
to Soviet force or subversion, and in no circumstances will I
subscribe to this betrayal of the world I live in ".

III

It has been shown that the world " peace " movement has no
independent policy other than that of the Soviet Government
and also that all the activities of the Soviet-controlled agencies
are geared to the " peace " movement.   It is therefore difficult
to discover whether there is any special type of activity which
is uniquely the task of the movement.

In general, it can be said that its function is to seek world
support for Soviet policy by dressing it up in a peace-like guise.
Sometimes a policy is initiated overtly by the Soviet Government
and dutifully echoed by the world " peace " movement.   At
others, the policy is launched through the Executive Bureau of
the " peace " movements, and then apparently taken up by the
Soviet Government.   These variations, however, are purely
tactical.   A few illustrations of the interaction of Soviet policy
and the activities of the world " peace " movement will suffice.

First, in 1948 Yugoslavia was expelled from the Cominform.
Yugoslavia was expelled from the World Peace Committee at
its first plenary meeting in Rome in 1949, and its place taken by
Communist China.

Second, ever since the United Nations set up the Atomic
Energy Commission, the Soviet Government has been trying
to overcome the obstacle to Russian policy caused by the
Western preponderance in atomic weapons.   In the meanwhile,
aided by German scientists and collaborators in the Western
world, Soviet Russia has made intensive efforts to build up its

own stock of atomic bombs. In the political sphere the Soviet delegation consistently rejected the plan evolved by the United Nations Atomic Energy Commission for the international manufacture and control of atomic energy, and has worked for the destruction of the existing American stock of bombs in advance of any system of international control which could ensure that Russia was not at the same time building up her own stock.*

No non-Communist Government would endorse the Russian plan, and the Soviet Government therefore tried to exploit the natural revulsion of world opinion against atomic warfare to obtain popular support for its own proposals. Accordingly, in March, 1950, the Second World Peace Congress issued the " Stockholm Appeal " for the banning of atomic weapons. This appeal was carefully calculated to attract the ordinary person who was unable, or unwilling, to examine its implications. The first clause invites the people of the free world to abolish an important and, according to Mr Churchill and others, the one weapon standing between them and conquest by Soviet Russia.

The second clause advocates a system of international control which, as the Russians showed by their attitude to schemes of international control during discussions at the United Nations, they would always veto if there were any risk of it being used to operate effectively on their own territory. The third clause condemns as war criminals not the Government which might unleash aggressive war, perhaps with every kind of atrocity, but the Government which, even if purely in self-defence, first uses the atomic weapon. A moment's thought will show that the Stockholm Peace Appeal was designed to operate to the exclusive advantage of Soviet policy.

Third, when the Communist North Korean Government attacked South Korea in June, 1950, the machinery of the world " peace " movement asserted that the South Koreans were aggressors, that the Americans were guilty of imperialist intervention in a private war on behalf of the South Korean aggressors, and that the United Nations was simply a pawn of imperialist, aggressive American policy. This display of Communist aggression by armed force led to greatly intensified defensive preparations in the free world.

The " peace " movement, as has been shown in the directives already quoted, countered by trying to organise strikes, sabotage,

* For further details see Appendix I.

L

industrial unrest, opposition to serving in the armed forces—anything that would weaken the will and capacity of the Western Powers to resist.

Next we find an example of the first overt move being taken by the " peace " movement, and the follow-up action being taken by the Soviet Government.   It had been apparent from the earliest meetings of the Security Council in 1946 that the Soviet Government had no intention of co-operating in the work of the United Nations on the terms prescribed by the Charter, but preferred to use the United Nations as a sounding-board for its own propaganda.   For a summary of Soviet Union policy at the United Nations see Appendix II.   As Soviet aims and methods in the United Nations came to be progressively better understood the value of the organisation to the Soviet Government was much diminished.   Finally, when in the summer of 1950 the absence owing to a tactical error, of the Soviet representative and his veto from the Security Council made it possible for collective action to be taken by the United Nations against the Communist aggressor in Korea, the Soviet Government realised that some other propaganda move was necessary to recreate the idea of unanimity between the five great Powers (including Communist China) on Russian terms.   Accordingly, in November, 1950, the Warsaw Peace Congress called for the signing of a peace pact between the five great Powers.   It has never been made clear what such a pact would contain, or what it could do that could not already be done by the five great Powers acting in concord in the Security Council.

The main object of the proposal appears to have been to get the Communist Government recognised as the legitimate Chinese representative on the Security Council, and otherwise generally to exploit the idea of " unanimity ".   After allowing the " peace " movement to make the running for a short period, the Soviet Government formally put forward the demand for a five-Power peace pact early in 1951.   The usual signature campaigns were then organised, and almost the entire populations of the Communist-controlled States have signed the required petition, together with the members of the Communist parties and anyone else they could persuade to sign in the free world.

Again, events in South-East Asia have always particularly interested the " peace " movement.   The attempts by Communist guerrilla warfare to win Malaya and Vietnam for the

Communist empire have been thwarted by the armed resistance
of the native peoples, aided by British and French troops. So
we find the " Warsaw Peace Appeal " in November, 1950,
calling for the end of hostilities in Vietnam and condemning
" violence employed to hold peoples in a state of dependence
and colonial subjection ". Similarly it called for the removal of
the barrier to the expansion of Communism in Japan by demanding withdrawal of occupation forces.

It would be simple, but tedious, to expand this list to cover all
the facets of Soviet propaganda which are duly reflected in
" peace " propaganda. Two further examples must suffice.

First, the Russian attack upon the United Nations. Fantastic
as it may appear that a group of 200 or 300 persons organised
to serve the Soviet Government should claim to be a substitute
for the United Nations, the fact remains that the World Peace
Council has made this claim. The World Peace Committee
turned itself into the World Peace Council (a change in name
only) at the Warsaw Peace Congress in November, 1950. It
modestly gave as its purpose the assumption of " the lofty task of
securing a firm and lasting peace that shall correspond to the
vital interests of all the nations ".

It then attacked the United Nations on the grounds that it had
been deflected from its path by influences not desiring peace.
This charge echoed the Soviet line that the United Nations had
failed because it had become the tool of the imperialist warmongers. A year later we find a member of the Executive
Bureau saying (at the World Peace Council in Vienna, November, 1951) :—

> " The United Nations has arrived at a stage at which,
> if it does not revert to its original principle of universality
> and to the Charter adopted in San Francisco, it will be
> unable to say or do anything which could serve the cause of
> peace."

At the same meeting a representative of the British delegation, Mr. D. N. Pritt, said :—

> " We are of the opinion that the World Peace Council
> should furnish a survey of all those tasks which the United
> Nations have taken on or promised to take on so as to
> ascertain to what extent the World Peace Council may

itself take over these tasks until such time as the Unite
Nations begin seriously to work in the sense originall
planned instead of acting as a branch of a group of nations.'

It will be apparent that in its organisation, its avowed aim
and the propaganda themes that it exploits, the World Peac
Council has no interest in peace unless it is peace on Sovie
terms, and that its principal function is to be an instrument c
Soviet policy and a sounding-board for Soviet propaganda
All these functions, and the methods by which it operates, ca
best be illustrated by the document printed in Appendix II
This is a draft " Teachers' Peace Appeal ", some copies of whicl
were sent to persons connected with the teaching profession i
The United Kingdom after a " Teachers' Peace Meeting,'
organised in France during the summer of 1951. It is
collector's piece!

CHAPTER XI

LIFE IN THE SOVIET UNION

A GREAT deal of nonsense has been written about the conditions of life in the Soviet Union; most of it by Communists or fellow-travellers, some of it by anti-Communists.

The first point to make is, that if we are to judge the issue as to whether Communism is good or bad solely by the standard of the change in the material conditions of life in Russia which have taken place since 1917, we are adopting a Marxian approach to the problem.

Admittedly—and we need not be ashamed to say so—material conditions, such as food, clothing and housing, are extremely important factors in life, and it is a mockery to tell a starving man that he is free to write a letter to *The Times*, which if not printed, he can then send to the *Manchester Guardian*! But man does not live by bread alone, and it is perhaps fair to say that as standards of living improve, non-material considerations become increasingly important.

The average inhabitant of the Soviet Union is better off to-day than he or she was in 1917—the same observation applies with equal or greater force to most of the inhabitants of the free world. Every effort is made by the rulers of Soviet Russia to conceal this fact from their people and lead them to suppose that the improvement which has taken place in the life of the Russian citizen represents the zenith—so far—of human endeavour. In view of the wonders which are to be seen in the Soviet Union and the prodigious production feat which Soviet Man has achieved, it is pertinent to ask why vital statistics automatically published in other countries are State secrets in Russia? The author has a vivid recollection of the curious fact that even in January, 1945, during his membership of a Parliamentary delegation to Russia, when—to be fair to the Russians—a great deal was shown which had never been shown before to visitors, the simple question to the manager of a factory: " How many workers do you employ here? " invariably met with an evasive answer, such as " A great many " or " It would be difficult to say exactly ".

Seven years later a British economist, Mr. Cairncross (see *Listener*, 23rd October, 1952), said, " I should have liked also to talk with some of the officials of Gosplan—the State Planning Department—but my efforts to arrange this were unsuccessful. My conversations about economic problems with Soviet economists were a great deal less illuminating than I had hoped." Mr. Cairncross then catalogued a list of specific questions to which he could get no satisfactory answers.

II

A decree of 8th June, 1947, " On liability for divulging State secrets and for losing documents containing State secrets ", laid down penalties of eight to twelve years' imprisonment for disclosing statistics on the following subjects:—

" industry as a whole and in its various branches;

" agriculture, trade and means of communication;

" the state of monetary reserves;

" the current balance of payments and the plans for financial operations of the U.S.S.R.;

" the location and the method of storing and transporting precious metals belonging to the State reserve, foreign currency and banknotes;

" plans and planning proposals relating to the import and export of different types of goods."

In Western countries all information of this nature is usually fully available. But in the Soviet Union:—

No figures (apart from percentages) are given for any important basic item of production such as coal, electric power, non-ferrous metals, oil, pig-iron, steel, synthetic rubber and chemicals.

For many years there have been no statistics for foodstuffs and many other basic consumer goods, with the sole exception of production figures for the grain harvest in 1948 and 1949.

As regards general consumption of consumer goods: No regular statistics have been published since the last issue of *Socialist Construction in the U.S.S.R.* (1936).

No references are made to the consumption of goods per head, or to total consumption, except for vague references to overall consumption and percentage increases in the retail trade in various communities which are to be found in annual reports on the fulfilment of the current Five-Year Plan.

In the important field of housing and allied subjects, no

basic statistics, apart from planned figures, are provided for average space per head of the population, or the average for centres such as Moscow or Leningrad. The only housing statistics issued are those which cover *all* living space made available over a given period. Repairs and construction are added together. Thus there is no true picture of new construction—far less of the newly built living-space per head.

A yearly statement of the percentage increase of investment in building is issued, as well as many vague statements on the situation in particular areas—*e.g.*, the amount of industrial building in the Ukraine since the liberation. These figures, however, are in terms of roubles, the value of which is uncertain and, in addition, not comparable with other valuta.

Until 1927 not only were total health statistics published, but there were also detailed statistics on such subjects as abortions, infantile mortality in backward regions, and the incidence of highly infectious diseases. These are no longer given. Indeed, since 1927 Moscow has issued no material statistics regarding health. Thus no figures are available for the incidence of venereal disease, typhus, leprosy, bubonic plague, beri-beri, chicken-pox, scarlet fever, and so on. Russia no longer provides the International Drug Control with statistics or any other assistance.

No statistics of population have been published since the results of the 1939 census. Although publication of the full returns was prevented by the war, yet to-day these returns have still not been published. Thus there are no figures for present population, war casualties or civilian casualties. Figures from which an estimate of the total working population can be made *are* published, but there are no figures from which the total population could be split up into its various occupational groups.

No statistics of cost of living have been issued since 1926.

III

There are now four main social classes in the Soviet Union. These are:—

    (*a*) State officials and employees;
    (*b*) urban and rural workers;
    (*c*) peasants;
    (*d*) people condemned to forced labour.

The top class of officials and State employees, though it i
not formally regarded as a " class ", is usually distinguishe
from the workers and peasants and described as the " intelli
gentsia ". It governs the State apparatus, administers th
country's economy, conducts the schools, runs the armed force
and the Press, and concerns itself with the advance of Sovie
science and arts. This class began its spectacular rise in 1936
when Stalin said, in his speech on the new Constitution, tha
the intelligentsia had become a fully-fledged member of Sovie
society and was participating with the workers and peasants i
building Communism.

The average earnings of the " intelligentsia " are at leas
twice the average earnings of the workers. But the top layer
of the " intelligentsia " earn far higher salaries than the average
Certain groups of engineers earn several thousand roubles
month (as against the worker's average 600–700). Mucl
higher are the earnings of the " ideological " writers, such a
Simonov, Ehrenburg and Fadeyev, and scientists, such a
Lysenko, the geneticist, who, in addition to salaries of tens c
thousands of roubles a month, receive all kinds of special grants
are given the use of cars and chauffeurs, and occasionall
exempted from paying taxes.

In Baku in 1945 the author had an interesting talk with th
composer of an opera. This man, whose opera was frequentl
performed by decision of a Committee of which he was chairmar
received 10 per cent. on the gross takings. Stalin had approve
of the opera and ordered its translation into the Russia
language. My friend conceded that he hoped soon to be
millionaire, but added, " Alas ! the taxes are awful ".

The aristocracy of the Soviet Union consists of the highes
Government officials, directors, chairmen of trusts, plan
managers, planning economists, the service chiefs, " idec
logical " writers, journalists and artists, professors, part
leaders and heads of trade unions. They number fror
800,000 to a million people, and their standard of living
incomparably higher than that of the workers, or even that c
the lower " intelligentsia ".

Furthermore, the custom of awarding large cash prizes t
certain artists, writers and engineers, ranging from 25,000
200,000 roubles, the presentation of cars and country homes
prizes, and salaries of 5,000 roubles or more per month, hav

created enormous social differences between the higher Government official and the ordinary worker. Members of the Soviet aristocracy have segregated themselves into a social group, which has been steadily seizing an ever-growing share of the national income. This class is extremely conscious of its differentiation from the " common man ", as a result of its many privileges, some of which are the following:—

(i) Its members enjoy decent accommodation (an entire and respectable flat to one family), as compared with the six or more families of workers crowded into a single flat, often, especially in the smaller cities, little more than a filthy and insanitary hovel.

(ii) They can afford to eat well, both at home and in first-class restaurants—with the abolition of rationing there is no limit on food—whereas the worker usually cannot afford even butter, meat, milk and cheese.

(iii) They can afford to buy clothes and furniture— items which the average worker can rarely afford during his whole life.

(iv) They ride in first-class railway compartments.

(v) They enjoy vacations in " homes of rest ", to which, in practice, few of the average workers can hope to obtain admission.

(vi) In theatres the best seats are allotted to members of this class.

All these privileges give the " intelligentsia " a feeling of superiority. These are the people with whom visiting delegations are most in contact. It is not surprising that visitors gain from them a favourable impression of life in Russia.

The ordinary semi-skilled worker, such as a joiner, a truck-loader, a locomotive fireman, a worker in a ball-bearing factory, may be taken as typical. Such a worker would be paid about 600–700 roubles a month (a fairly high figure—an unskilled worker such as a cleaner gets about half this). Six to seven hundred roubles a month is the equivalent in buying capacity to about £2 to £2 10s. a week in English money.

The legal entitlement for housing accommodation is rather less than 3 yds. by 3 yds. of floor-space per person. A worker with a wife and two children should get a room (or part of a room) about 18 ft. by 18 ft. in size. A few feet larger than this would bring him above the legal *maximum*, and he would be liable to give up any extra space. But, in fact, by no means all workers have even the minimum legal entitlement. The very poorest live in wooden hovels which can be seen even in the heart of Moscow. And the ball-bearing worker would consider himself reasonably housed if he had 15 ft. by 15 ft. for his family.

This average worker's room includes no facilities for washing or cooking, which are normally done in a kitchen shared by four or five families. The worker, on getting up, must queue for tap and basin, then for the lavatory and then for the kerosene or wood-stove on which to cook his breakfast (probably a cup of tea, a slice of black bread and a couple of potatoes). He must queue again to wash up. Rent, however, is very low, as indeed it should be.

Food prices were raised about 300 per cent in September 1946. In December 1947 rationing was abolished and monetary reform took place. The consequent reduction in food prices left their real level well above that ruling before September 1946. If the worker has the money he can get the goods. With a wife and two children he must spend about 750 roubles a month to obtain the bare necessities of life. Rent, income tax, forced contributions to the State loan, other taxes, trade union dues, etc., will bring his expenses up to about 1,000 roubles a month, leaving about 200 roubles for all other expenses out of the combined incomes of himself and his wife, assuming that, like most Russian wives, she also works and is in the same grade as her husband. Clothes are, proportionately, even more expensive than food.

To compare real wages we must consider how much longer than British men and women of the same status the Russians must work to buy the same necessities:—

> For a cotton dress, about three times as long;
> for a pound of bread, about four times as long;
> for a man's suit, five times as long;
> for a pound of butter, seven times as long.

The ratios are similar for other products. The quality of clothes bought by the Briton is much higher than that bought by the Russian; and in the U.S.S.R., the price of consumer goods is inflated by a very high " turnover tax " which is re-

uired by the State to pay for its bureaucracy, Secret Police
nd armaments. These figures are for the period since the
rice cuts of 1950 and 1951.* It is noteworthy that the heaviest
uts were in the prices of caviare, cameras, gramophones and
ther commodities only within reach of the Soviet rich. In
ict they amounted to a subsidy for the rich.

The Soviet trade union leader, Lozovsky, in his *Handbook
n Soviet Trade Unions*, published in 1937, said:—

> " In the U.S.S.R. there is no struggle between the workers
> and the administrative bodies for higher wages as there is
> under capitalist conditions, nor can there be such a
> struggle."

And the present chairman of the Soviet trade unions,
Kuznetsov, wrote on 20th February, 1947, in the newspaper
Trud that, as far as wages were concerned, it was well-known
hat the rates were established only by the Government.

Up to 1929 factories in the Soviet Union were run by a
Committee of Three ", which included, in addition to the
nanager, the secretary of the Communist Party cell of the
ictory and a representative of the trade union. In 1929,
owever, the director became sole master. The Committee
ost its authority and was later abolished. Promotion of
vorkers to the rank of factory director, which had been common
ractice in the early days of the régime, practically ceased.
Heads of factories began increasingly to form part of a closed
aste, of that " intelligentsia " of which the bureaucracy above
hem, consisting of experts, technicians and administrators,
vas an even more important part. The factory manager does
ittle more than carry out instructions from above. But in his
elationship with the worker below he has far greater authority
han a manager in capitalist countries. His disciplinary
owers are not limited or controlled by the workers' representa-
ives, and Soviet law compels him to be ruthless in securing the
ccurate fulfilment of all tasks. He himself can be called to
ccount if he does not enforce these orders: for example, if he
oes not prevent the production of sub-standard goods he can
e sent to a labour camp or sentenced to as much as eight years
n prison. On the other hand, his basic income is several times

* In April, 1952, further price reductions were made, ranging mainly
om 10 to 20 per cent.

higher than the average worker's, and he also receives bonus
on the successful completion of tasks—bonuses usually share
with only a few foremen and " shock " workers, while th
ordinary worker very rarely receives any substantial bonus.

Labour Discipline

A decree of 18th January, 1941, which is still in force, defin
absenteeism for the Soviet worker as being twenty minutes la
for work (or taking twenty minutes too long in the lunch brea
or leaving twenty minutes early), or being late for even a less
period three times in one month, or four times in two successiv
months. The punishment for absenteeism is six month
" corrective labour "—*i.e.*, work at the usual factory at long
hours and for reduced pay. Transport workers are subject
particularly strict discipline, certain breaches of which a
punishable by sentences of up to twenty-five years' forc
labour.

The normal Soviet method of increasing output at th
workers' expense is by raising the " norms ". The " norm
is the output the worker must achieve to get his wage. Gre
encouragement is given to those who manage to do more tha
the " norm ". Those who do very well receive special faciliti
—higher wages, new machines, assistants, the best raw materia
the best lighting and so on—and are encouraged to do bett
still. The new records they set up later become the "norm" f
the ordinary worker, who has to work at greatly increas
pressure to get the same wage as before. Another device is th
" Socialist competition "—when a factory is specially geared
for a certain period to work harder than usual so as to defeat a
arbitrarily nominated rival factory. After the " competition
both factories may have their " norms " raised to the hig
pressure competition level.

Under a decree of 20th December, 1938, all Soviet worke
have " labour books ". In these documents are entered ma
details about the worker and his record : his name, age, educ
tion, qualifications, type of work, efficiency, dates when
changed his jobs, the reasons for change, and so on. Witho
his labour book no worker can obtain employment. As the
is no unemployment benefit in the Soviet Union, the man wh
is blacklisted has no legal alternative to starvation. A decree
26th June, 1940, which is still in force, forbids workers to lea

their jobs without special authorisation. This is given only on medical grounds or if the worker is required for special training.

Soviet trade unions are now not trade unions as understood in the West. Kaganovich, as long ago as 1933, was able to say that " the Party is the controlling force in all these organisations ", while in 1951 Moscow Radio was saying, " the Party is responsible for the general line adopted by the trade unions ". President Shvernik, when head of the Soviet trade unions in 1943, using Lenin's and Stalin's simile, described them as " schools of Communism, the transmission belt from the Party to the masses ". In fact the trade union's sole rôle is to impose the Party's industrial policy on its membership. When Tomsky was removed from leadership of the trade unions in 1928 and the last relics of their independence were extinguished, the official pronouncement condemned him and his associates because, " instead of extensively working to enlist the mass of working men and women in the work of economic reconstruction and Socialist nationalisation, *the raising of labour production and the strengthening of labour discipline*, they attempted to act as a screen for class interests and the sentiments of the backward sections of the working-class ". In fact they tried to protect their members' interests and respect their wishes.

The Communist Party provides all the leading full-time trade union officials, the secretaries of some seventy unions and the Soviet delegates to international trade union conferences. It also dominates all trade union congresses held in the U.S.S.R. For seventeen years, from 1932 to 1949, however, no such gatherings took place, which meant that during this period the reputedly highest organ directly representing the workers was unable to elect its leaders or discuss far-reaching changes which the Politburo had introduced into labour policy. If the congress had met it would have had to obey the Politburo's orders, but the fact that it was not called shows the attitude of the Party leaders to the unions.

Besides being dominated entirely by the Communist Party the unions have become the home of a privileged bureaucracy. Their pre-war budgets showed that they maintained over 50,000 paid officials. This does not include such people as the employees of social clubs and the like under trade union control whose salaries were not paid from membership fees. Since the war the Soviet unions have failed to produce any figures about their staffs nor have they published their budgets in full. Individual unions are completely without independence and the Central Council of the Trade Unions abolishes or merges unions whenever it thinks fit.

Unemployment

There is a considerable turnover of labour in the Soviet Union, and this naturally involves the workers concerned in at least short periods of unemployment. In the United Kingdom there is unemployment pay to cover such gaps. None exists in the Soviet Union, since the official line is that unemployment does not exist.

But the existence of seasonal and turnover unemployment is admitted in certain official instructions on the calculation of " work stages ". Thus a document entitled " Clarification of Instructions by the A.U.C.C.T.U., confirmed by the Council of People's Commissars of the U.S.S.R. on 28th December, 1940 ", points out that a worker may count his " work stage " as uninterrupted when he starts employment at a new place of work, if he has been dismissed as a result of cuts in staff or the closing down of an enterprise or establishment, provided the break in his employment does not exceed one month.

The peasants, who comprise nearly half the working population of the Soviet Union, endure a standard of living lower than that of the industrial workers. The forcible and unscrupulous collectivisation which took place in the early thirties represented, in effect, a return to the old order of peasant serfdom. The peasant is now required to work a minimum amount of time for his collective farm—to which he is bound as the former Russian serf was bound to his master. For this compulsory work he is very poorly paid, and manages to keep body and soul together by working the small allotment of up to half a hectare [1¼ acres] which he is allowed for his private use. For his work on the collective farm he is paid on the piece-work system, according to the number of " labour-days " he has put in.

Social differentiation is also found on the collective farms. Officially there are seven classes of collective farm " workers ", ranging from ordinary farmhands down to watchmen and cleaners. While the highest of these classes are credited with two or more " labour-days " for each day's work, the ordinary armhand must fulfil a given norm to qualify for payment for one " labour-day ", even though it may take him more than a day to do that work.

There is an enormous apparatus of officialdom in the Soviet villages. In 1938 there were some 400,000 presidents and vice-presidents of collective farms, some 250,000 book-keepers, and 30,000 chairmen of inspection committees—all whole-time employees. The total number of rural officials, who are paid from the proceeds of peasant labour and at much higher rates than the peasants themselves, was some 2½ millions.

The Communist Party obtained the peasant support which enabled it to come to power in 1917 by approving or sponsoring the handing-over of the land to the peasants. When the Party had established its grip properly, however, Stalin launched the collectivisation programme. In the years following 1929, in spite of their stiff resistance, the Russian peasant masses were forced to hand over practically all their land, livestock, implements and buildings (except dwelling-houses) to the collective farms.

The intentions of the Soviet leadership in this matter appear to have been as follows:—

(a) On general, doctrinal grounds it was expected that at some stage the co-operative farming of the land must come about.

(b) So long as the large agricultural section of the economy was under private control " capitalism was born every hour " in a small way in each village. Not only capitalist economy, but the habits of mind based on it received continual encouragement and support so long as no change was made.

(c) The food harvested by the peasant remained outside the stocks under direct control of the State and the Party, and either had to be seized by force, as in the 1917–21 period, or extracted by economic pressure (as in the 1921–29 period). Once the collective farm was set up Party control became direct.

(d) Similarly the peasant himself was brought under direct control.

(e) A large programme of industrialisation was about to be launched. It required a very much larger number of industrial workers than then existed. Collectivisation of

the land, accompanied by the provision of tractors an
other machinery, was expected to make possible th
harvesting of crops as large or larger, with a considerabl
reduced labour force, thus releasing workers for industry

Collectivisation was put through in the course of a fierc
struggle directed particularly against the five million or so mor
prosperous peasants or " kulaks ". Peasant resistance took th
form of the destruction of their corn and the slaughter of the
livestock. Between 1929 and 1933 Russia's livestock wa
reduced by half. Very large numbers of people died of starva
tion and the Soviet Government ceased the publication of birt
and death statistics in the middle of this campaign. Millio
of " kulaks " went to forced labour. But by 1935 practicall
the whole agricultural sphere had been collectivised, an
only a few hundred thousand nomad shepherds in Centr
Asia avoided the " kulaks' " fate by escaping with their her
into China and Afghanistan.

However, peasant resistance had gained one concessio
The collective farm member in most regions was official
allowed to retain for his own use in addition to his plot of lan
a cow, and/or certain other livestock. The peasant made th
best of this concession, and by the end of the 1930's the Gover
ment ordered the confiscation of all land and cattle which th
peasants had acquired above the maximum limits. Similarl
after the war, the collective farm system had practically brok
down over large areas of European Russia—including tho
which had not been occupied by the enemy, such as the low
Volga Basin—and had to be forcibly reimposed.

The peasant has once more become a serf. He owns practi
ally no land, and he has very large obligations in labo
towards the collective farm, just as the feudal serf had to t
landlord. Meanwhile, rural Russia is as greatly differentiat
by class and economic status as any other country in the worl
First come the personnel of the " machine tractor stations
whose wages compare favourably even with the most skill
workers in the cities, and then the new agricultural Stakhan
vites (shock workers), bureaucrats, and the chairmen of t
collective farms, who can earn three or even five times as mu
as the ordinary peasant. Above everybody are the local Par
officials.

In the Army, too, where most male Soviet citizens spend several years of their lives, the class system prevails. The life of the Soviet conscript is a hard one. He is well fed and his boots and other clothing, though not of first-class quality, are considerably better than those of the civil population. But discipline is extremely harsh. Even in peace-time the commander has almost unlimited powers. The disciplinary code states: " The commander has the right to apply all measures of coercion up to, and including, the application of force and firearms." The Army paper, *Red Star*, wrote on 22nd October, 1940:—

> " Comradely relations between soldiers and officers are no more. The hail-fellow-well-met spirit in relationships between a commander and a subordinate can have no place in the Red Army. Discussion of any kind is absolutely prohibited among the subordinates."

Such outward forms of discipline as saluting are enforced to the extent that the soldier even salutes his N.C.Os. Absence without leave for three hours may entail punishment of up to ten years in a labour camp. *Pravda* on 6th October, 1940, at a time when the last remnants of the earlier and more democratic system in the Army were being replaced by the present rigidity, wrote:—

> " No more group declarations, no more joint discussions— whether concerning an order or bad food or any other topic—all this comes under the heading of ' insubordination ' and for it a soldier may be shot on the spot without a court-martial hearing or investigation if a superior officer solely and personally decides."

Differences in pay in the Army are very great. A private gets 360 roubles a year: a Marshal 40,000. Senior officers, especially in the occupied countries, live in great luxury, while in East Germany, for example, all private soldiers are now permanently confined to barracks. The differentiation in pay and conditions is part of the general building-up of a privileged class which is going on throughout the Soviet Union. But it is clear that special importance is attached to the military sphere.

In 1943 this tendency was greatly assisted by the setting up of special institutions—the " Suvorov " military cadet schools.

M

By the decree of 22nd August, 1943, nine of these, each with 500 pupils, enrolled boys at the age of ten for " military service with the rank of officer ". There are also preparatory classes for children aged 8 to 10, and similar schools have been established to train officers for the Navy.

Taxation and Social Welfare

The taxation system in the Soviet Union probably bears harder on the poorer sections of the population than any other taxation system in the world. In the 1950 Budget estimates, the total revenue amounted to 447,000 million roubles. Of these the main item was the " turnover tax ", which accounted for 239,100 million roubles. The turnover tax is basically the same as the purchase tax. But it is employed on a far wider scale and its aim is not to prevent inflation, but to secure revenue.* It affects everything produced, manufactured and delivered through trade channels, though not in the same degree. For example, it is 1 per cent. and even less on raw materials and manufactured goods, but 100 per cent. on tobacco and alcohol, while on fats it is 50–80 per cent., on vegetable oil 33–35 per cent., on meat 77–87 per cent. and on salt 35–88 per cent.

In Russia the largest item of consumption is bread, especially by the poor. The State buys grain compulsorily for low prices and sells it for very high prices in the form of flour or bread. In 1937 the tax on cereals amounted to a third of the total revenue in the turnover tax. This tax is paid several times, e.g., on grain at the time of its delivery at the mill, and on flour at the time of its delivery to the baker.

Social Welfare

" The whole practice of social insurance must be transformed with a view to securing a privileged position for the shock workers and those with long service. We must handle the social insurance weapon so as to promote the attachment of the worker to the undertaking ".†

Nearly half the working population of the Soviet Union is not covered by the State social insurance legislation. Article

* British purchase tax is now (1953) open to the same criticism.
† *Questions of Insurance*, Nos. 7–8, 1933, p. 12. Shvernik.

75 of the Soviet Labour Codex states that " social insurance covers all persons engaged in *hired* labour ". This excludes collective farm workers, who are defined as communal owners of property working not for hire but on a co-operative basis. There are over 33 million of them as against nearly 41 million industrial and office workers.

Soviet factories and enterprises have to pay a specified proportion of their wages expenditure into the State social insurance fund. This proportion must be large enough to cover all expenditure for the enterprise concerned in the field of social insurance.

The compulsory contributions paid by Soviet enterprises and institutions vary from 3·7 per cent. of the wages fund for ' artistic " concerns to 10·7 per cent. for more dangerous enterprises, such as those in the nitrogen industry.*

As the wages of Soviet workers are calculated on the basis of the profits remaining after the various appropriations are made by the State (*e.g.*, turnover tax and for capital investment), any further deduction from those profits in effect involves a deduction from wages.

Free medical treatment is provided under the State medical service. In practice, however, this is so slow and inadequate that those who can afford it seek private treatment. The Soviet authorities, recognising the inadequacy of the State service, have established " Commercial Polyclinics ", where the wealthier classes can obtain preferential treatment against payment. Specialists and doctors, practising in their spare time, also provide paid treatment. Well-informed students of Soviet affairs estimate that, over the whole Soviet Union, one person in 100 may be able to afford paid treatment: in the capital towns, about one in twenty.

Men have the right to old age pensions at 60, but not unless they have worked without a break for twenty-five years. Women receive the old age pension at 55, if they have worked continuously for twenty years. For workers in certain harmful occupations the qualifying periods are shorter.

Persons guilty of absenteeism and condemned to forced labour at their place of work automatically lose all right to benefits for six months from the beginning of the sentence.

* See the Directive of the Council of People's Commissars of the U.S.S.R., 23rd March, 1937.

They also lose their " working stage "—the period of continuous work previously accumulated.

Stalinist propaganda has made great efforts to extol the merits of Soviet sanatoria and rest homes. The oft-quoted Article 119 of the Soviet Constitution states that " the right to rest and leisure is ensured by the establishment of an eight hour day for factory and office workers . . . by the institution of annual vacations with full pay for factory and office workers, and by the provision of a wide network of sanatoria, rest homes and clubs for the accommodation of the working people."

The administration of welfare, including sanatoria and rest homes, has been entrusted to the trade unions since 1933. An order of the A.U.C.C.T.U. dated 29th May, 1948, lays down the conditions of admission as follows:—

> " Twenty per cent. of all tickets for sanatoria and prophylactoria and 10 per cent. of tickets for rest homes are issued free by the trade union organisations at the expense of the State Social Insurance funds. The remaining 80 per cent. of tickets to sanatoria and prophylactoria and 90 per cent. of tickets to rest homes are issued on payment of 30 per cent. of their cost. Free tickets must be issued, in the first place to persons with the best production record, war invalids who are working, juveniles employed at enterprises, pregnant women, and nursing mothers. All earlier instructions of the Presidium . . . as regards the provision of free tickets to sanatoria . . . and rest homes are hereby annulled.
>
> " Central, provincial, factory and local trade union committees must ensure that Stakhanovites, and engineering and technical personnel engaged in production have priority in obtaining tickets to sanatoria and rest homes."

This provision applies to tickets for accommodation at sanatoria in general, not merely to the free tickets.

An instruction of the secretariat of the A.U.C.C.T.U. and the Ministry of Finance, dated 8th June, 1948, reads:—

> " The Social Insurance Council . . . hands over the tickets to the worker or employee only on presentation of a receipt showing that part-payment has been made. . . ."

The official Soviet press has boasted that in 1951 more than four million workers and employees visited Soviet sanatoria and rest homes. As there are nearly 41 million workers and

mployees, this means that, on an average, the Soviet worker
vould have the opportunity to visit such a resort only once every
en and a half years. Agricultural workers are not normally
ligible for accommodation at State-run sanatoria or rest
omes. In practice, the majority of Soviet workers never have
he opportunity to visit a rest home or sanatorium, but members
f the privileged minority are fairly regular visitors.

Of the 41 million citizens eligible, the sanatoria and rest
omes annually admit on *free* tickets only about 400,000 and
00,000 privileged persons respectively (the statutory 10 per
ent., and 20 per cent. of four million). Observers who have
nown the Soviet Union are mostly agreed that the great
najority of these favoured few are Party officials and members
f the administrative classes and their favourites. The
emainder have to pay.

Religion

The official Communist attitude to religion is that it is a
ostile force which must be opposed and eradicated. However,
n the Marxist view, religion will disappear of its own accord
nce the economic and social causes of it are removed. The
etting up of a Socialist and eventually a Communist society is
upposed to remove these causes. Therefore it should not be
uppressed by force, though a continuous propaganda against it
hould be maintained.

In practice the Communist campaign against religion in the
oviet Union has gone through various stages, some of them
nvolving the use of violence.

The original Soviet Constitution of 1918 guaranteed " free-
om of religious and anti-religious propaganda ". This
lause, liberal in appearance, actually represented a consider-
ble blow to religion, since the religious propaganda was to be
ndertaken by a weakened and isolated Church, while the anti-
eligious propaganda was pursued with vigour by the con-
rollers of all the machinery of the State and its propaganda.
)n 2nd January, 1918, a decree ordered the seizure of all
Church-owned property without compensation. Local Soviets
vere empowered to leave in the hands of religious organisations
uch of their property as was absolutely essential to them;
uildings, chalices, vestments, etc. Monasteries and convents
vere closed down. No church was permitted to own private

property. Priests were disfranchised and their children not admitted to secondary schools and universities, and other oppressive conditions were laid upon them. During this period the Soviet authorities encountered considerable resistance to these measures from the population, and by 1923, twenty-eight bishops and about 1,000 priests had been executed, though of course many of them had probably been involved in political resistance.

In May, 1922, the Communists supported an artificial schism in the Church and turned over a large proportion of the Church's offices to their own faction. The Patriarch was arrested. However, for lack of support among Church people the schism failed and it eventually broke up after the second World War.

Direct attack on the Church having failed, the Party went over to more orthodox propaganda methods. In February, 1922, a journal called the "Godless" was published, and in the same year an anti-religious museum was opened in Leningrad Christmas, 1922, saw the organisation of an anti-Christmas carnival, when various doctrines of the Church were held up to mockery. In 1925 the League of Militant Atheists was formed, and conducted powerful anti-religious propaganda During this time various administrative measures, mostly of an economic nature, put the churches in an extremely unfavourable position compared with other bodies. On the death of the Patriarch in 1925, the authorities prevented the election of a new Patriarch and arrested successive Acting Patriarchs until in 1927, a compromise was reached.

Beginning in 1929, and synchronised with the forced collectivisation of the peasantry, a fresh campaign was launched against the Church. Throughout the country the Communist called meetings which "voted" for the demolition or conversion of the churches. A further wave of arrests and persecutions fell on the priesthood. A decree of the 8th April, 1929, imposed fresh restrictions on the religious groups, who were forbidden to use any of the funds except for purposes directly connected with worship—that is to say, all mutual assistance between them or charity was prevented. Most other activities such as Bible classes, the opening of reading-rooms and so on were also forbidden. They were also forbidden to organise collections; donations had to be spontaneous. In the autumn of 1929 the Central Committee of the Printers' Union ordered its members to refuse to print religious works, and various other unions concerned with transport and communications prevented these services being used by the Church.

This further direct attack also failed, and the position became regularised by the 1936, " Stalin " Constitution, which permitted " anti-religious propaganda " and " religious worship ". That is to say, it remained illegal to attempt to convert people to a religious belief, or to give religious instruction to children, but worship was permitted in the few churches which had been able to maintain themselves under the heavy economic pressure put on them.

A further wave of violent persecution coincided with the great purges. During the Second World War considerable concessions were made to the Orthodox Church, honours were paid to its dignitaries and the election of a Patriarch was permitted. The influence of the Church on the population was at this time vital to the régime in helping it to raise enthusiasm for the war against Germany. And even since the war ended the practice of using high Church dignitaries to influence the other Slavonic and Orthodox populations of Eastern Europe and the Middle East has been continued. The State, however, did not abandon its Marxist views, and kept up its persecution of those religious bodies which would not serve its purposes. And in 1946 a fresh " educational " campaign emphasising the importance of scientific materialism began to gather momentum.

On 18th October, 1947, the newspaper *Young Communist Truth* found it necessary to deny the possibility of any reconciliation between religion and Communism. To prove its point it quoted Stalin, who had said :—

> " The Party cannot be neutral regarding religion, and it conducts anti-religious propaganda against all religious prejudices, because it stands for science, and religious prejudices are opposed to science, since any religion is contrary to science."

The quotation continued :—

> " There are cases in which some members of the Party occasionally hinder the thorough development of anti-religious propaganda. If such members of the Party are expelled, this is very good, since there is no room in the ranks of our Party for such ' Communists '."

Among later pronouncements on the official Communist attitude to religions were the following:—

(a) " The outstanding Soviet teacher entrusted by the party with the education of youth, cannot and must not be neutral to religion or assume a policy of non-interference, the position of a detached observer, in circumstances in which believers sometimes try to infect children with the poison of religious dope. . . . He is obliged not only to be an active propagandist of Godlessness among others but also to be the bearer of ideas of militant proletarian atheism." *

(b) " The struggle against religious prejudices and scientific atheist propaganda form an inseparable and, moreover, an extremely vital part of the Communist education of the masses of the people." †

(c) " It is clear that religious beliefs are profoundly alien to our convictions and opinions and fundamentally contradict the tasks of Communist education. That is why the Komsomol obliges its members to fight against religious prejudices and to explain their harmful nature to the youth." ‡

(d) " Religion cannot help hindering the building of Communism for it represents an anti-scientific, reactionary ideology. Religion gives a fantastic, false and perverted idea of nature and society. . . . Why then . . . do churches exist in our country, why is not religious preaching prohibited? . . . For the very reason that neither closing down churches nor prohibiting the performance of church ceremonies are effective measures for combating religion nor are they recognised by the Communist Party and the Soviet State. The attitude of Marxism–Leninism toward such means of combating religion was always sharply negative.

" The Party, as has been pointed out time and time again by Lenin and Stalin, combats religion by the only correct ideological means of educational work, conviction, elucidation, wide-scale propaganda of political and scientific knowledge. This work must be carried out without offending the feelings of those who believe. . .

" Assisting the Party in the Communist education of

---

* *Teacher's Gazette*, 26th November, 1949.
† Article in *Science and Life*, February, 1950.
‡ Editorial answer in *Young Communist Truth* of 21st March, 1950, to letter from a Komsomol member asking whether he should agree to his fiancée's wish to be married in a church.

young people, the Young Communist League is expected
to fight to overcome survivals of the past in the minds of
the young, including religious survivals. This work must
not be carried out as a campaign, but day in and day
out, purposely and persistently. . . .

" For the Young Communist League member, just at
for the Communist, attitude to religion can in no way be
a ' personal matter ', since religious conceptions are
foreign to our Communist outlook. . . .

" The Young Communist League member is an advanced, cultured person, and his task is to wage an irreconcilable struggle against survivals of the past and for
Bolshevist education of vigorous and high-spirited young
builders of Communism."*

From these quotations from official Soviet publications, it is
obvious that a large-scale struggle is in progress for the minds of
Soviet youth between the Communist organs of mass con-
ditioning and the Orthodox Church.

The Soviet Constitution clearly gives the advantage from
the start to the Communist Party.

Political Rights and Freedoms

It is necessary for the rulers of the U.S.S.R. to keep their
population under constant supervision with the application of
terror methods to prevent the natural reasoning power of man
from drawing conclusions hostile to the régime and expressing
them in word or deed.

Three types of document are obligatory for Soviet citizens—
military service documents, the labour book and the internal
passport. The last is the most important.

The internal passport system now in force was introduced by
a decree of 27th December, 1932. It restricts freedom of movement within the U.S.S.R., it assists the direction of labour of the
State, and it serves as one of the many weapons against suspect
elements, while providing the authorities with an easy reference
to case-histories. At present possession of a passport is necessary
for (a) everyone over 16 years of age permanently living in towns
and locations where tractor stations are situated; or (b) anywhere in the Moscow region, within 100 kilometres of Leningrad, or 50 kilometres of Kiev, or in zones adjacent to the

* Extracts from editorial replies to readers' questions in *Young Communist
Truth*, 25th April, 1951, p. 3.

borders; or (c) working on construction projects, transport or State farms.

There are three types of passports:—

(i) the indefinite passport, for people over 55 years old, Heroes of the Soviet Union, invalids and pensioners;

(ii) the five-yearly passport, the normal type;

(iii) the temporary passport for those who have lost their passports, or are entering a region where the system is in force from a rural area where it is not.

Any change of domicile for a period of twenty-four hours or more entails registering one's passport with the militia at the place of arrival. Absence from one's place of residence for more than a month and a half (except for official trips, medical treatment or leave), any change of address or death, involves de-registering. Those without passports are expressly forbidden (with exceptions for those under 16, those in hospital, Servicemen and seasonal harvest workers) to reside in areas where the passport system is in force. That is to say, most rural workers are deprived of the right to a passport and not normally allowed to enter the passport area. The concession is made that they are permitted to visit towns within their local province for a period not exceeding five days, though even then they are required to register such visits with their own local officials. Any other form of unofficial visit to a region or area would require a passport not normally given.

The *Large Soviet Encyclopædia*, Volume 44, states:—

" The issue and registration of a passport serves as a means of administrative count, control and regulation of movement of the population according to a given system determined by class interests."

All those employed in the defence industry, the coal industry, railway transport and certain banking jobs are required to surrender their passports in exchange for special certificates issued by the chief administration of the militia.

The Soviet internal passport is no mere identity card. It can only be issued on production of the following documents:—

(i) birth certificate;

(ii) military service draft certificate;

(iii) certificate of domicile;

(iv) work certificate.

It carries, among others, the following details: name, date of birth, nationality, social position, and military service. And entries are made in it on the following occasions:—

    (i) registration with the militia;
    (ii) (by the employer) engagement for or dismissal from work;
    (iii) marriage or divorce;
    (iv) entry into a frontier zone.

Article 29 of the 1940 Passport Law lays down that:—

" Officials of establishments, enterprises and organisations are liable by administrative process to a fine of up to 100 roubles for the engaging of citizens for work without passports or without duly registered passports, for the failure to make entries in the passports of workers and employees about their engagement and dismissal."

Entry into a frontier zone is forbidden by a decree of 17th June, 1935, for those not domiciled in these areas, except by special permission of the M.V.D. In an earlier decree the M.V.D. frontier guard are responsible for the administration of a 22-kilometre belt all round the frontiers. At present very much larger areas are regarded as frontier zones from the point of view of the passport system. By the 1935 decree any infringement of the frontier regulations may entail a sentence of three years' imprisonment in a camp.

Penalties for breaches of the ordinary passport regulations are as follow: the initial offence—of engaging a worker without a passport, of allowing infringement of residence regulations by a caretaker or house-owner, or of non-registration, registration no longer valid, or lack of passport by the passport owner— entails a fine of only 100 roubles. The second offence involves corrective labour for a period of up to six months for infringement of the registration rules; and for being passportless in an area where a passport is required—deprivation of freedom for a period of up to two years.

Visits by Soviet citizens to foreign countries are unknown except for those sponsored by the Party and the State. The only category allowed abroad, except on official business, are the members of so-called " delegations " sent to attend congresses of various sorts, or make certain visits, mainly of a propaganda nature, at the instance of the Soviet authorities. How carefully these are selected may be seen by the numbers allowed out of the U.S.S.R. in 1950, when a total of 1,893 " delegates " went to various parts of the world. The total includes those who went to satellite countries and who probably comprised the majority.* An interesting comparison is that there were 600,000 visitors to France from Britain alone during the same period—notwithstanding currency restriction!

The main personal interference to which the Soviet citizen is exposed at any hour of the day or night is the violation of the sanctity of his home either directly by visits from the Secret Police or indirectly by its agents. Owing to congested housing conditions members of families are nearly always forced to spy and report on other families or even on other members of their own family. The tales of these informers make it impossible for the Soviet citizen to enjoy privacy as it is known in the West. Even the more privileged Party members, with rooms and flats to themselves and cars at their disposal, have all their movements shadowed and their conversations recorded by servants or chauffeurs. Conditions in factories or offices are no better, and every worker or official knows that his colleagues may be following his actions and informing on him. Every factory and office of a reasonable size, without exception, contains a " secret department " run by the Security Police, which maintains files on every individual employed in the establishment. These " secret departments " are quite openly provided for in published Soviet legislation.

Soviet legislation includes one staggering provision for the victimisation of a family which can well be mentioned here. It is included in the ferocious deterrent provisions against frontier-crossing by members of the Soviet armed forces. Those members of the family who fail to denounce their relatives are condemned to forced labour, while members who have no knowledge of their relatives' plans, and thus are entirely innocent, are deprived of their electoral rights and exiled to Siberia. That is to say, they are treated as hostages without even the pretence that they were in any way guilty. The decree—of 8th June, 1934, supplementing Articles 58 and 59 of the Penal Code—runs as follows:—

* These figures were given by M. Malik in conversation with a Quaker delegation in July, 1951.

" If a person in military employ takes flight across the frontier by air or otherwise, any member of his family who is of full age and who assists him in preparations for or in committing treason, or who, having knowledge of it, fails to bring it to the knowledge of the authorities, is liable to deprivation of liberty for a period of from five to ten years and confiscation of the whole of his property. Any other member of the traitor's family who is of full age and was living with or dependent on him at the time when the crime was committed, is liable to deprivation of electoral rights and exile to remote regions of Siberia."

The Rights of Minorities

This question is dealt with briefly, and with reference to the theoretical teachings of Stalinism on the subject, in Chapter VIII.

The Soviet Constitution provides on paper for the most elaborate system of satisfying national aspirations by the institution of " sovereign " republics for the larger nations of the Union and of " autonomous " republics for the smaller ones. Article 15 of the Constitution states that " the sovereignty of the Union republics is limited only in the spheres defined in Article 14 of the Constitution ". Article 14 reserves to the Central Government matters of war and peace, diplomatic relations, defence, foreign trade, State security (which, of course, overrides everything else), changes in the mutual frontiers of Republics, economic planning, credit and currency, education, criminal and civil codes, and many other matters.

In fact, these reserved powers are so much wider than in any other federal system in the world that the Union republics are left with no autonomy except in trivialities,—and even these, it appears, often have to be referred to the Central Government. For example, in the accounts of the 1950 budget debates published in the Soviet Press we read that even such matters as plans and estimates for building a bridge in the " autonomous " republic of Bashkiria,* for " new water pipes and drains and a trolley-bus line " in Nalchik, capital of the Kabardin Autonomous Republic, for the construction of schools and hospitals in the Tadzhik Soviet Socialist Republic † and municipal development and the financing of an opera and ballet theatre in the Turkmen S.S.R.‡ have

---

* *Izvestia*, 18th June, 1950.   † *Izvestia* and *Pravda*, 18th June, 1950.
‡ *Izvestia*, 18th–19th June, 1950.

to be referred to the Central Government before funds are
released. Even an increase in the number of hospital beds in
the Georgian S.S.R. has to be " considered " by the State
Planning Commission under the Central Government and the
Ministry of Health of the Central Government.*

But, apart from this centralisation, a far more effective
stranglehold is exercised on the Union republics through
the organisation of the Communist Party—for the Party i
explicitly and openly organised on a centralised, non-federal
basis. In other words the Party organisations of the Union
Republics are strictly subordinated to the Party Central Com
mittee in Moscow. And the Soviet Union openly admits (as
in Article 126 of the Constitution) that it is the Party which
provides the leadership and direction which permeate all
public and private life.

It is also clear that the alleged equality of these nations is
mere propaganda, as can be seen from the fact that according
to figures published in the Soviet Press there are at least as
many Russians as natives in the local Communist parties. For
example, we read that in 1949 there were 55 per cent. of
Russians among the leading Party workers of the Kirgiz S.S.R.
Even in district and town Party Committees the number of
Russians was 40 per cent. Of appointments of responsibility in
the Party apparatus, 47·7 per cent. were held by Russians in
Kirgizia in 1949.†

Similarly, among Central Asian Government officials
Russian control is exercised behind a façade of " national "
leadership. There are Russian deputy-chairmen in the local
Supreme Soviets and Councils of Ministers. In most cases
Ministries are headed by local nationals with at least two
Russian deputies. Russians hold most of the leading positions
in the sphere of security and justice, and all the procurators are
Russian.

In Kirgizia the first Party secretary, Bogolyubov, admitted
at the end of 1949 that the percentage of local nationals holding
prominent positions in industry was only 17·8; in planning
finance and trade 27; and in agriculture 28.†

The position in the Governmental Ministries is even worse
and it is quite clear that administrative and specialist posts in

* *Izvestia*, 21st June, 1950.
† *Sovetskaya Kirgizia*, 29th October, 1949.

ocal Ministries are monopolised by Russians to a very large extent. For example, in 1948, the percentage of administrative posts occupied by local nationals in the following Kazakh Ministries were stated by the Soviet Press to be:—

> 14·0 per cent. in the Ministry of the Meat and Dairy Industry.
> 11·7 per cent. in the Ministry of State Farms.
> 10·0 per cent. in the Ministry of Agriculture.
> 2·0 per cent. in the Ministry of Public Health.
> 2·0 per cent. in the Ministry of Local Industry.*

In other words, Russians (with possibly one or two other non-Kazakh nationals) occupy from 86 to 98 per cent. of the posts in the Kazakh Ministries. In Kirgizia the situation was apparently the same.

In the sphere of education a similar situation prevails. In Kazakhstan, for example, from 1945 to 1948, of all the students in the factory and trade schools less than 25 per cent. were natives *; in Uzbekistan in 1946 the figure was 35 per cent. The record for higher education is equally bad. In March, 1949, the rector of the Kazakh State University in Alma-Ata publicly admitted that " during its entire existence i.e., since 1934) only 17 per cent. of the University's graduates had been Kazakhs."

In 1951 it was admitted at the " Congress of the Communist Party of Kazakhstan that only 37 per cent. of the students in local institutes of higher education were Kazakhs, while of the 102 Doctors of Science working in the Republics only seventeen were Kazakhs." † These facts may be explained by the circumstance that a comparison of the census figures of 1926 and 1939 shows that during this period 800,000—or nearly one third—of the Kazakh nation had " disappeared ".

The Soviet destruction of the freedom of the Baltic nations now incorporated in the U.S.S.R. and of other smaller Muslim groups has been mentioned on page 74. Izvestia of 26th June, 1946, published a decree abolishing the Chechen-Ingush and the Crimean Autonomous Soviet Socialist Republics, and ordering the mass deportation of those races on the grounds that many of them assisted the Germans while " the main mass of the

---

* Kazakhstanskaya Pravda, 13th August, 1948.
† Ibid., December, 1951.

population . . . took no counteraction against these betrayer
of the Fatherland".

This monstrous punishment of a million souls was on purel
racial grounds.   The crime alleged against a given individua
was not that he personally had done anything illegal but tha
he belonged to a racial group some of whose members wer
accused of illegal activities.

The Volga-German Autonomous Soviet Socialist Republi
had similarly been abolished in 1941, and the fact mad
public.   In addition the autonomous republics and regions c
the Kalmyks, the Balkars, and the Karacha disappeared, th
peoples being deported without any public announcemen
being made.   Their fate became clear only when new edition
of the *Soviet Gazetteer* showed that their administrative areas n
longer existed and when the new volume of the *Soviet Encyclo
pædia* revealed that their names are now omitted from the lis
of races of the Soviet Union, and that they are no longe
represented in the Soviet of Nationalities.

Perhaps the most interesting aspect of this series of genocid
operations by the Soviet Government is that they show in
disputably that the nationalities of the U.S.S.R. are no
deceived by, or reconciled to, the illusory apparatus of auto
nomy.   The fact that almost all the small nations which cam
within the grasp of the German armies used the opportunit
to revolt, effectively disposes of Soviet claims.   Such revol
were even more remarkable when we consider that thes
peoples had been entirely cut off from all sources of informatior
except those of the Soviet propaganda machine, for severe
decades.   They knew nothing of the Nazis except that Sovie
propaganda described them as fiendish oppressors.   Th
seems to have convinced these races that the Nazis must b
good people, a mistake which some of them are known to hav
regretted when Nazi policies became evident, but whic
nevertheless reveals most significantly their attitude to Sovie
rule.

Similarly Soviet propaganda about " the limitless devotio
of the working people of the Volga-German Autonomou
Soviet Socialist Republic to the cause of Communism " * c
about " the indestructible foundation of the Kalmyk sociali
edifice ",* is seen for what it is worth.

* *Large Soviet Encyclopædia.*   Vol. 41, p. 596 [Moscow, 1939].

It is also noteworthy that although the deportation of a million people is confirmed in a published Soviet decree—such deportations have often been described by Communist sympathisers in the free world as " fantastic " and " impossible ".

Justice, the Police and Forced Labour

Article 127 of the Soviet Constitution lays down that " no one can be subjected to arrest except by order of a court or with the consent of the procurator ". Like many of the other provisions of the Soviet Constitution this is meaningless in practice.

In the first place there exist valid legal provisions which have not been repealed that are inconsistent with this article. By a decree of 16th October, 1922, the G.P.U.* had the power of banishment to forced labour camps of " activists of anti-Soviet parties " and in 1934, when security was organised under the N.K.V.D.,† that body was given even wider powers.

In the second place, in the absence of an independent judiciary the requirements of an order of the court or of the procurator is no safeguard for the individual. It is obvious, for example, that where banishments to forced labour camps have to be reckoned in millions, such a preliminary order, even if in practice it is obtained, can hardly be more than a rubber stamp formality. Further, the Soviet citizen has no protection against persecution by the Secret Police, on whose powers no statutory limitations have been placed. No reference, of course, is made in the Constitution of the U.S.S.R. to its existence, but it cannot be doubted that this force, estimated by some authorities to be about 600,000 strong, with far-reaching extra-judicial powers, is a constant menace to the lives and liberties of Soviet citizens.

The enormous police force which maintains this rule is assisted by an army of informers. The M.V.D.‡ maintains a large force of part-time assistants in the villages. They are called "rural executives". According to a decree of 1935 they are supposed to assist the police in protecting the social

* " Political direction of the State " which replaced the *Cheka* founded 20th December, 1917, as " The all-Russian Special Commission for the fight against counter-revolution, sabotage, and speculation ".
† All Union Commissariat for the Interior.
‡ The new name of the N.K.V.D.

N

order and State and collective property and to escort arrested persons to prison. Every place in the Soviet Union must have at least one informer and larger villages must have one for every 300 inhabitants. In both towns and villages the M.V.D. maintains " Police Assistance Brigades " which are organised in the farms and the factories, universities and other institutions. Their rôle is to give active co-operation to the police and they may be provided with firearms for the execution of special operational assignments under the guidance of the M.V.D., though even they are not permitted to keep their arms when the assignments are finished.

Whether arrest is made by the Secret Police or by the ordinary civil police acting on the local prosecution's orders, there is no right of *habeas corpus* which the citizen may invoke, and he may be held without trial for an indefinite period while his case is being investigated. The procedure laid down in the case of such arrest and imprisonment is open to all kinds of interpretation in accordance with the requirements of the authorities.

As a result of the arbitrary powers of the Secret Police, millions of Soviet citizens have been torn from their homes, with or without trial and sequestered, without hope of legal redress, in the notorious concentration camps of the Soviet Union.

Again, Soviet Administrative Law distinguishes *detention* from *arrest*. Whereas *arrest* requires the sanction of the court or of the procurator, *detention* is of two kinds.

> (1) Where the person detained is suspected of having commited a crime and attempted to evade justice. In this case the procurator must be informed and the detention confirmed by him within forty-eight hours.
>
> (2) " The usual form of personal detention " (Soviet legal textbook). Here the reasons for detention are " highly varied in their nature and relate to all cases where public order and security is threatened." In such cases there appears to be no provision limiting the period of detention or requiring confirmation of the detention by any other authority.

The ordinary police also have a fairly limited power of detention, but they have extensive rights of search on suspicion alone without any warrant. The only legal safeguard against detention which is not in conformity with Administrative Law is Article 115 of the Criminal Code, which makes such illegal detention punishable by a year's imprisonment.

Under a decree (dated November, 1934, published in Collection of Laws, 1935, No. 11) the Special Council of the Ministry of Internal Affairs has power to inflict on persons " regarded as dangerous to the community " banishment to places under supervision or detention in forced labour camps for a period up to five years, and to expel foreigners. These powers are exercised without any order from a court.

And under the Corrective Labour Codex Article 8 runs:—

> " Persons are directed to corrective labour who have been sentenced thereto by
> (a) a sentence in a court of law;
> (b) the decree of an administrative organ."

Millions have been so sentenced by " administrative organs " —the " Troikas " of the Secret Police.

Even if the protection of the courts was actually procurable it would be of little avail to the accused. For though the paper Constitution, in Article 112, states that the judges are " independent and subject only to the law ", they are in fact the nominees of the Communist Party.

Although all judicial posts are nominally elective and any citizen entitled to the vote may be elected judge or assessor of any court, the Party exercises the closest supervision over nominations and ensures that only reliable servants of the Party can be elected. Moreover, the judges themselves can be prosecuted and sentenced for " giving an unjust judgment out of personal or interested motives ",* which clearly lends itself to very wide interpretation. The Minister of Justice is a member of the plenum of the Supreme Court.

Soviet legal text-books stress the rôle of the judges' " Bolshevik conscience " in the formulation of their decisions. In practice this means that the decision on the merits of any given case may be determined extrajudicially, since the final authority on points of " conscience " is, of course, the Communist Party.

The general purpose of the Soviet Courts, as defined by the Law on the Judiciary of the U.S.S.R. (August, 1938), is " to educate the citizens of the U.S.S.R. in a spirit of devotion to the Fatherland and to the cause of Socialism, in the spirit of an

---

* *Criminal Code Article* 114.

exact and unfaltering performance of Soviet laws, a careful attitude to Socialist property, labour discipline, honest fulfilment of State and public duties, and respect towards the rules of the Socialist Commonwealth." In other words, the avowed purpose of the Soviet legal system is not so much the regulation of relations between citizens of the U.S.S.R., in accordance with ethical principles which are regarded as having an absolute value, as the coercive organisation of the working masses for the fulfilment of the political aims of the State. The *Soviet Encyclopædia* admits that the judicature of the U.S.S.R. is " a means of strengthening the Socialist régime, guarding the rights of citizens and repressing the enemies of the people and the Trotskyist Bukharinist agents of foreign espionage organisations."

It was M. Vyshinsky who summed up this position in November, 1948. Addressing the Political Committee of the United Nations, he declared, " We say that the law has no independent rôle ".

The victim of police rule who is not shot goes to the labour camps. These represent such an astonishing mass phenomenon that it is worth while to examine their working in some detail.

The *Large Soviet Encyclopædia* * states : " Forced labour is one of the basic measures of punishment of Soviet Socialist criminal law . . ."

The Corrective Labour Codex of the R.S.F.S.R. of 1st August, 1933, discloses that legislation dealing with forced labour is part of the basic law of the Soviet Union. The " basic proposition " of the Corrective Labour Codex, photostatic copies of which were submitted by Britain to the ninth session of the United Nations Economic and Social Council on 22nd July, 1949, is as follows :—

> " The task of the penal policy of the proletariat . . . is the defence of the dictatorship of the proletariat and the Socialist construction being carried out by it against encroachments by class-hostile elements. In accordance with this the corrective labour policy pursues the following aims :—
>
> > (*a*) to put the condemned in conditions which debar them from committing acts which inflict harm on Socialist construction, and

* Vol. 47, p. 36.

(*b*) to re-educate and adapt them to the conditions of the labouring community by means of directing their work and by organising their labour on the principle of the gradual approximation of forced labour to voluntary labour based on Socialist emulation and the shock-brigade system. The basic type of places of deprivation of freedom are the labour colonies of different sorts to which the condemned are sent . . ."

Those sentenced do not usually even go before the Soviet courts, but are punished at the decision of the police themselves, as the following quotations from Soviet documents make clear:—

As we have seen, the Corrective Labour Codex (Article 8) states:—

" Persons are directed to corrective labour who have been sentenced thereto by:—
(*a*) Sentence in a court of law;
(*b*) *Decree of an administrative organ.*"

Article 45 reads:—

" For reception into a place of deprivation of freedom, it is obligatory to have a sentence or an order by organs legally empowered thereunto, *or an open warrant.*"

The " Principles of Criminal Jurisdiction " (Article 22) as cited in the Criminal Codex of the R.S.F.S.R. states:—

" Punishment in the form of exile can be applied by a sentence of the *State prosecutor* against persons recognised as being socially dangerous, without any criminal proceedings being taken against these persons on charges of committing a specific crime or of a specific offence and also even in those cases where these persons are acquitted by a court of the accusation of committing a specific crime."

The Criminal Codex Commentary on this states that a plenary session of the Supreme Court ruled that these provisions had been superseded by later legislation *as far as court proceedings were concerned.* But it is quite clear that " administrative " proceedings and sentences remain unaffected.

The *Large Soviet Encyclopædia* * says: " The right to apply

* Vol. 52, p. 523, published in 1947.

deportation (Sylka) as an administrative measure is granted to
the Special Council under the Ministry of Internal Affairs . . ."
Article 3 of the Corrective Labour Codex states:—

> " The basic type of places of deprivation of freedom
> are the labour colonies of different sorts to which the
> condemned are sent in accordance with their labour habits,
> their degree of class dangerousness, their social positions,
> and the success with which they are being corrected."

Article 29 says that only persons under " investigation or
trial " are sent to solitary confinement.

The others work mainly in:—

> (1) Factory and agricultural colonies, places at which
> " people deprived of freedom " are " trained and
> disciplined "; *
> (2) Colonies for mass-work, which are of two kinds—
> those in " distant regions " for " class-dangerous elements "
> who require " a more severe régime " and " other
> colonies "; †
> (3) Punitive colonies for the " strict isolation " of
> convicts who were " previously detained in other colonies
> and showed persistent insubordination ".‡

Article 62 says:—

> In " places of detention, 75 per cent. of (the prisoners')
> earnings are put at the disposal of the detainees . . . the
> remainder is given to them on their release."

Economic Value of Forced Labour

The " State Plan for the Development of the National
Economy of the U.S.S.R. in 1941 ", presents official data on
the contribution of forced labour to economic activities in the
U.S.S.R.

According to this plan, the total volume of capital construction in the U.S.S.R. for 1941 was fixed at 46–47 billion
roubles expressed in terms of 1926–27 prices. The Ministry of
Internal Affairs (M.V.D.), formerly the N.K.V.D., which
administers forced labour in the U.S.S.R., was responsible for
6·81 million roubles' worth of capital construction, or 14 per
cent. of the total.

The 1941 plan shows that this body was to produce 34·73
million cubic metres of industrial timber and firewood out of a

* Article 33.   † Article 34.   ‡ Articles 35 and 37.

planned total of 191 million cubic metres. It also stated that the "Main Administration of Corrective Labour Camps" (Gulag) was expected to produce 40·5 per cent. of the total Soviet output of chrome ore. This sufficiently indicates the economic importance, and the mass nature of these camps.

This is but the dry bones, the statistics, the legal phraseology of the most fearful and continuous human tragedy. In the deserts of Kazakhstan, the forests of Arctic Russia, the mines of Northern Siberia, the road projects of the Soviet Far East, millions of people who have had the misfortune to catch the eye of the security forces are sweated to death, with meat rations officially stated to be lower than the rations of the dogs maintained to hunt them down if they escape.*

The terrible sufferings of these people have been described in detail in a number of moving books, written by people of all types who have managed to get to the West after serving sentence. These books, which should be read by anyone wishing to form an opinion of the labour camps, include *Under Two Dictators* by Frau Buber-Neumann, wife of a leading German Communist, who fell from favour with her husband and was eventually handed over by the Russians to the Nazis and suffered at their hands also; *Eleven Years in Soviet Prison Camps*, by Frau E. Lipper who worked in the Kolyma mines in North-East Siberia; *The Dark Side of the Moon* in which the experiences of the thousands of Poles sent to these camps after the Russian invasion of Poland in 1939 were described; *A World Apart*, by Gustav Herling, and *Le vie et la mort en l'URSS*, by Gonzales (El Campesino), the former Communist General in the Spanish Civil War.

These and other books, and the statements of other ex-prisoners which appear from time to time, give an absolutely consistent picture of these places. They are conducted in a completely inhuman fashion, the only important consideration being the maintenance of the camp's output. Just as the Soviet worker's wage is dependent on sweated norms, so here the same system is applied and greatly intensified. The entirely

* See *Regulation for the Supply of the Ukhta–Pechora N.K.V.D. corrective labour camp*, issued in May, 1937. By these regulations dogs receive: 250 grammes of meat [prisoners receive 22 grammes] per day. "Detective dogs" receive 400 grammes of meat a day. Prisoners get twice as much vegetables as dogs and a little more salt. But the dogs get "scraps left over from rations of the guard".

inadequate rations are made dependent on the fulfilment of norms which only the healthiest and strongest can perform. The result is that as soon as the inevitable weakness through overwork sets in and the prisoner starts to produce less, his ration is immediately reduced and the vicious circle leads inevitably to death from fatigue and starvation.

A large proportion of the camps are in the coldest areas in the world, which adds considerably to the misery of the prisoners. Medical conditions are bad, deficiency diseases are rife, and the loss of toes and fingers through frostbite is extremely common, though measures are taken to prevent epidemics—which might affect the health of the captors. In some camps the death rate is so high that a turnover of 80 or 90 per cent. in the year is not uncommon.

The inmates of the camps form the lowest and most oppressed class in the Soviet Union, the class of slaves. They have no rights and are used by the State as entirely expendable people from whom, before they die, some economic benefit must be squeezed at the expense of appalling suffering.

In November, 1952, the government of the U.S.A. presented a report to the United Nations Committee on forced labour, in which it was stated that there was evidence that there had been some improvement in conditions. This fact, which was based on evidence in the form of affidavits from 105 people, some of whom had emerged from the camps as recently as May, 1952, was attributed in part to the attention which continual criticism in the United Nations had directed towards conditions in camp and partly to the fact that:—

> " There is continual conflict among Soviet forced labour functionaries as to whether forced labour should be used for punishment and liquidation of ' undesirable elements ' or for the exploitation of apparently cheap prison labour. Since the Soviet economy is presently geared largely to war production, the exploitative factor would seem now to be dominant, requiring that the labourers be fed, clothed and housed at survival level."

Nevertheless, this report added:—

> " Many of the brutal procedures and methods of the early purge days continue to be used . . . in apprehending, sentencing, and transporting their victims to forced labour camps. Midnight arrests, baseless accusations

physical and psychological torture, confessions signed under duress, and transport, sometimes for thousands of miles, in overcrowded and unhygienic cattle-cars are still part of the standard routine suffered by the unfortunates selected to work in the Soviet forced labour battalions."

Estimates of the number of prisoners vary. From documents which were brought out and the evidence of inmates it is possible to some extent to deduce the number of camps and the average number of inmates. For example, Dr Margolin, a former prisoner now in Israel, was in several camps in the Baltic-White Sea group between 1940 and 1945. He found that this group included a Division No. 28, and that each division had at least ten to fifteen sites. It is not difficult to deduce that the whole group must have held about half a million prisoners: this estimate may be wrong by a fair margin, but it at least reveals the magnitude of the undertaking. Other prisoners have given similar information about other groups of camps. In addition, it is possible from the Budget figures to work out the proportion of the economy under control of the M.V.D., *i.e.*, work by forced labour. Taking this in conjunction with the known average numbers employed in certain types of labour in proportion to the capital investment, it is also possible to form an estimate of their numbers.* To the minimum of 5 million in the U.S.S.R. should be added hundreds of thousands in the six satellite states if the whole picture is to be seen.

Education, Culture and Science

The principles of Stalinist education are well covered in the official Soviet publication *Pedagogy*, by Yesipov and Goncharov, 3rd edition, published in Moscow in 1946, and approved by the Ministry of Education of the R.S.F.S.R. for use in teachers' training schools—the schools which turn out teachers for the Soviet elementary schools.†

The authors of *Pedagogy* explain in detail how the various school subjects should be presented to comply with the purposes of Soviet education. Thus they say that " physical education as a whole promotes the development of those qualities which

* Mr Mayhew (British Under-Secretary of State for Foreign Affairs) gave a figure of 5 to 12 millions in an official statement in the House of Commons, 3rd May, 1949.

† See also *I Want To Be Like Stalin*, published in London by Victor Gollancz in 1948.

are essential to the future warriors of the Red Army ", and must consequently include " kinds of exercise designed to give specific mastery of certain forms of knowledge and habits related to military training, such as the elements of military formation, the use of gas masks and mastery of ski-ing. . . . Simple military games leading to the acquisition of the ability to overcome various obstacles and to the development of strength, agility, ingenuity, endurance, and other such qualities of particular value."

The teaching of history must give the children " an awareness of the need for the vigilant defence of the accomplishments of the Revolution and the fruits of the valiant Red Army over the Fascist robbers," and must prepare them to " realise the great historic rôle of the Party of Bolsheviks in the struggle for the liberation of the workers of all peoples of our land from exploitation and oppression." History must also inspire children " with deep love for the highly gifted leaders of the proletarian revolution—Lenin and Stalin."

" In the teaching of geography, attention should be given to the development of the ability to define cardinal points, to use the compass, to understand a topographical plan, to read a map, to grasp the relations of the various elements of relief. This is an essential part of military study."

" Mathematics should provide training in the use of the scale, the divider, the caliper, and other instruments used in the making of a simple survey of locality. Knowledge of mathematics is extremely important for the mastery of military technique."

It is clear from a study of *Pedagogy* that Soviet education places an enormous stress on the inculcation of national patriotism of an extreme kind. This is shown in such passages as the following :—

(*a*) " A morally educated individual, according to our understanding, is one who in his conduct subordinates his own interests to the service of his Fatherland and his people. Such service presupposes wrath and hatred towards the enemies of the Fatherland who imperil the battle-won rights of the people and all that has been created in the realm of material and cultural life by both the older and the younger generation."

(*b*) " Stalin, disciple of Lenin, is our own beloved Father of the Workers, leader of the people, organiser of victory over the Fascists and enemies of our Fatherland.   Children can easily understand this.   They associate with the concrete images of Lenin and Stalin the Party of Communists, the Party of Bolsheviks, created by the great leaders.   They quickly begin to perceive that under the leadership of the Party of Lenin and Stalin we both build and defend our Soviet State, our Fatherland.   And then they are able to see the relation of their work and their study to the tasks of the State.   This association of the immediate activity of the children with the social life of the country as a whole facilitates the development in them of genuine patriotic feelings, of a sense and awareness of their duty to the Fatherland."

(c) " Pupils must come to know that in our Soviet country the interests of the people are inseparable from the interests of their Government. . . . And the natural attachment to the native country is strengthened by pride in the Socialist Fatherland, in the Bolshevik Party, in the leader of the workers of the entire world—Comrade Stalin.   It is a great honour to any individual to be a citizen of and to defend such a Fatherland."

(d) " The services of the Russian people are exceptionally great, not only to the peoples of the Soviet Union, but also to all mankind.   The Soviet Union by its example inspires the workers of the entire world for the struggle against exploiters and ravishers.   The history of the Russian people proves to all mankind their political wisdom, their military valour, and their genius.   These facts from the past of our heroic people must be skilfully presented to the pupils in order to awaken in them a feeling of just pride in everything progressive and revolutionary which has so enriched the history of our country."

(e) " The pupils of the Soviet School must realise that the feeling of Soviet patriotism is saturated with irreconcilable hatred towards the enemies of Socialist society. Hatred gives birth to class revolutionary vigilance and creates a feeling of irreconcilability towards the class enemy;   the weakening of such vigilance undermines the cause of the Socialist revolution.   It is necessary to learn not only to hate the enemy, but also to struggle with him, in time to unmask him, and finally, if he does not surrender, to destroy him."

The current regulations governing the acceptance of students into universities and institutes are published annually in a

Soviet publication entitled *Handbook for Entrants to High*
Educational Establishments of the Soviet Union, which contains th
following significant regulations and remarks: " On th
Conduct of Entrance Examinations to H.E.E.":—

(*a*) With regard to examinations in literature: " th
articles of Lenin, included in the programme for literatur
having immense methodological and educational import
ance for youth, must be mastered by the examinee in al
their profundity.

" A profound and full acquaintance must be shown b
examinees with the outstanding models of Soviet literatur
and the important guiding documents on literary question
(the Ordinance of the Party Central Committee o
literary questions and Zhdanov's report on the journal
Zvezda and *Leningrad*); this is one of the principal require
ments in conducting examinations in literature."

(*b*) With regard to examinations in Soviet History:—

" Particular attention must be paid to knowledg
and understanding of current events and of the leadin
rôle of the Soviet State in the struggle for a lastin
peace and democracy."

(*c*) With regard to examinations in Physics, examinee
must know all about the " outstanding Russian scientist
and inventors: Lomonosov, Polzunov, Petrov, Lodygin
Yablochkov, Stoletov, Yakobi, Zhukovsky, Popov, Tsiol
kovsky, and their significance for world science."

The significance of many of these names lies in the fact tha
the Soviet authorities now claim that they were the original in
ventors of such things as electric light, wireless telegraphy
and jet propulsion. The list has recently been considerabl
extended, and one may prophesy with confidence that the en
is not yet.*

Literary Gazette of 3rd September, 1949, stated:—

" It is in the school, at the desk, in the first class, tha
the foundations for a Communist outlook are laid in futur
Soviet citizens. The country entrusts the school with it
most treasured possession—its children, and no one shoul
be allowed to indulge in the slightest deviation from th
principles of the Communist materialistic upbringing o
the new generation."

Discipline is extremely strict. For instance if a Sovie

* News is to hand that baseball has joined the list, 1.1.53.

youngster leaves a trade school against orders, he is punished by imprisonment in a labour colony. The Criminal Code lays down:—

> "Voluntary departure from the school or systematic violation of school discipline by students of trade and railroad schools and factory and plant training schools entails expulsion from school and imprisonment, pursuant to trial, in a labour colony for one year." *

The Cultural Field

Many Soviet writers have suffered execution or disappeared since the execution of the poet Gumilev. Such leading figures as Pilnyak and Bebel have certainly been shot. Practising writers whose works do not satisfy the Central Committee of the Communist Party are censored. During the war a certain relaxation of pressure made possible large printings of the works of some of the great writers of the older generation. Many of the other works which the Party had not seen fit to publish circulated widely in manuscript. They enjoyed an enormous popularity both in the Army and at the rear. After the war the Central Committees of the Party launched an attack on the defects of the main cultural magazines, on the activities of the Union of Soviet Writers, and on a number of writers by name— in particular on the great poet Pasternak, the poetess Anna Akhmatova, on the writers Zoschenko and Tikhonov (the latter for his responsibility, as chairman of the Union of Soviet Writers, for the " ideologically unsound " literature published) and on many others of lesser repute. The first three mentioned have now practically ceased to publish. Writers who flourish are entirely second-rate, who write purely to the Party line, as for example Simonov and Fadeyev. Even in their cases extraordinary servility is imposed. For example, Fadeyev has recently had to rewrite his hack war novel *The Young Guard* because it exaggerated the merits of the Komsomols (Young Communists) as compared with their seniors the Communist Party members, and of partisans as compared with the Red Army. Several new chapters have now been added, the Komsomol partisans rendered more ignorant and incompetent, the Communist Party officials wiser and more masterful, and some brand new Red Army heroes introduced.

* Criminal Code of the R.S.F.S.R., Moscow, 1948.

In music a similar trend is visible. Again the Central Committee of the Communist Party took it upon itself to issue criticism, *e.g.*, a decision published in *Pravda* on 11th February, 1948, condemned Muradeli's opera *The Great Friendship*. Other attacks were made by Party spokesmen on Shostakovitch, Prokofiev, Khachaturian, to mention only the most famous.

In science the great biological purge has become notorious. A theory, regarded as untrue in world biological circles, has been imposed on Soviet science. But even more significant is the fact that the final arbiters of truth or falsehood were not scientists at all, but the Central Committee of the Communist Party.

At least twelve leading biologists, all but one members of the Soviet Academy, were dismissed, as a result of the notorious Lysenko " packed " debates in the summer of 1948, and seven biological institutes and laboratories closed. In addition, three leading medical research specialists were dismissed. One of the world's leading biologists, Vavilov, is known to have died in a labour camp in the early part of the last war, some years before his, perhaps more fortunate, successors.

Since 1948 some leading Soviet atomic physicists have also been criticised. The main attack on them has been that they followed the methods of certain leading Western physicists, of whom Bohr, Geisenberg and others were specially condemned. Considerable attacks have also been made, on ideological grounds, on Einstein's theories.

Press and Publishing

" The central newspapers are called upon to be an all-Union propaganda tribune of Marxism–Leninism." *

> " It is pertinent to recall a Party directive of 1922 concerning editorials in provincial newspapers. . . . The editorial must give ' leadership, guidance, and indicate the basic line of behaviour.' . . . Inasmuch as the editorial is called upon to express the point of view of the Party, the thesis of the article cannot be contestable, or a subject for debate [there are other types of newspaper for such materials]. The editorial of the newspaper is accepted as a directive and consequently must be particularly profound, well-grounded and in any event, not confusing." †

* Leading article in *Culture and Life*, 20th September, 1946.
† *Culture and Life*, No. 4, 30th July, 1946.

An article by D. Zaslavsk in *October* of January, 1948, reveals the present Soviet conception of the rôle of the Press and demonstrates that a word such as " freedom " has for the Stalinist a meaning totally different from that normally used. This view begins with a definition of the basic principles of freedom of the Press. These are quoted as:—

" (i) The organisation of a fight for the principles of democracy, for the unmasking of Fascism and for the eradication of Fascist ideology in any form.

" (ii) The unmasking of warmongers and the organisation of an active campaign against the organs of the Press and other channels of information engaged in inciting to war and aggression.

" (iii) The development of friendly relations between nations on the basis of respect for the principles of independence, equality and self-determination of peoples."

The writer continues. " The resolution of the Soviet delegation [at the U.N.] further proposes that freedom of the Press be recognised as the right of all citizens *except those preaching Fascism, war and aggression.*" It also " provides for the passage of laws punishing those owners of press organs and means of information which disseminate false and slanderous reports and confuse public opinion in order to worsen relations between countries, to provoke conflicts and incite to war ".

Since the Soviet definition of a warmonger or a Fascist is anyone who holds different political views from those of the Communists, these limitations are a complete negation of Press freedom (*e.g.*, to advocate a Soviet attack on Finland or a Nazi–Soviet Pact in 1939 was not warmongering: to criticise such action is. Attacks on the Western Powers do not harm " friendly relations between nations ": criticisms of the U.S.S.R. do.)

Article 124 of the Soviet Constitution runs as follows:—

" In conformity with the interests of the working people, and in order to strengthen the Socialist system, the citizens of the U.S.S.R. are guaranteed by law:—

(*a*) Freedom of speech.

(*b*) Freedom of the Press.

(*c*) Freedom of assembly, including the holding of mass meetings.

(*d*) Freedom of street processions and demonstrations."

" These civil rights are assured by placing at the disposal
of the working people and their organisations printing
presses, stocks of paper, public buildings, the streets, communication facilities and other material requisites for the
exercise of these rights." [From Article 125.]

The first nine words of the preamble to this Article, " in
conformity with the interests of the working people ", remove all
real content from the article's liberal provisions. For the
interests of the working people of the Soviet Union must be
determined by the Communist Party, since in the words of
the first paragraph of the " Statutes of the All-Union Communist Party ": " The All-Union Communist Party is the
foremost, organised detachment of the working class of the
U.S.S.R., the highest form of its class organisation."

It is not illogical to suggest that the interests of the working
class are decided by the " foremost organised detachment "
of that class. For, in reality, in the U.S.S.R., freedom of
speech, Press, assembly and demonstration are guaranteed
only when they conform with the interests of the Communist
Party. Soviet citizens are free only to speak, print and demonstrate their agreement with the pronouncements and actions
of the Party, and of the State.

It should be pointed out here that Soviet propaganda,
internal and external, makes great play of what it describes
as " Bolshevik criticism and self-criticism ". That this has
nothing in common with what we understand to be criticism is
apparent from the inclusion of the preliminary epithet. In
practice it consists of encouraging rank-and-file members of
the Communist Party or some other " public or State organisation " to express dissatisfaction with the way in which the
orders of the Soviet leaders are being carried out. As a result
of such " criticism " heads have often been known to fall from
minor bureaucratic shoulders. The system is not without its
uses to the Soviet leaders, since any discontent as a result of
inefficient or mistaken planning from above can effectively be
diverted to break over subordinate heads. There has never
been any example of rank-and-file criticism of the wisdom of
plans and orders emanating from the Soviet leaders—such a
thing is, indeed, unthinkable in the Soviet Union.

The final paragraph of Article 125 indicates the exact
methods whereby these civil liberties are ensured. Presses

stocks of paper, public buildings, the streets, communication facilities and other material requisites are "placed at the disposal of the working people and their organisations". This means in practice that they are placed at the disposal of organisations (*not* of individual working persons); and Article 126 clearly indicates how these organisations are controlled, and hence at whose disposal the Press really is.

> "Citizens of the U.S.S.R. are ensured the right to unite in public organisations . . .; and the most active and politically most conscious citizens in the ranks of the working people unite in the Communist Party of the Soviet Union (Bolsheviks) which . . . is the leading core of all organisations of the working people, both public and State."

It is useful to contrast this decree with the administrative regulations which deal with the right to acquire any form of hand-duplicating machine. Here a licence must be obtained from the local police authorities, and it must be issued in the name of the head of the so-called "secret department" (*i.e.*, the department responsible for security to the Security Police) of the undertaking or organisation applying for the licence, or in the name of the organisation if there is no "secret department". Licences are not issued to individuals.* The machine must be registered with the State Publishing and Censorship Department. The licence must be produced each time before replacements, accessories or materials for the machine can be purchased. Everything produced on the machine is subject to preliminary censorship by the local branch of the State Publishing Department before it can be distributed.

The hand-out of news in the U.S.S.R. is controlled by Tass, and all newspapers and periodicals are owned by the Communist Party or other official or Government bodies. Therefore all news for home consumption reflects only the Party view.

Radio

The Soviet Government maintains a vast broadcasting system with 100 high-powered regional stations and over

---

* See Decree "Concerning the opening of polygraphic concerns . . . sale of print duplicating apparatus and accessories" of 26th June, 1932, in which it is laid down *inter alia* that supervision of "the correct employment of duplicating apparatus is exercised by the appropriate organs of the militia".

O

10,000 low-powered relay stations in smaller towns and villages.
In 1947 there were a million receiving sets in the country, but
there were seven million loud-speaker points—which means
that 80 per cent. of the listening facilities were controlled by
the authorities. Even those in possession of a set, however, are
indirectly controlled by the fact that the Government maintains
a vast and expensive system for jamming foreign broadcasts.

This simple and well-known fact is—even in isolation—a
formidable piece of evidence in support of the view that there
must be something rather unnatural about the whole Soviet
system and the relations between governors and governed.
It may seem an elementary question to ask, but it is worth
considering: "Why, if there is so much contentment and
happiness in the type of society which exists beyond the Iron
Curtain, do the inventors and masters of this society make such
extraordinary efforts (substantially increased in 1952) to prevent
the people listening to broadcasts, whether they be answers
on the part of the Western Powers to Russian accusations, or
even straightforward factual accounts of the conditions in
Western Society?" No Communist has ever been able to
give a satisfactory reply to this answer, since it would be absurd
(and untrue) for him to argue that the Russian people are
incapable of rational thought.

What is broadcast would astonish a Western listener. An
extraordinary amount of ordinary propaganda is put over; for
example, statements by Soviet delegates at the United Nations
are broadcast in the form in which they appear in the Press
and a single speech may take as much as ninety minutes to
read. The same applies to Government announcements and
decrees. A decree on the Afforestation Plan, a highly intricate
and technical document, full of subsections and scarcely under-
standable even by the expert without reference back to earlier
points, was once broadcast for two hours.

Even so, more than half the time is devoted to recognisably
cultural material—music, plays, etc.—which is more than can
be said of the Soviet Press. It is true that this material is often
politically angled, and is always politically censored. Never
theless, it must be extremely refreshing. There are about 20,000
television sets in Moscow. A set costs 2,000 roubles. They will
become cheaper, since television has advantages for internal pro
paganda; until the West can televise through the Iron Curtain

" Agitprop "

The Communist Party maintains, in addition to its control of the public media of propaganda, elaborate machinery whereby the decisions of the leadership are passed down to local cells and branches, which are then bound to call meetings at factories, farms and every other suitable place and the decisions passed on to the people in the form regarded as most suitable. Attendance at these meetings is in effect compulsory. The worker, who also has to attend lectures of routine political indoctrination, is here submitted to long harangues at which the Party " Agitator ", basing himself on specially issued speakers' notes, attempts to link the most unlikely events with the sins of the imperialists and the necessity for working harder, in an atmosphere of enthusiasm for the régime.

It is difficult to make clear how pervasive and penetrating is this constant attempt to press the Party's views down the ordinary man's throat. But the Party is quite open about how it is done. *Bolshevik*, the official Party journal, wrote in its fourth issue for 1947 :—

> " The Soviet State determines the behaviour and activity of Soviet citizens in various ways. It educates the Soviet people in a spirit of Communist morality by the system which it introduces of legal norms regulating the life of the population, imposing interdictions, establishing encouragements, and warnings of punishment for violation of these norms. The Soviet State stands guard over these legal norms with all its power. The conduct and activity of the Soviet people is also determined by the force of public opinion which is created by the activity of numerous public organisations. In creating public opinion the decisive rôle is played by the Party and the Soviet State which through various media, first of all through ideological work, formulates public opinion and educates the workers in a spirit of Socialist awareness."

Conclusion

This, then, is the Soviet Union. There are, of course, many gaps in our knowledge. This is inevitable because of the reluctance of the Soviet leaders to allow the facts about the Soviet paradise to become known—a reluctance far more revealing than any selection of information allowed to pass through Soviet-controlled channels. Nevertheless, the salient features of life in Russia are known, and cannot be controverted or seriously modified by material still undisclosed. After all, it is not in the Soviet Governments' interest to conceal anything which would commend life in a Communist State to the free world.

The facts about Russia give rise to countless questions which are beyond the scope of this book to discuss. There are, however, certain aspects which have to be faced. In the first place, it may fairly be asked what concern it is of ours how the Soviet Union conducts its affairs? If they choose to conceal their way of life from the outside world, have we the right to be curious about it?

The reply is, that internal conditions in Russia are a matter of major interest and importance to the free world. The Soviet régime is the model for that which is progressively imposed upon any State which falls under the domination of a Communist Party. Czechoslovakia, for example, was a well-developed democratic State, perfectly capable of conducting its own affairs and providing normal human rights and freedoms until the Communist *coup d'état* in February, 1948. Since that time all the apparatus of the police State, censorship and the control of knowledge, Secret Police, concentration camps, Communist Party-controlled justice and the substitution of hatred for understanding in all State relationships, has steadily been reducing the Czechs to the Russian level of misery. Precisely similar conditions would soon exist in Britain, France or Italy if these nations ever fell under Communist control. Life in Russia, the bastion of the Revolution, is the model which all Communist parties subordinate to the Kremlin have to copy.

Secondly, it may be asked whether the misery of life in Russia is an ephemeral thing, and whether the workers' paradise is just around the corner. The answer to this has to be sought in official Communist doctrine, which makes it clear that as long as there has to be a machinery of government in a Communist State that is what the machinery is. Moreover, the necessity for such machinery—*i.e.*, the police State—must, according to Communist doctrine, continue as long as there are nations in the world which reject the Communist system and the resultant subservience to Russia which it demands. Worse still, even if every nation had a Communist Government, the Secret Police, spies and the travesty of justice would still be necessary to deal with individuals or groups within the State who took exception to details of official policy until, under full Communism, such " remnants of capitalist mentality " were finally liquidated. But since it is contrary to human nature to be a slave at all times, the Communist State must be, according to the implications of Soviet doctrine, a police State for ever.

The third point of interest is the reaction of the professional apologists for the Soviet Union to the facts from which they cannot escape. They have a regular technique for dealing with this problem, which may be summarised as follows:—

(i) To make irrelevant counter-attacks, inventing or exaggerating some fault of Western Governments. For instance, Soviet genocide against the Chechens may be defended by the statement that some British colony has not yet reached full independence.

(ii) To say that all this is slander. It would be more convincing if an attempt were made to refute the facts.

(iii) To reverse the rational order of argument by asserting that the U.S.S.R. is a workers' State or a democracy, and that hence the rights and freedoms do exist, or that where they are missing or take strange forms, it is in the interests of the workers and of democracy. [It would be more convincing to argue from the facts upwards. Our view is that since these rights do not exist, the Soviet Union is not a workers' State or a democracy in any sense except for the verbal one that it describes itself as such.]

It would be more impressive if the Soviet apologist did not always answer on the basis that the U.S.S.R. is a democracy, *therefore* the Communist totalitarian dictatorship is democratic; or that it is a workers' State, *therefore* ruthless discipline and sweating of the workers are in the workers' own interests; or that its freedom is freedom in the highest form, *therefore* the Communist monopoly of the means of expression constitutes freedom of expression.

The Soviet line is always the same; they take some defect in Western life—it may well be a real defect, for no social system is perfect—and inflate it into an accusation that one of the recognised human rights is suppressed in the West. They then turn to the situation in their own country, where it is not a question of a mere defect, but of a total absence of the right in question, and apply the *name* of that right to its opposite. A common example of this verbal trick may be seen in discussions on the freedom of the Press. The facts are not disputable: in the United Kingdom a man may freely buy and read newspapers of every point of view, from Conservative to Communist, and may form his opinions accordingly. In the U.S.S.R. he can read the events of the day only as interpreted through the machinery of a single dogma. That is the simple issue between a free Press and an unfree Press. Soviet argument evades the issue by saying that some of our Press is owned by capitalists, and therefore cannot be free. This is a purely *a priori* statement and is quite meaningless unless supported by evidence. The ownership of some newspapers by capitalists may be undesirable on other grounds or not, but unless it actually has resulted in the suppression of the freedom of publication of newspapers of various opinions it is quite irrelevant. And it has not so resulted. Furthermore, in, for example, Great Britain there is constant and public discussion about the relationship between the Press, the public and the State, and a Royal Commission has reported to Parliament on this matter. Whether or not one agrees with various measures which have been proposed to remedy defects real or imaginary in the British Press, it is indisputable that all are agreed that, within the limits of human failings, the Press must be free. Similarly, to call the Press monopoly of the U.S.S.R. " freedom of the Press " because, allegedly, the papers belong to what are called " working-class organisations " is mere verbiage, because no papers opposed to the policies of the ruling party can actually be published and sold. To say in effect that someone is free because he is free to do what he is told is tyranny saucily masquerading as freedom.

The same sort of thing can be said about the other " rights " and " freedoms " of the Soviet citizen. His political democratic rights consist of the obligation to provide from time to time a 99 per cent. vote for the candidate put before him by the ruling group. His right to work consists of the duty of working under heavy discipline for pay constantly reduced by cutting the rate for the job, without the right to strike. His right to national autonomy consists of the right to say what he is told to say in his native language, to be dragged off with all his compatriots to the wastes of Siberia if his nation happens to be geographically situated in the " wrong " place, or offends or opposes the leaders in Moscow. His personal liberty consists in the liability to be seized without trial by the omnipresent secret police and sent to the deadly labour camps of Karaganda or Magadan. Words, as the Communists use them, have ceased to have meaning, except often to mean the opposite to what they mean to us.

The final salient point about the Soviet State is that when it is laid bare to the foundations, whatever may be the pleasant aspects of the edifice that are disclosed to suitable visitors, its foundations are fraudulent. The fraud which is the foundation of this sinister tyranny over the minds of millions of men is, where necessary, supported by the use of force to create fear. As already mentioned, this author spent seven weeks in 1945 travelling about Russia in circumstances of freedom to contact the people (with the aid of a British interpreter) and to go to places and see things which were unprecedented and have never been since repeated. The author has spent as long as eight hours in succession in free discussion with (for example) students at Sverdlosk. They were, of course, not unlike any other group of young people, except in some of the extraordinary ideas they held about life in the West. The great question upon which the peace of the world may depend can be put as follows : There is not the slightest doubt that since the October revolution there has been a very considerable advance in Russia in technical education, in which is included the virtual abolition of illiteracy. It is worth noting that the claims made in this respect by Communist propaganda are exaggerated. In 1914 of the school age population, 90 per cent. in towns and 70 per cent. in the villages could read and write. The previous generation were illiterate, and the Communists attacked this defect with marked success. There are to-day hundreds of thousands of young technicians in the Soviet Union who have had a good scientific education. The deep problem confronting the Soviet system is not the " Imperialist Powers "; they have not the slightest intention of launching a military attack upon Russia, although it is always possible to find within the freedom of opinion in the West foolish advocates of a preventive war. The long-term problem which in the opinion of the author may defeat the Communist leaders will be how to keep under control the natural instincts and desire for freedom of millions of people whose standards of living are rising. People cannot be taught to think and be generally instructed in order to make a more efficient Communist State without also causing them to enquire whether this State, its methods and its theories, are so essential to the well-being not only of the Russians but of all mankind, as is laid down by the leaders. The control by the Communist Party over the Russian people is dependent on the maintenance in the minds of those people of a crisis mentality. In a crisis, as was seen in the U.S.A. in 1933 and in Britain in 1940, even peoples well accustomed to freedom are willing to entrust enormous powers to the State. It remains to be seen whether, if and when the Communist leaders find it difficult to keep up the crisis atmosphere based on the twin pillars of an internal struggle to raise standards of living and an external struggle against imperialist enemies, they will receive from their people that degree of support, the product of propaganda backed by tyranny, which the Soviet leaders at present enjoy.

It is possible that the XIXth Congress of the Soviet Communist Party, held in the autumn of 1952, may in retrospect be seen as an event when certain considerable changes in Soviet policy were set in motion.

Immediately prior to the Congress, M. Stalin [who only appeared in person at the end in order to give some rousing words of comfort to the foreign delegations] published four essays on the economics of Socialism.

These essays, described as of the utmost significance, provide the party with a new ideological springboard. This was the voice of the Almighty. In these essays M. Stalin explained that the wonderful achievements of the Soviet State may have led some people to indulge in false hopes that the ideal in which the apparatus of the State will wither away, in which there will be super-abundance for all, a kind of utopia, is just round the corner. This is not so. Much remains to be done. There must be a great increase in production; all collective farms must be transferred to the State, and their production increased, and the working masses must become more politically educated, and in order that they shall have the time in which to be suitably indoctrinated, the working day must be reduced from eight to six hours! All this was in the best Churchillian tradition of "blood, sweat and tears". But M. Malenkov, who was chosen by M. Stalin to present the report of the Central Committee, dwelt on a less lofty theme. He indicated that though armaments will still have priority, there is also to be (in the new five-year plan) a considerable increase in consumer-goods. This statement, taken in conjunction with M. Stalin's remark on the international situation in which he indicated his faith in the probability of war between the capitalist States, and especially a revolt by Britain and others against American imperialism, and his advice to foreign Communist Parties to be non-violent, leads this author to the following speculative conclusions.

The hold of the Communist Party upon the Russian people is dependent upon the acceptance of two propositions.

(a) That the Russian State as now constituted offers (in due course) Everyman a degree of material and spiritual happiness not yet known in human society.

(b) That the considerable improvements which have been made since the revolution in the lot of the Russian people are logically and inevitably menaced by the imperialist and capitalist Powers.

May it not be that the men of the Kremlin have reached the conclusion that a new situation is arising due to the progress which has been made in raising the educational level, literary and technical capacity of the Russian people? That in this situation a concession must be made to the natural desire of the people to see a large share of the national income devoted to consumption? Hence Malenkov's speech. Secondly, that it is difficult to keep up the propagandist pressure about imminent aggression by the Western imperialists and a day may come when Russian public opinion (their country *not* having been attacked) will begin—however furtively—to enquire whether the enormous armaments expenditure is strictly necessary? Hence M. Stalin's apparent return to a policy of "peaceful co-existence" with capitalist Powers inevitably doomed to decay, and almost certain to leap at each other's throats in a struggle for survival. These are summarised speculations, but some instinct seems to tell this author that something may be on the move in Russia which may prove one day to be fissionable political material. If this surmise proves to be correct, then a very dangerous moment in world history will arrive when the Communist Party, if it is to survive in control of the Soviet State, might be faced with the necessity of inverting itself and becoming democratic in the sense in which that word is used in the West. As, in fact, it could not survive in these conditions, desperate men might be driven to desperate deeds.

Faced with this dilemma, the Communist Party, in order to reinforce its hold over the Russian people, might seek escape from an internal contradiction by indulging in external adventures disguised as crusades for peace or as necessary precautionary actions of self-defence against Imperialist aggressors. Such policies might take the form of telling the satellites to attack Yugoslavia, or the East German Communists might be instructed to seize Berlin. The Kremlin would be ready to disown these adventures if they collapsed or intervene with the formidable Russian military machine " in the interests of peace " if that course of action seemed likely to be profitable. It is to guard against this possible development (amongst others) of the Communist conspiracy that the western world must become much stronger militarily and much more united politically than it now (1953) is.

To think otherwise is to be in a dream world from which a horrible awakening is inevitable, unless we are to assume that everything the Communists have done, are doing, and say they intend to do to overthrow freedom on a world scale is not fact but fiction.

CHAPTER XII

THE SOVIET UNION AND THE WEST, 1944–53

BETWEEN the two wars the author of this book wrote a two-volume study of contemporary history called *Our Own Times 1913–1934*. It was well received, and ran through many editions until the story was taken up to 1938. Other activities have prevented any attempt to carry on the story, but if it were now possible to bring this work up to date it would include the chapter the reader is now beginning.

The Communist conspiracy is so far flung and so complex and, one should add, so strange and incredible to men and women nurtured on democratic ideas, that it is hard for some people to believe that what has been put into a pattern in this book is not the product of a diseased mind.

This may indeed be the reply of Communists, notwithstanding the care which has been taken to support the argument by plentiful and sometimes—it is to be feared—rather boring extracts from Communist sources.

There is, however, another way of approaching the whole question, and that is to present the reader with an objective and undeniably true account of what has happened in the world since 1944 so far as relations between the Soviet Union and the West are concerned, and then ask ourselves whether it has all been a great big accident or misunderstanding, or whether the events now to be recorded may reasonably be attributed to the begetters of a vast conspiracy against the free world.

.   .   .   .   .

The events referred to above fall into two periods of time: first from 1944 to 1947 and then from 1947 to the present time—1953. During the first period the Western Powers appeared to be incapable of doing anything to avert, or to defend themselves from, the menace which was in part creeping and in part rushing at them. In truth, the statesmen in London, Paris and Washington (or some of them) were not blind to what was happening, but democratic public opinion had to be allowed to learn through the actions of the Russians that the war-time

co-operation between the Soviet Union and the West (so far as
it *was* co-operation) was merely a marriage of convenience from
the point of view of Moscow.

By 1947 it became possible for political leaders in the West to
begin to call upon their electorates to bestir themselves in the
defence of the free way of life, and the second period began.
The Russian tactics were different in the two periods, for in the
first the allies were almost the conscious, or at any rate the
helpless, agents and co-belligerents in the Soviet Union's plans
whilst in the second period the cold war began.

In 1944 and 1945, in the course of the war against Germany
Soviet troops occupied the countries of Eastern Europe. When
the leaders of the three great Powers met at Yalta in February
1945, the Russians had already installed the puppet Lublin
Committee as the Government of Poland, and had been an
accessory to the massacre by the Germans of the genuine Polish
Liberation forces during the siege of Warsaw. In Bulgaria and
Rumania coalitions including the Communists were in power
in Yugoslavia, Communists controlled a large part of the
country; in Hungary, partly occupied by the Red Army, a coali
tion including Communists administered the liberated territory
Part of Czechoslovakia occupied by Soviet forces, was dominated
by Communist-controlled committees, and the genuine Czecho
slovak Government, under Soviet pressure, had admitted
Communist Ministers to the key positions of power.

In Greece a large-scale Communist effort to seize power had
been frustrated by British troops, and there the first Western
victims of Communist violence had already been slain. In
Belgium a confused Communist effort to gain power had come
to grief.

The position at the time of Yalta was that, except in Poland
and Yugoslavia, the established Governments were, if not
strictly representative, at least broadly based. The aim of the
Western Powers was to secure a broadening of the Polish and
Yugoslav Governments and to ensure that in the whole area
free elections would be held as soon as possible to ensure full
representative régimes. Both these points were agreed at Yalta
when the three Governments pledged themselves to " form
interim governmental authorities broadly representative of
all democratic elements in the population, and pledged to the
earliest possible establishment through free elections of govern

ments responsible to the will of the people, and to facilitate where necessary the holding of such elections ".

The Lublin " Government " in Poland and the Tito Government in Yugoslavia were in fact broadened during the year, and were recognised by the Western Powers. The declarations at the Potsdam Conference in August, 1945, " took note " of the Polish Government's agreement to " hold free and unfettered elections " with universal suffrage and secret ballot. But in both cases complete control of the police and army remained in Communist hands, while Soviet forces remained in Poland, as they remain to this day, ostensibly to guard their lines of communication to Germany.

In no case were the free elections guaranteed at Yalta carried out. In fact, during the next two years all genuinely non-Communist elements were forced out of the coalitions, and replaced by stooges of the Communist Party. During this period some opposition parties were tolerated, but they operated under severe disadvantages.

The Yalta Conference was held in February, 1945. The first major breach of the provisions of the Yalta agreement was made in March, 1945, when Vyshinsky forced King Michael of Rumania by direct threats to give power to the Communist-controlled " National-Democratic Front " and to exclude the Liberal and National Peasant Parties, which represented the vast majority of the nation.

In May–August of that year the Communists squeezed the Agrarians—by far the largest and most democratic party—out of the Bulgarian Government. In Hungary this stage did not come until 1947, when Soviet troops arrested the secretary of the majority Smallholder Party, Bela Kovacs, and later secured the dismissal of Prime Minister Nagy. In Poland Mikolajczyk left the Government in the summer of 1946.

The second stage was the destruction of the great democratic parties which had been forced into opposition. This ended, except for mopping-up operations, in the autumn of 1947 with the execution of Petkov in Bulgaria, the imprisonment of Maniu and abdication of the King in Rumania, and the flight of Mikolajczyk from Poland.

In February, 1947, peace treaties were negotiated and signed between the Western Powers and the Soviet Union on the one hand, and Bulgaria, Rumania and Hungary on the other. It is symptomatic that they were broken in the following important respects as soon as they came into force:—

(i) They guaranteed political freedom and human rights and were followed by the immediate suppression of the remnants of these rights.

(ii) They guaranteed respect or compensation for former financial interests of the Western Allies in these ex-enemy States. This was ignored.

(iii) They guaranteed reparations to the Allied States— Yugoslavia, Greece and the U.S.S.R. No reparations were paid to Greece, and payment of reparations due to Yugoslavia was stopped when that country left the Soviet bloc. Payments on an enormous scale were, however, made to the U.S.S.R.!

(iv) They limited the armed forces permitted to these States, but their forces remained far above the permitted level and have since continually increased.

(v) They provided a mechanism whereby the diplomatic representatives of Britain, the United States and the U.S.S.R. should investigate alleged breaches of the treaties and secure their enforcement. Soviet refusal to participate rendered this a dead letter.

Thus in Eastern Europe a combined operation by Soviet diplomacy and the thugs of local secret police backed by the Soviet Army, secured complete control in the hands of Soviet agents, and these agents secured recognition and peace treaties from the West, while rival centres, such as the Yugoslav and Polish Governments in exile, lost such recognition and were disintegrated.

Western Europe

Throughout the world during the whole of this period Soviet propaganda exploited prestige built up during the war; it utilised the false impression successfully given by Communist propagandists that the war-time resistance movements were mainly Communist; it exploited the desire of the Western peoples for more egalitarian policies; and it played on the general reluctance after such a bitter struggle, to face another threat to peace.

At the end of the war, with two of the world's major military and industrial Powers, Germany and Japan, knocked out, the

Soviet leaders saw themselves faced with only two major rivals, Great Britain and the United States.

It has naturally been a matter of considerable concern to the Soviet Union to prevent the revival of the two defeated Powers, except on her own terms and under her control, or, at worst, neutralised in some way. It would probably not be going far wrong to say that the Soviet leaders regard the German problem, in particular, as the key to further major advance. The original idea which animated the Western Powers of a four-Power guarantee of a united but peaceful Germany, which would have involved the Russians in trusting others and themselves honouring treaties, has long since gone.

At Potsdam, in July, 1945, Britain, the United States and the U.S.S.R. agreed to the economic unity of Germany, and to the extension of full democratic rights to Germans in all four occupation zones. In reality Soviet obstruction on the Control Commission prevented the realisation of economic unity (which would have hampered the absorption of East Germany into the Soviet economic bloc) while all the clauses about political freedoms have been completely flouted.

However, while breaking all four-Power agreements on the administration of the Eastern Zone, the Soviet Union attempted to use four-Power agreement to interfere in the Western Zones, and in particular to obtain a share in the control of the important Ruhr industrial area.

The Council of Foreign Ministers failed to reach agreement, and by the end of 1947 the division, which had been a reality since 1945, became formal and definite.

Middle East

During the war Stalin had proposed to Hitler that the U.S.S.R. should have bases covering the Dardanelles and the Bosphorus. On 8th August, 1946, a Soviet Note to Turkey made the same proposal, in the form of a demand for the revision of the Montreux Convention to include the regulation of the Straits by Black Sea Powers only and joint Russo-Turkish defence of the Dardanelles. Turkey rejected this dangerous proposal, and was then for some time subjected to a war of nerves, including propaganda on territorial claims against her. She stood firm.

In Persia the position was different. British and Soviet

troops were in that country as a result of the war, and the Soviet Army had set up under its protection an " autonomous " Communist Government in the border Province of Persian Azerbaijan. The Soviet Union was under treaty obligation to Britain and to Persia to withdraw her troops by 2nd March, 1946.

In January, 1946, Persia complained to the Security Council of Soviet interference in her internal affairs. On 27th March, demands presented by the U.S.S.R. to Persia were made public; they provided for the indefinite stay of Russian troops in parts of Persia, Persian recognition of the " autonomy " of Azerbaijan, and the setting up of a Soviet–Persian Oil Company in which the Soviet Union would own 51 per cent. of the shares.

After considerable negotiations, in which the Security Council was involved, the U.S.S.R. agreed to withdraw her troops (the question of their stay, she declared, was unconnected with the other negotiations), while Persia provisionally agreed to the oil proposal, which was, however, later rejected by the Majlis. The Azerbaijan Communist régime fell shortly after the withdrawal of its protectors.

Far East

In the period 1944–47 the Soviet Union obtained territorial concessions and the restitution of the former rights of Tsarist Russia in Manchuria, including the lease of Port Arthur and control of the main railway, in return for its brief campaign against Japan, but its main immediate gain was colossal loot in machinery and goods from industrial Manchuria.

At the same time the territory of Tannu Tuva (officially part of China, an ally of the U.S.S.R.) was annexed and Outer Mongolia, which had long been under Soviet domination, was granted " independence " by the Chinese. Soviet penetration of Sinkiang completed the great arc of Soviet-controlled territory to the north of China. In Korea a Communist régime was set up in the northern part, occupied by Soviet troops.

It does not appear that at this time the Russians had any serious expectation of the success of the Chinese Communists. Nevertheless, by turning over to them arms captured from the Japanese Kwantung Army, they greatly assisted their eventual success.

II

The Cold War

By 1947 public opinion in Britain and the United States and in most of the other Western countries was awake to the Russian threat and prepared to back measures required to hold it. The Communists in France, and to a lesser extent in Italy, showed no signs of coming to power: their vote had settled down and was too small. Finally, the launching of the Marshall Plan in June, 1947, showed that the United States was not going to permit the economic collapse of Europe.

It was true that Soviet military superiority was vast. But the atomic weapon and Anglo-American air power were sufficient to provide a formidable retort, and local and immediate successes would not guarantee final Soviet victory in an all-out war. By the industrial and economic criteria which the Communists usually apply, the United States had all the real potentialities of victory in such a struggle.

The Soviet leaders therefore were faced with the need for a decision. They could accept the position, and settle down to " peaceful co-existence " on the basis of existing spheres of influence. Or—and this was the decision they took—they could launch a powerful, world-wide offensive, making use of every method and tactic short of large-scale war, to prevent the political and economic consolidation of the free nations, and to extend their own power.

During the period since mid-1947 this cold war campaign, waged with complete ruthlessness and disregard for honesty and truth, has been the essence of the international situation.

The activities undertaken, under the general control of the political general staff in Moscow, to implement this plan of disruption in the free world have been numerous and have assumed many different forms.

In Russia itself a series of great ideological purges associated with the name of Zhdanov, a great administrative tightening up, and a wave of chauvinist propaganda, put an end to the slight relaxations of the war period.

In the satellite States the Communists were finally established in all positions of power, and campaigns were launched against the last of the independent organisations, the Churches. A Soviet economic programme designed to increase industrial

P

productivity on Soviet Stakhanovite lines and to bring the peasantry under direct control by forced collectivisation got well under way.

At the same time the satellite Communist parties were brought under rigid Kremlin control, and great purges and trials removed many of the leading figures of the party.

In Yugoslavia, however, the attempt to impose complete Kremlin control failed, and resulted in the Yugoslav secession from the Soviet bloc. The attempt to eliminate Yugoslav independence was in full swing in March, 1948. By June behind-the-scenes action had failed to shake Tito, and the Cominform made its public denunciation, which the Russians appear to have thought would bring about the fall of the Yugoslav leaders. It failed entirely, and left the best-organised army in the Balkans outside Russian control.

Together with this consolidation of the base went the attack on the West. The Marshall Plan, which had been launched in June, 1947, was denounced by the Russians as an attempt to submit Europe to American economic domination, and some of the satellite states who had welcomed the generosity of the U.S.A. were forced hastily to reject the plan. A few months later, in September, 1947, the Cominform was established to co-ordinate the Communist Parties of the U.S.S.R., of Eastern Europe, and the two leading ones of the West—those of Italy and France.

In fact the Cominform has met only occasionally to launch some specially important Soviet initiative, though its journal, *For a Lasting Peace, for a People's Democracy*, is published fortnightly, and comments on the activities of Communist parties throughout the world, and serves to convey Soviet directives to every country for the operation.

The Cominform was set up, according to its original manifesto, to conduct the work of the Communist parties in the " conditions of sharpened struggle which characterise international relations in the post-war period ". Zhdanov, in his inaugural speech, re-enunciated the doctrine of " the two camps ", and made an ideological declaration of war on the " reactionary imperialist camp" of the West. At the same time, with the usual Communist double-talk, he spoke of Soviet interest in peace.

The launching of the Cominform may be regarded as the formal ending of " Big-Four co-operation " in foreign policy, and of co-operation with Socialist and Catholic parties in the Western countries. The "popular front" idea was not abandoned, but was now limited to parties which accepted, or did not reject, all the various Soviet views on current affairs.

Before considering the results of this new Soviet assault, it is necessary to recall the foundation of the other main political weapon of Soviet policy, the World Peace Congress, whose predecessor, the Wroclaw Congress, was held in Poland in August, 1948. The history of this movement has already been dealt with in Chapter IX, but it is worth reiterating that it works in close co-ordination with the Cominform journal, which carries its pronouncements and, in its issue of 29th November, 1949, published a Cominform resolution that " the struggle for stable and lasting peace, for the organisation and consolidation of the forces of peace against the forces of war should now become the pivot of the entire activity of the Communist Parties and democratic organisations ".

This interlocking into the " peace " campaign of the Communist parties, with their varied and almost invariably highly *unpeaceful* activities, has been carried to such lengths that workers in armaments factories in Eastern Europe work extra " peace shifts ", that slowing up of uranium deliveries from East Germany to Soviet atomic bomb plants is punished as warmongering, that armies launched on wars of aggression, as in Korea, sign " peace appeals ", and so on. The essence of " peace " propaganda is that " peace " is a popular and pleasant word and is applied to any action undertaken in the Soviet interest, including war.

The decision to reject peaceful co-existence once taken the new Soviet assault went into action on a wide front.

In the spring of 1948 a Communist-sponsored body called the German People's Congress launched the appeal for " German Unity " which has since been the main Soviet propaganda weapon in Germany. In June came the separate currency reforms in the two zones and the beginning of the Berlin blockade.

A complete blockade was instituted, absolutely contrary to the spirit of the Potsdam agreement granting the Western Powers unconditional access to the city. At the same time a conference of the Foreign Ministers of the U.S.S.R. and Eastern Europe, held in Warsaw, accused the Western Powers of reviving

Germany's military potential for imperialist aims, and demanded four-Power control of the Ruhr and a single " democratic peace-loving " Government for all Germany, with the signature of a peace treaty and the withdrawal of all foreign troops within a year. Thus a purely illegal and aggressive action was bound up with a typical bit of " peace " and reasonableness in Soviet propaganda.

The Berlin blockade was maintained, even after the airlift had clearly shown its futility, apparently in the hope that hard winter weather would stop the lift or that the Allies would tire. But Soviet determination had met its match in allied doggedness, and eventually the Russians had to admit defeat. Seventy allied airmen lost their lives in carrying out the airlift.

In the following year the Russians set up the " German Democratic Republic " in East Germany, which undertook the formation of a National Front in West Germany, to agitate for unification.

By 1952 the East German zone was a fully organised Russian satellite State separated from West Germany by the usual fortified and police-patrolled zone across which (but excluding Berlin) numbers of East Germans continuously risked their lives in order to escape to the West. The immediate consequence of the partition imposed by Russian policy on Germany and of Russian aggression in general in the cold war has been greatly to accelerate the growth of an independent West German Republic invited to play a full part in the plans for the defence of the West, now further menaced by growing East German forces.

Austria. The subsidiary problem of Austria, with whom a peace treaty should long ago have been negotiated, is slightly different. Though the Russians have obtained considerable financial loot (a reasonable word, since most of it was unjustified on reparations or other grounds), just as they have from Germany, Hungary and Rumania, the main reason for their stay seems to be to prevent Austrian recovery, to keep the situation fluid for further advances, and to maintain the legal basis under which Russian troops are present in Hungary and Rumania to hold the lines of communication to Austria. There has long since been no real reason why the occupying Powers should not have withdrawn and peace signed.

Greece. In Greece sporadic guerrilla fighting had already started late in 1946, with the Communists receiving support and arms from Greece's northern neighbours. A United Nations Commission visited the area, and Belgrade and Sofia. Later a semi-permanent sub-commission was established, in spite of Soviet vetoes, to watch the frontiers. But the Communist activities were more of a nuisance, intended probably to keep trouble going, than a major campaign. The Communist Party and its Press remained legal in Greece until the autumn of 1947.

In December, 1947, however, the rebels announced the formation of a " Democratic Greek Government ", and the following year attempts were made to capture towns and change from guerrilla to regular warfare. A Government offensive in the summer of 1948 drove the rebels into Albania, from where they re-emerged in other areas. It was not until the summer of 1949, when Yugoslavia was no longer prepared to help the rebels, that they were again driven over the frontiers and gave up the struggle.

Czechoslovakia. In Czechoslovakia the Communists had obtained control of the police forces after the war, and the other main positions from which the fight for power is carried on, though they had not broken with the democratic parties, and Czechoslovakia was often looked on as a bridge between East and West, where Communists played a major, but not tyrannical part. Late in 1947, however, it became apparent that the methods of their police had alienated the other parties, and that public opinion had shifted away from them, so that their chances in the forthcoming elections were poor. In February, 1948, in the presence of Zorin, the Soviet Assistant Foreign Minister, Gottwald, now Communist President, but at that time the Prime Minister, carried out his " police revolution ". Within a few months the country was in the same condition as the other East European States. A bloody purge closed the year 1952.

Finland. In 1949 came the Communist attempt on Finland. Soon after the war the Communists secured the key Ministry of the Interior, but their attempts to infiltrate the police had not had decisive success. In 1949, when the new Finnish Government was formed and the Communist Leino was excluded from the Ministry of the Interior, the party attempted to reinstate him and to gain further power by street demonstrations and strikes on the Prague model. These completely failed in their object.

Assault in Asia : Insurrection and War

In Asia, however, which has always been regarded by the Communists as the back door route to any attack on " imperialism ", events have proved, so far at any rate, that the Soviet Union has found a more promising field than Europe.

China. The Chinese revolution was, of course, accelerated by Soviet help, and even more by complete Kuomintang incompetence, but it was an indigenous product. Since its success, however, the Soviet Union has naturally made every effort to get it fully under control and seems to have been successful, at least to the extent of securing complete co-ordination of Soviet and Chinese efforts in foreign policy. The Communist victory in China, in any case, is obviously of enormous world significance.

Indo-China. The nationalist movement which came to the fore at the end of the war was, unlike such movements in other parts of the East, led by a Communist, though not entirely under Communist control. The years of fighting, however, have naturally proved useful to the party, and its control now seems fairly complete. The Vietminh, which it controls, occupies a large proportion of Annam, and although it cannot expel the French, its own forces seem to be in a very strong position, particularly as they now have Communist China as a neighbour. From the point of view of Soviet policy, they are providing a possible spring-board for further advance and tying up and wearing down large French forces which might otherwise be strengthening Western Europe. In addition, they constitute a constant threat to the Red Delta, the rice bowl of South-East Asia.

Malaya. The jungle has so far proved difficult territory for operations against the fairly small bands of the Malayan Communist revolt, as the mountains did, to a lesser extent, in Greece. The benefit to the U.S.S.R. of this revolt, which can never hope to obtain power except as the result of a major war, is that it ties up British troops and hampers production of strategic materials, especially tin and rubber.

Other Far Eastern Territories. A similar revolt has taken place in the Philippines, and in Burma prolonged civil war, combined with political intrigue, has enabled a small Communist army to maintain itself. In India agrarian revolts have given way to parliamentary tactics after firm action by the Indian Government. But Tibet has now come under the control of Peking.

Korea. In June, 1950, the North Korean attack against South Korea was launched in the one area, it seemed, in which an important advance might be achieved without Western intervention. This miscalculation brought, after the Communist loss of most of North Korea, the added threat to world peace with the launching of Chinese armies to turn the scale. Their failure has blocked the Russians in yet another direction, but the long and typically Soviet-style negotiations which followed the failure in 1951 of the last Chinese offensive, which was launched under the public prediction by Stalin that: " the war in Korea can only end in the defeat of the interventionalists ",* are not complete at the time of writing, and a renewal of the war on a large scale is by no means impossible.

This survey of the Soviet attack on the free world is designed to lay before the reader in perspective, all these and similar actions of Communists everywhere, as part of one single, flexible but unremitting campaign for world domination. The North Korean conscript firing a Soviet machine-gun, the New Zealand longshoreman striking against the State, the police thug beating up an old Communist in the Pankrac jail in Prague, the woman speaking on a " peace " campaign platform in Hammersmith, are all taking part in actions planned in the Kremlin for the consolidation and extension of their rule over the whole world. Some carry out their tasks voluntarily, some under compulsion: others are dupes.

The first step in stopping the assault on world freedom is to understand its nature and to recognise its manifestations; the next is to spread this knowledge.

There is also the third need, which is to maintain in the West, through united democratic policies, sufficient physical force to remove from the minds of the Communist leaders any hope that by threats of armed aggression they can frighten free nations into accepting Communist domination, or that by such aggression itself they can extend their economic, psychological and political dominion.

But the willingness of the free peoples to make the necessary and, in a material sense, the unproductive sacrifices needed for this purpose, depends on public opinion in the free countries

* *Pravda*, 17.2.51.

appreciating what is at stake and the formidable nature of the menace. Late, but, better late than never, the North Atlantic Treaty Organisation came into existence, but its effectiveness depends on its being supported by public opinion, and much needs to be done to make N.A.T.O. (within the general framework of an effective United Nations) something more than a defensive military arrangement; but to discuss this problem in detail would take us far beyond the already extensive horizons of the subject of this book.

It is hoped that the facts published in this book will assist in the task of spreading knowledge about this Communist Conspiracy. But the concluding thought must be, that essential though it is, that the peoples of the free world should understand the peril in which they stand, such understanding—still very imperfect in many quarters *—will not, even when it is reasonably complete, be sufficient to overthrow the menace to the free way of life. The fundamental fact about this menace is that it is an idea from which (in accordance with the relationship between ideas and actions) spring certain actions which are the visible menaces to freedom and the supreme importance in society of the personality of MAN the individual. The defeat of the evil idea at the root of Communism cannot be achieved simply by the use of physical force. This is not to say that the physical re-armament of the West can be dispensed with, but there is a danger that the free peoples will suppose that armaments are in themselves the whole answer. They are not; and

---

* As an example of lack of understanding even in quarters where might least be expected, I recollect the astonishment with which I read a broadcast printed in the *Listener* in 1951. It was the last of a series called " On the Conditions for an East–West Settlement ", and was delivered by Professor Arnold Toynbee, who is Director of Studies at the Royal Institute of International Affairs and Research Professor of International History in the University of London. As part of his argument in favour of the view that peaceful co-existence between the Soviet Union and the West was not only possible but desirable, Toynbee said, " In order to keep morally fit, human nature needs to be exercised and kept in training by some devil or other, and our western world to-day is having this indispensable, though very disagreeable service performed for it by Russia ".

It would be interesting to hear comments on these words by the millions in the Soviet Labour camps who may feel together with—for example—some of Professor Toynbee's friends who may still be in Prague or Warsaw, that they are paying rather a high price to keep the Western world " morally fit ".

I pointed out in a letter published in the *Listener* that according to this doctrine we must regard Hitler and the Nazis as having been our benefactors and " training devils " and asked Toynbee to comment on whether we had been foolish to destroy them. There was no reply.

they are probably not half the answer. Physical armaments have their place in the Communist strategy—as we have shown in this book—but they have certainly not, up to date, been used as the spearhead of the Communist Conspiracy, and indeed there are some reasons for supposing that the Master Conspirators realise that if they used their armaments to precipitate a third world conflict of an atomic character, this gamble, unless it were immediately and completely successful, might lead to the collapse of the whole conspiracy, and certainly the collapse of the Russian bastion. It is equally true that if the cold war degenerated into world-wide fighting, even a military victory would probably result in such chaos that the free way of life would disappear.

What is required in the free world is a more alert appreciation of the issues which are at stake, and something of that passion for and belief in the supreme importance of our cause which is characteristic of the devotees of the Communist creed. The correct reply to the Communist Conspiracy is first to expose it for what it is, and then to so practise and preach democracy that the psychological campaign carried on by the Russian-controlled Communists is powerless to affect the minds of men. The object of this book is to expose the nature of the Communist Conspiracy by using, so far as possible, Communist statements. But, in contrast to the certitudes of Stalinism, it is appropriate that this book in aid of democracy should terminate upon a humble note. Let it therefore be noted and taken to heart by all those who cherish freedom that this formidable and fundamentally wicked conspiracy was, and only could have been, born because of certain failures in the democratic way of life. We need not follow Professor Toynbee in seeking external devils; there are plenty within the free world. The Communist turns to the teachings of Marx–Lenin–Stalin for guidance in his behaviour; it must be our duty in the West to seek our guidance in the teachings of Christ.

SUMMARY OF COMMUNIST POLICY AND THE CONTROL OF ATOMIC ENERGY

THE General Assembly of the United Nations set up the Atomic Energy Commission in January, 1946. It met in June, 1946, and considered two plans, one American, one Soviet, for the control of atomic production. The Baruch Plan put forward by the United States proposed the setting up of an International Atomic Authority with full powers of control and inspection throughout the world and not subject to great Power veto. The Soviet plan proposed the immediate banning of the atomic bomb and the destruction of stockpiles within three months, punishment for violators of the convention under the domestic legislation of each State, and an incomplete system of control and inspection subject to great Power veto.

It will be apparent that the Soviet plan would have ensured the destruction of the stocks of the one weapon which, at that time, enabled the United States to nullify the Soviet superiority in all other weapons, but would not enable a serious check to be made on Soviet developments in the same field.

After a deadlock the matter was referred to a Scientific and Technical Committee, which included Russian and Polish scientists and the French Communist Professor Joliot-Curie. This Committee reported in September, 1946, unanimously holding that inspection and control over the whole process of production was desirable and technically possible.

Further attempts were made in the Atomic Energy Commission, the General Assembly and the Security Council, on the basis of this report, to reach agreement on an effective plan, but the majority view was rejected by Mr Gromyko on 5th March, 1947, on the grounds that the Atomic Central Authority's proposed rights of control would constitute a violation of Soviet sovereignty. This line was maintained until, on 23rd June, 1948, the Soviet delegate in the Security Council vetoed the reports of the Atomic Energy Commission and negotiations broke down.

Though the Soviet Union's propaganda has continually urged the abolition of the atomic bomb it does so in general terms, such as those of the so-called "Stockholm Appeal" and of Stalin's statement of 6th October, 1951. Its record in the negotiations proves that its real intention is to secure, if possible, the destruction of the American stock of atomic bombs on terms which leave the U.S.S.R.'s secrecy precautions intact to conceal its own retention of the weapon.

Since there is universal repugnance for this terrifying weapon, such propaganda has been able to play upon and make use of the feelings of large numbers of honest people. But the Stalinists' hypocrisy in their appeal to humane feelings on this matter is all too obvious.

At the time when the first bombs were dropped in 1945, when a considerable part of the Western Press was expressing the real misgivings that most of us feel about this weapon, the French Communist Party organ *Humanité* at the beginning of August featured the Hiroshima explosion on its front page with a photograph of Professor Joliot-Curie (now one of the leaders of the Communist anti-Atomic Bomb Movement), and stated: " The work of Professor Joliot-Curie was of enormous assistance in the realisation of this wonderful conquest of science." It went on to say: " The repercussions of the discovery are considerable. And yet the Vatican makes bold to disapprove of it. We permit ourselves to express astonishment."

At the same time the Italian Communist organ *Unita* was writing:

> " News that the American Air Force has used the atomic bomb, news that has evoked an enormous impression throughout the world, has been received in some quarters with a sense of panic and with expressions of blame. This, it seems to us, is a curious psychological kink, schematic obedience to an abstract humanitarianism. . . . We do not, therefore, share the sense of dismay evident because we consider in its concreteness, the use of this formidable weapon of destruction."

These statements make it clear that the bomb is only regarded as objectionable when used by or in the possession of Powers opposed to the Soviet Union.

Now that the Soviet authorities (after a period in which they claimed that though they held the secret of atomic energy they were using it only in its peaceful applications) have admitted that they possess and are testing the atomic bomb, Communist objections to it have changed in emphasis. The Soviet admission that the U.S.S.R. had developed a bomb was greeted by the Communist Press and radio with acclamation. For example, Prague radio on 18th October, 1951, said that " Vyshinsky's statement in 1949 that if necessary the Soviet

Union would have as many atomic bombs as were needed has evoked a very a joyful response. Hence also the deep satisfaction at Stalin's recent assurances." The Rumanian Communist organ, *Scanteia*, in its editorial of 7th October, 1951, had said :—

> " Peace-loving people all over the world felt tremendously relieved to learn that atomic energy and the atomic bomb are possessed also by the Soviet Union "; and, " We can recall the boundless enthusiasm aroused throughout the world by the Tass communiqué on September 25th, 1949, which announced that the U.S.S.R. had the secret of the atomic bomb and possessed this weapon."

Stalin, in his statement on 6th October, 1951, described the atom bomb in Soviet hands as a weapon which would be used " in accordance with the plan for the defence of our country ", and stated that it was necessary " in order to meet the aggressors fully prepared ". Previously Communist propaganda had described the atomic bomb as a weapon usable only for the mass extermination of civil populations; as soon as the Russians had theirs it became a legitimate defensive weapon.

General disarmament also has always been delayed by similar Soviet tactics. The United Nations Commission on Conventional Armaments was set up by the Security Council in February, 1947. It took over a year to cover the first two items in its plan of work. The British and other delegates maintained from the start that disarmament must be preceded by the establishment of an effective international security system and by a system of international control. To this the U.S.S.R. would not agree.

It is clear that the alternative—for the free world to disarm without any method of checking that disarmament was also taking place behind the Iron Curtain, and without the establishment of any machinery for coping with aggression—means merely laying ourselves open, without any *quid pro quo*, to Soviet attack.

The Soviet Union has made much general propaganda " in favour of " disarmament. Its proposals at present are that complete atomic disarmament must come first (that is, that the United States must abandon the one field in which it certainly has a lead), and that the great Powers should then each cut down their other arms by two-thirds, which would mean that the Soviet superiority in them would be maintained.

COMMUNIST POLICY AT THE UNITED NATIONS

THE Soviet Union subscribed to the United Nations Charter, as it had to the Atlantic Charter, but as in all similar cases, whenever a clause in the Charter was phrased in general terms, Soviet interpretation was quite different from that ordinarily understood.

The United Nations Charter provides a satisfactory basis for world peace and world organisation. But the United Nations has succeeded as far as it has only by waging an unremitting struggle to prevent its being rendered useless by Soviet tactics and Soviet interpretation. The Soviet aim has been on the one hand to prevent United Nations actions, and on the other, to retain the United Nations as an unrivalled propaganda forum.

The main Soviet weapon has been THE VETO. When the United Nations was formed in 1945 the Security Council was set up to take immediate and effective action to keep the peace where any danger of war appeared. The great Powers were made permanent members so that those able to act would always be represented on the Council.

Each of these Powers was given the power to veto actions recommended by the rest of the Council because it was felt that in the case of a major conflict between the great Powers matters should not be allowed to go to extremes, since the support and goodwill of all these Powers were essential for world peace. Mr Attlee told the House of Commons on 23rd October, 1946, that it was always understood that the veto should be used " only in the last resort in extreme cases when the great Powers might be involved in conflict. It was never conceived as a device to be used constantly whenever a particular Power was not in full agreement with the others."

The first Soviet veto, on 10th February, 1946, was in stark contrast to this idea. The Security Council was debating the withdrawal of British and French troops from Syria and the Lebanon, and a resolution acceptable to and accepted by all the parties concerned was vetoed by Vyshinsky, who put forward a much stronger resolution. The troops, however, were finally withdrawn satisfactorily in general accordance with the vetoed resolution. The Soviet object in this matter, in which they had no conceivable direct interest, was to prevent a goodwill solution and to obtain propaganda prestige in the Arab world as a protector of Arab interests. The attempt backfired.

By 1952 the U.S.S.R. had used the veto fifty-five times in all. Typical Soviet vetoes have been:—

(a) 25th March, 1947: a veto on the attempt of Britain to obtain redress from Albania for the mining of a British destroyer in the Corfu Channel.

(b) 20th September, 1946; 29th July, 1947; 19th August, 1947 (2); 15th September, 1947 (2): vetoes in connection with the Greek complaint that the Communist rebellion in their country was assisted from Bulgaria, Albania and Yugoslavia; and after the report of the United Nations special Commission on the Balkans established that the accusation was true, to prevent any action, even that of setting up a Commission of Conciliation. The Soviet motive was clearly to prevent the suppression of the violent and underhand activities of its agents, dangerous though they were to peace.

(c) 24th May, 1948 (2): vetoes on an attempt by Chile to have investigated alleged Soviet interference in Czechoslovak affairs, a reference to the Communist seizure of power in February, 1948.

(d) 22nd June, 1948: veto on the approval of the report of the Atomic Energy Commission.

(e) 29th October, 1948: veto on the proposed draft settlement of the Berlin dispute put forward by six neutral Powers.

(f) A whole series of vetoes on the admission to membership of the United Nations of Italy, Ceylon, Ireland, Portugal, Austria, Finland and other countries. The admission of these States has been made conditional by the U.S.S.R. on the simultaneous admission of Bulgaria, Hungary and Rumania, whose refusal to carry out the terms of their peace treaties renders them unsuitable for membership, of Albania [she has already flouted the United Nations on two occasions], and of Outer Mongolia, whose independence is non-existent even compared with the other four.

The Soviet Union has obstructed, or attempted to obstruct, the Security Council in a number of other ways. For instance, at the time of the Azerbaijan venture the Soviet representative withdrew from the Security Council. The Security Council did not take any strong action, and this may have been the reason for the Soviet delegate's withdrawal again in June, 1950, when the North Korean aggression came before the Council. On this occasion, however, his absence enabled the Council to take satisfactory and energetic action which he might otherwise have vetoed, and judging from past events certainly would have vetoed.

That action to preserve peace should depend on this sort of chance was intolerable, and the next session of the General Assembly set up machinery whereby action by the United Nations can be taken without the risk of a Security Council veto.

The United Nations Charter (Art. 43) also provides for armed forces to be placed at the disposal of the Security Council to enforce peace, and in February, 1946, a Military Staff Committee was set up under the Security Council to recommend methods of providing these forces. Later that year the General Assembly recommended the Security Council to speed up " the placing at its disposal of armed forces ". The Security Council directed the Military Staff Committee to report by 30th April. But no unanimous report could be produced because of the failure of the Soviet delegation to agree even on minor issues. In August, 1948, the Commission reported that it could make no progress until divergencies of general principles were resolved. There has since been no progress, and in January, 1950, the Soviet delegate withdrew from the Committee.

Thus the attempt to give the United Nations the " teeth " whose absence had resulted in the failure of the League of Nations was, as far as lay in their power, frustrated by the Soviet delegates. As all aggressions since then have been Soviet-sponsored it is clear why the Soviet Union did everything possible to obstruct the establishment of effective machinery to counteract aggression.

Soviet action as regards the United Nations specialised agencies has also been aimed at the disruption of peaceful world co-operation in such matters of common interest as trade, health and education.

The Russians refused to join the International Monetary Fund or the International Bank for Reconstruction and Development and do not participate in UNESCO, one of whose aims is to secure a free exchange of cultural knowledge, a procedure incompatible with the maintenance of the Iron Curtain.

In the economic sphere, they refused to join the International Trade Organisation or the Food and Agriculture Organisation; they do not belong to the International Labour Office, the International Maritime Consultative Organisation, the International Civil Aviation Organisation, or the International Refugee Organisation.

They joined the World Health Organisation on its inception in 1948 and left in 1949, declaring that they were "not satisfied" with its work. The Director-General of the organisation offered to visit Moscow for discussions, but without avail.

The Russians are, however, members of two of the Economic and Social Council's regional Commissions, the Economic Commission for Europe and the Economic Commission for Asia and the Far East. But they use both almost solely as sounding boards for propaganda.

A COLLECTOR'S PIECE

DRAFT FOR AN APPEAL BY TEACHERS AND SCHOLARS IN FACE OF THE THREAT OF ANOTHER WORLD WAR. [1]

" Having learned from the painful experience of two world wars that a race for armaments can end only in war; [2]

" Being shocked in our consciences by the thought that the new means of destruction can annihilate all life on our planet, or would at all events turn into deserts immense areas now peopled by hundreds of millions of human beings; [3]

" Being aware of the responsibility weighing on us whose task it is to spread knowledge, at a time when the most magnificent discoveries of science are being used for the destruction of mankind; [4]

" Realising that in the face of the threat of another world war our work as teachers would become futile, and that despair might then be our only reaction at the thought of our pupils and students being doomed to massacre; [5]

" Convinced, however, that war is neither inevitable nor necessary,

WE, TEACHERS AND SCHOLARS,

solemnly declare that both as men and as educators we cannot remain passive in the face of the fearful catastrophe threatening all human beings without exception.

" We deem it possible for different economic and social régimes, in particular socialistic and capitalistic ones, to exist in peace side by side, and consider that peaceful competition alone can allow the peoples of the world to judge these régimes objectively. [6]

" We ask that all people be free to have the régime of their own choice, and condemn all interference and armed intervention in their internal affairs. [7]

" We believe that all differences between nations can be settled peacefully, that this is possible within the structure of the U.N.O., and that a solution for the present crisis can be found only in disarmament. [8]

" We denounce as a delusion the opinion that the rearmament of any part of Germany could make an effective and lasting contribution to the restoration of peaceful relations between peoples. [9]

" We strongly condemn all propaganda in favour of wars of aggression and particularly in favour of preventive wars. [10]

" We are firmly resolved to do our utmost and to use all our moral and intellectual authority in order to save our children, our countries and the forms of civilisation to which we are attached, and we pay tribute and appeal fervently to those Powers—especially India—which have thus far given evidence of a desire to act as mediators. [11]

WE REQUEST:

" 1. The immediate cessation of all current military operations, [12] and the peaceful settlement within the framework and according to the spirit of the Charter of the United Nations of all present and future conflicts; the admission of the People's Republic of China to the U.N.O. [13]; and the drafting between all Powers concerned of peace treaties with Germany and Japan. [14]

" 2. A meeting of the five great Powers (U.S.A., France, Great Britain, People's Republic of China, U.S.S.R.) in order to draft a Peace Pact which would be open to all nations, this being indispensable for a return to a state of international normality and confidence. [15]

" 3. The opening of negotiations for progressive universal disarmament affecting all weapons, permanently supervised in all countries and allowing all nations finally to devote their resources to peaceful endeavours and particularly to education. [16]

" 4. An increase of cultural exchanges and of trade between countries having different social structures, and a return to free international circulation of men and printed matter, in order to encourage intellectual disarmament through mutual understanding. [17]

" 5. The organisation of a vast campaign among the youth of all countries in order ceaselessly to denounce the horror and futility of another war, and to protest against the passive acceptance of the idea of war." [18]

This is a collector's piece, an admirable specimen of its kind, so devised that many of its finer points are not appreciated until a second or third reading. In studying this document, it must be remembered that since there is no free public opinion in the Soviet Union or the Communist States which could influence the policy of its government, the draft appeal is designed exclusively to influence public opinion in the free world, and, through public opinion, the governments of the free world.

With these facts in mind, the following are the comments on the text that suggest themselves, numbered to correspond with the numbers inserted in the text itself.

One: the title and the appeal as a whole assume that the threat of another world war is becoming more acute, and that an appeal such as this, addressed to free governments and free society, can diminish this threat. The basic assumption of the appeal is therefore fundamentally wrong. If there is a threat of another world war, it is due to the aggressive policy of the Soviet Government since the end of the Second World War.

The threat was most acute after the three most clearly defined acts of aggression of the Communist empire: the political aggression against Czechoslovakia; the blockade of Berlin, and the Communist invasion of South Korea. The threat has on each occasion been diminished by the growing realisation of Russian aims and methods, by the growing unity of action of the non-Communist world, and the decision to lessen the likelihood of the use of force by Russia through increasing the defensive strength of the free world.

Two is irrelevant and untrue. It is a falsification to say that the Second World War was caused by the defensive preparations of the Western Allies in the face of German rearmament in the 1930's. It would be nearer the truth to say that the outbreak of war was caused by the fact that the Allies were too slow in starting to rearm; but fundamentally what matters is not armaments but the policy that these armaments are designed to serve.

Three, four and **five** are part of the standard technique of building up the fear of war. Nobody denies the truth of these propositions, but as a contribution to averting war they are quite useless unless teachers and scholars in Soviet Russia are using them as an argument for pressing the Soviet Government to renounce the basic aggressive aims of their political philosophy. Anyone who tried to do so would be sent straight to his death or a concentration camp.

Six: this is the standard current Soviet propaganda line about peaceful co-existence. As has been shown, the Soviet Government regard this as a necessary interlude before the final downfall of non-Communist society. The proposition of the teachers and scholars would only be true if they could persuade the Soviet Government to try peaceful co-existence on free and equal terms, *i.e.* with freedom of access to all sources of knowledge and opinion inside the Soviet Union itself, and the right of the Soviet people to control the policy of their government.

Seven is an admirable general principle, the effect of which is spoiled by the interpretation which Soviet-controlled agencies and their collaborators put upon it; by employing a series of half-truths, misinterpretations and errors of fact, they seek to relate such generalisations to the situation inside the North Atlantic Treaty Organisation, the Middle East, and Korea (where Soviet Russia has always tried to justify the North Korean aggression by calling it " an internal affair " and the United Nations the aggressor).

Meantime they keep silent about the internal conditions of the Communist States. The teachers and scholars could make a useful contribution to peace by examining the freedom of the peoples of the Soviet Union or Satellite States to have a régime of their own choice and the degree to which the Russian people can at present control the policy of their government.

Eight contains three disconnected points. The first, that all differences between nations can be settled peacefully, is obviously true, and that is what the United Nations is for. The difficulty has been that the United Nations can only operate on principles of tolerance, compromise and a genuine desire for understanding, qualities which Soviet policy has lacked ever since the United Nations was set up. That is the cause of the present crisis, and disarmament would follow its solution.

Nine is again a standard Soviet propaganda line, based on the natural reluctance of the peoples of Western Europe to see Germany rearmed. The problem here is that the Soviet Zone of Germany has already been sufficiently armed to constitute a threat to Western Germany, and the general Russian threat to Western Europe is such that the whole of free Europe has to be called upon to contribute to its own defence. Denunciations of the German defence contribution are designed to strengthen the Soviet position in Europe.

Ten: Comment as in **seven** above. This must be examined in the light of the Soviet attitude towards peace and war; this generalisation is never applied to Communist hate propaganda, but to the misdeeds of a mythical group of war-mongers.

Eleven means nothing unless the action which teachers propose to take to give effect to it is specified. If the implication is that teachers should try to find some middle position between the foundations of Soviet policy and the policy of the Western Governments, they may find themselves in a very curious moral and intellectual position. Assuming, however, that they support the principles of the Charter of the United Nations, they could make a useful contribution to peace only if they were in direct contact with a similar group of equally free and independent teachers in Russia, equally free to press upon the Soviet Government an identical interpretation of these principles.

Twelve: this means in effect that the Communists and bandits must be left to overrun Malaya and Vietnam without resistance, while its bearing upon the Korean situation is obscure, where the Russians are sabotaging the armistice negotiations.

Thirteen: the first part of this request should be addressed to Moscow, whose representatives have consistently sabotaged the work of the United Nations. The second request can be answered by the British with the remark that having recognised the Chinese People's Government two years ago, this government has responded by confiscating all British property in China and keeping our representative on the doorstep. In addition China has intervened in the Korean War.

Fourteen: the Japanese Peace Treaty has already been signed, and the Russian obstruction of all attempts to make a peace treaty with a united Germany is too well known to be worth repeating. It is noteworthy that there is no mention of an Austrian treaty, where Russian obstruction has been even more obvious.

Fifteen: this Russian attempt to by-pass the United Nations has already been discussed on pages 217–220.

Sixteen: now under discussion in the United Nations. It would be much more useful if the teachers would examine the advantages and disadvantages of the various proposals for disarmament and the control of atomic energy which have already been put forward.

Seventeen comes straight from the Warsaw Peace Appeal. Teachers could contribute to peace here if they would insist upon free access by the peoples of Russia and Eastern Europe to the world's knowledge and culture without censorship and governmental control of publishing and the Press; the point is worthless unless it is addressed directly to the totalitarian governments.

Eighteen—this activity seems scarcely necessary in view of the universal hatred of modern war. What is much more important is to spread knowledge of the real sources of the tension in the world to-day which might lead to war.

The general position about peace appeals such as this is that unless the governments principally concerned—in this case the Communist bloc on the one hand and the free world on the other—are equally susceptible to pressure from their public, the

Q

contribution to peace that these appeals are likely to make is to be assessed solely by their impact, if any, on the world situation.

The effect of the teachers' appeal, analysed above, upon the Soviet Government would be non-existent; whereas if it attracted enough adherents in the free world it would merely be weakening the free world against Soviet political or military aggression.

SELECTED BIBLIOGRAPHY

I. COMMUNISM

What is Communism? John Plamenatz (K-H Services, 1947), 3s. 6d.

The Theory and Practice of Communism, Carew Hunt (Geoffrey Bles, 1950), 12s. 6d.

The Practice and Theory of Bolshevism, Bertrand Russell (Allen and Unwin, 1951), 7s. 6d.

The Communist International, F. Borkenau (Faber and Faber, 1938), 12s. 6d.

Three Who Made a Revolution, Bertram D. Wolfe (Dial Press, New York, 1948), $5.

Lenin, D. Shub (Doubleday and Co., New York, 1948), $5.

History of the Communist Party of the Soviet Union. [*Bolsheviks*]; short course.

Problems of Leninism, Stalin.

Lenin, Selected Works.

Handbook on the Soviet Trade Unions, A. Lozovsky.

(The above four books are published in Moscow and can be obtained in the United Kingdom through Colletts Bookshops.)

Stalin, Boris Souvarine (Secker and Warburg, 1939), 15s.

Stalin, A Political Biography, I. Deutscher (Oxford University Press, 1949), 25s.

Stalin, Nikolas Basseches (Staple Press, 1952), 18s. 6d.

Stalin, Leon Trotsky (Harper and Bros., New York and London).

Capital, Karl Marx (Everyman Edition, 2 vols., J. M. Dent, 1951), 5s. each.

Fundamental Problems of Marxism, Plekhanov.

Karl Marx, I. Berlin (Home Universities Library, 1949), 6s.

The Open Society and its Enemies, 2 vols., Karl Popper (Routledge, 1945), 42s.

Marxism and the National and Colonial Question, Stalin (Lawrence and Wishart, 1947), 6s. 6d.

Marx and Engels, *Selected Works*, 2 vols. (Lawrence and Wishart, 1942), 6s. 6d. each.

Paths in Utopia, Martin Buber (Routledge and Kegan Paul, 1949), 15s.

On Literature, Music and Philosophy, A. A. Zhdanov (Lawrence and Wishart, 1930), 3s. 6d.

The Yogi and the Commissar, Arthur Koestler (Jonathan Cape, 1947), 10s.

The Soviet Constitution, (Soviet News, London, 1950).

II. THE SOVIET UNION

The Foreign Policy of Soviet Russia, Max Beloff (Royal Institute of International Affairs, 1945), 36s.

The Real Soviet Russia, David Dallin (Hollis and Carter, 1946), 18s.

Russian Purge and the Extract of Confessions, F. Beck and W. Godon, (Hurst and Blackett, 1951), 10s. 6d.

The Russian Peasant and Other Studies, Sir J. Maynard (Gollancz), 15s.

Musical Uproar in Moscow, Alexander Werth (Turnstile Press, 1951), 6s.
Soviet Trade Unions, I. Deutscher (Royal Institute of International Affairs), 7s. 6d.
Soviet Politics, Barrington Moore (Harvard University Press, 1950).
The Bolshevik Revolution, Vols. II and III, E. H. Carr (Macmillan, 1952 and 1953).
The Scared Men in the Kremlin, John Fischer (Hamish Hamilton, 1949), 10s. 6d.
In Anger and Pity, R. Magidoff (Doubleday, New York, 1949), $2.95.
Stalin versus Marx, K. Mehnert (Allen and Unwin, 1952), 8s. 6d.
Development of the Soviet Economic System, A. Baykov (Oxford University Press, 1946), 30s.
Soviet Economic Development, M. Dobb (Routledge, 1948), 18s.
U.S.S.R., A Concise Handbook, E. J. Simmons (Cornell University Press, 1947), $4.50.
Soviet Genetics and World Science, Julian Huxley (Chatto and Windus, 1949), 8s. 6d.
Russia Puts the Clock Back, John Langdon Davies (Gollancz, 1949), 7s. 6d.
Scientists in Russia, E. Ashby (Penguin Books).
The Socialised Agriculture of the U.S.S.R., Naum Jasny (Oxford University Press, 1950), 60s.
How Strong is Russia? T. Zavalani (Hollis and Carter, 1951).
Russia's Soviet Economy, H. Schwatz (Jonathan Cape, 1951).
Dateline Moscow, Don Dallas (Heinemann, 1952), 21s.
Stalin's Russia, Suzanne Labin (Gollancz, 1949), 2s.
British Students Visit the Soviet Union (K-H Services, 1951), 5s.
Marx Against the Peasant, David Mitrany (Weidenfeld and Nicolson, 1951), 25s.
The Soviet in World Affairs, Louis Fischer, 2 vols., (Oxford University Press), 63s.
Conspiracy in Silence, Alex Weissberg (Hamish Hamilton, 1952), 21s.
Invitation to Moscow, Z. Stypulkowski (Thames and Hudson, Ltd., 1951), 15s.
Stalin's Slave Camps (International Confederation of Free Trade Unions), 5s.
It Happens in Russia, V. Petrov (Eyre and Spottiswoode, 1951), 21s.
Under Two Dictators, Margaret Buber (Gollancz, 1949), 21s.
The Inhuman Land, Joseph Czapaki (Chatto and Windus, 1951), 16s.
A Reluctant Traveller in Russia, Tadeusz Wittlin (Hodge, 1952), 15s.
Eleven Years in Soviet Prison Camps, Elinor Lipper (Hollis and Carter, 1951), 18s.
A World Apart, Gustov Herling (Heinemann, 1951), 16s.
Forced Labour in Soviet Russia, Dallin and Nicolaevsky (Hollis and Carter, 1946), 25s.
Political Power in the U.S.S.R., 1917–1927, Julian Twister (Oxford University Press, 1948), 35s.

III. COMMUNISM OUTSIDE THE SOVIET UNION.

FAR EAST:

Revolution and Counter-Revolution in China, M. N. Roy (Calcutta, 1947), 15s.

New China: Three Views, O. B. van der Sprenkel, Michael Lindsay and R. Guillain (Turnstile Press, 1950), 9s. 6d.

The Rise of Russia in Asia, David Dallin (Hollis and Carter, 1950).

China and the Soviet Union, Aitchen K. Wu (Methuen, 1950), 25s.

The Chinese in South-East Asia, Victor Purcell (Royal Institute of International Affairs), 50s.

The Autobiography of Mao Tse-tung, translated from the Chinese by Edgar Snow (Truth Book Co., Canton, China).

Revolution in China, C. P. Fitzgerald (Cresset Press, 1952), 21s.

Chinese Communism and the Rise of Mao, B. I. Schwartz (Oxford University Press, 1925), 25s.

NEAR EAST:

Russia and the West in Iran, 1918–48, Dr. G. Lenczowski (Oxford University Press, 1951), 36s.

EUROPE:

The Curtain Falls, edited by Denis Healey (Lincolns-Prager, 1951), 4s. 6d.

East Wind over Prague, Jan Stransky (Hollis and Carter, 1950), 10s. 6d.

Who's Next, the Lesson of Czechoslovakia, John Brown (Hutchinson, 1951), 12s. 6d.

The Soviet-Yugoslav Dispute (Royal Institute of International Affairs, 1948), 2s.

Tito v. Stalin, Jan Tindrich (Ernest Benn, 1950), 8s. 6d.

Tito and Goliath, H. A. Armstrong (Gollancz), 18s.

East European Revolution, H. Seton Watson (Methuen, 1950), 22s. 6d.

The Secret Army, T. Bor-Komorowski (Gollancz, 1950), 21s.

Stalin and the Poles, Dr. Borislaw Kusnierz (Hollis and Carter, 1949), 16s.

East of the Iron Curtain, Vernon Bartlett (Latimer House, 1949), 8s. 6d.

Czechoslovakia Enslaved, Hubert Ripka (Gollancz, 1950), 18s.

Oh, My Country, Josef Josten (Latimer House, 1949), 14s.

From Christmas to Easter, Alexandra Orme (Wm. Hodge and Co., 1949), 15s.

The Katyn Wood Murders, Joseph Mackiewicz (Hollis and Carter, 1951), 15s.

Stalin and German Communism, Ruth Fischer (Harvard University Press, 1948).

Nazi–Soviet Relations, 1939–41 (U.S. Government Printing Office, Washington, D.C., 1948), $1.

The Russo-German Alliance, A. Rossi (Chapman and Hall, 1950), 12s. 6d.

The Struggle Behind the Iron Curtain, Ferencz Nagy (Macmillan, New York), 45s.

The Pattern of Soviet Domination, Stanislaw Mikolajczyk (Sampson Low, 1948), 15s.

Soviet Trade with Eastern Europe 1945–49 (Royal Institute of International Affairs, 1951), 8s. 6d.

The Captured Archives, Bernard Newman (Latimer House, 1948), 8s. 6d.

Demetrov Wastes no Bullets, Michael Padev (Eyre and Spottiswoode, 1948), 5s.

The Eastern Zone and Soviet Policy in Germany, J. P. Nettl (Oxford University Press, 1951), 21s.

News from Soviet Germany, Fritz Lowenthal (Gollancz, 1950), 18s.
A Communist Party in Action, A. Rossi (Geoffrey Cumberlege, 1952), 25s.
The Communist Technique in Britain, Darke (Penguin Special, 1952).

IV. COMMUNISM AND CHRISTIANITY

Christianity and Communism, John C. Bennett (S.C.M. Press, 1949), 7s. 6d.
Communism and Christian Faith, H. Ingli James (Carey Kingsgate Press, 1950), 6s.
Communism and the Churches, *A Documentation*, J. B. Barron and H. Waddams (S.C.M. Press, 1951), 4s.
Commentary on Communism, Edward Rogers (Epworth Press, 1951), 17s.

V. MISCELLANEOUS

The Russian Idea, N. Berdyaev (Geoffrey Bles, 1947), 18s.
Defence in the Cold War (Royal Institute of International Affairs, 1950), 5s.
The Burden of Our Time, H. Arendt (Secker and Warburg, 1951), 30s.
Sociology of Communism, Jules Monnerot (Allen and Unwin, 1953).
Lost Illusion, Freda Utley (Allen and Unwin).
Strange Land Behind Me, Stephen Pollak (Falcon Press, 1952), 15s.
I Believed, Douglas Hyde (Heinemann, 1950), 10s.
I Chose Freedom, Victor Kravchenko (Chas. Scribner, New York, 1946: Abridged version Robert Hale, London), 2s. 6d.
Truth Will Out, Charlotte Haldane (Weidenfeld and Nicolson, 1949), 12s. 6d.
The God that Failed, edited by R. H. S. Crossman (Hamish Hamilton, 1950), 12s. 6d.
Soviet Atomic Spies, Bernard Newman (Robert Hale, 1952), 15s.
Report on the Canadian Spy Trials (published by the Canadian Government, Ottawa, 1946).
Assassins at Large, Hugo Dewar (Wingate, 1951), 12s. 6d.
Russia and her Colonies. Walter Kolarz (George Philip, 1952), 25s.

SOME FOREIGN BOOKS:

Lénine et la IIIe Internationale, B. Lazitch (Neuchatel, 1951).
Histoire économique de l'URSS, S. N. Procopovicz (Paris, 1948).
Le Glacis Sovietique, N. Clarion (Paris, 1948).
Histoire du Parti communiste français, G. Walter (Paris, 1948).
Die KPD in der Weimarer Republik, O. K. Flechtheim (Offenback am Main, 1948).

FICTION:

Animal Farm, George Orwell (Secker and Warburg, 1944), 6s.
Nineteen Eighty-four, George Orwell (Secker and Warburg, 1949), 12s. 6d.
Darkness at Noon, Arthur Koestler (Jonathan Cape), 12s. 6d.

INDEX

Printed in Great Britain by
RICHARD CLAY AND COMPANY, LTD.

BUNGAY

SUFFOLK